THIS SHEBA, SELF

THE JOHNS HOPKINS UNIVERSITY STUDIES IN HISTORICAL AND POLITICAL SCIENCE

NINETY-SECOND SERIES (1974)

J. E. CROWLEY

THIS SHEBA, SELF

THE CONCEPTUALIZATION OF ECONOMIC LIFE
IN EIGHTEENTH-CENTURY AMERICA

THE JOHNS HOPKINS UNIVERSITY PRESS
BALTIMORE AND LONDON

This book has been brought to publication with the
generous assistance of the Andrew W. Mellon Foundation.

The Johns Hopkins University Press, Baltimore, Maryland 21218
The Johns Hopkins University Press Ltd., London

Library of Congress Catalog Card Number 73-19334
ISBN 0-8018-1579-7
Manufactured in the United States of America

Library of Congress Cataloging in Publication Data will be
found on the last printed page of this book.

For Mary

CONTENTS

ix

ACKNOWLEDGMENTS

It is a pleasure to have this opportunity to thank publicly those persons and institutions which played crucial roles in the preparation of this book. The graduate schools of the University of Michigan and the Johns Hopkins University provided both formal training in the study of history and invaluable informal opportunities for bringing that training to life. Both universities gave financial assistance through their administration of National Defense Education Act, Title IV, fellowships. The Woodrow Wilson Foundation provided assistance through a dissertation fellowship. A Fulbright fellowship from the United States–United Kingdom Educational Commission enabled me to spend a highly profitable year of research and writing in the congenial and stimulating atmosphere of Churchill College, University of Cambridge. A fellowship at the John Carter Brown Library introduced me to an indispensable resource for early American history, and I shall long value the expert helpfulness extended by the librarian, Thomas R. Adams, and the staff there. From this study's beginnings as a dissertation, Professor Jack P. Greene has given it patient encouragement, searching criticism, and illuminating suggestions about the argument's context in early American history. Gabrielle M. Spiegel gave the penultimate draft an incisive and painstaking reading which resulted in numerous beneficial recommendations.

THIS   SHEBA,   SELF

This Sheba, SELF, has blown the Trumpet of Rebellion.

John Danforth, *The Vile
Profanations of Prosperity* (1704)

From whence, then, arises that emulation which runs through all the different ranks of men, and what are the advantages which we propose by that great purpose of human life which we call bettering our condition? . . . It is the vanity, not the ease, or the pleasure which interests us.

Adam Smith, *The Theory
of Moral Sentiments* (1759)

PROLOGUE

W HEN I BEGAN THIS STUDY, I anticipated finding that during the eighteenth century American attitudes toward work changed from a communally oriented ethic suited for a clearly articulated, traditional society to a highly individualistic set of values appropriate to social changes following from a rapidly expanding economy. Such an expectation depended on a hypothetical relationship between values and behavior, in which values tagged along with, "reflected," and accommodated themselves to changes in "basic" aspects of social life, especially economic activity. The plausibility of this expectation derived from a conventional model of early American social development which takes the diffusion and increase of wealth, the expansion of commercial life, and an increase in secularization to be the most significant phenomena of the period.[1] I now think that the initial proposition was wrong on both counts: seventeenth-century America, and contemporary England a fortiori, cannot realistically be painted as an economic never-never land where the poor but unambitious folk pooled their resources and their miseries and lived in timeless

---

[1]For examples, see William S. Sachs and Ari Hoogenboom, *The Enterprising Colonials: Society on the Eve of the Revolution* (Chicago, 1965), pp. 68, 73, 85, 104; Max Savelle, *Seed of Liberty: The Genesis of the American Mind* (New Haven, 1948), pp. 223-25. A more sophisticated version of this interpretation is found in Rowland Berthoff, *An Unsettled People: Social Order and Disorder in American History* (New York, 1971), which takes the retention of traditional values in early America to be a tempering of explosive forces to be unleashed in the nineteenth century.

communities without recourse to monetary exchange and its vicissitudes. From the start the American colonies were societies with enormous potential energy for commercial endeavors and the pursuit of self-interest: early Virginia was the scene of fierce exploitation of labor to meet overseas demand for tobacco, and the settlement and social development of Plymouth were shaped in basic ways by changing opportunities for trade.[2] Nor was intellectual and psychological accommodation to conditions of prosperity and social boundlessness the most significant cultural development of the eighteenth century. On the contrary, it became apparent to me while reading early American social commentary that the relationship between changes in values and behavior is dialectic, not isomorphic. I have come to see values as responses to behavior, as efforts to understand, define, and shape it, and therefore as manifestations of the mediation of experience and consciousness.

In the eighteenth century Americans often wrote about work, their livelihoods. Peculiar to them, as to any culture, was their way of talking about their work. This book is a study of the terms Americans used to express themselves publicly about work; it defines the limits within which economic action could be given meaning. I have examined two values, industry and frugality, in relation to an ideal of community solidarity. Most discussions of industry and frugality have stressed that the problem explained by an examination of the application of these values to work is a Christian one, involving the relationship between the self and the material world. I would argue that the more important problem by the eighteenth century was an ethical one, concerning the relationship between the self and society, and that certain inferences about discontent can be made on the basis of the particular construction placed on the self (the insistence that it be treated in moral terms).[3]

In public discourse the usual valuation of work was a social and moral one: an individual's work was to be rationally harmonized with the interests of others in his community. This conception derived from classical notions of justice and from Christian ethics of self-denial and brotherly love, but its immediate intellectual sources were three strands of English thought: pietism, benevolist ethics, and the social analysis originating in opposition politics. Industry and frugality have usually been thought of as aspects of a supposed American individualism, but in the colonial period

[2]Edmund S. Morgan, "The First American Boom: Virginia, 1618 to 1630," *William and Mary Quarterly*, 3rd ser., 28 (1971): 169-98; Darrett B. Rutman, *Husbandmen of Plymouth: Farms and Villages in the Old Colony, 1620-1692* (Boston, 1967), chap. 2.

[3]Clyde Kluckhohn, after only a cursory reading in the sources, came upon a significant truth about the psychology of men at this time: "I have a hunch—from reading some of the literature on Puritanism in both its New England and its frontier forms—that the only way the American Puritan could lower his guilt level was by participating in a group—especially (but not exclusively) a religious group. To the extent that the Puritan Ethic has declined one would expect that the whole problem of conformity would be less compulsive and emotional in both its affirmative and its negative direction." "The Evolution of Contemporary Values," *Daedalus*, 87 (1958): 93n.

they were thought of simultaneously as social duties and as means for the preservation of autonomy.

These values applied to two apparent and persistent results of work in America: excessive consumption, which fostered irrationality and a loss of self-control in personal and social obligations; and destructive competition, which unleashed self-interest and displaced social ties with economic ones. Luxury and self-indulgence had connotations of emasculation and passivity for the colonists, who referred to these vices as "unmanly," "base," and a form of "subjection." Idleness, by contrast, implied an oedipal aggression against the proper order of things. Idleness, wrote Cotton Mather, was "the most *concealed,* and yet the most *violent,* of all our passions. . . . It lays adamantine chains of death and of darkness upon us."[4] At the very beginning of the eighteenth century, John Danforth, long-time minister at Dorchester, made one of the fiercest colonial attacks on extravagance and the sins of indulgence in a sermon entitled "The Vile Profanations of Prosperity." By identifying the wicked self of New Englanders with Sheba, he reminded his listeners that their economic life was leading them into the rebellion of sin, for, in addition to referring to the Benjaminite who rebelled against David after his restoration as king, Sheba also represented the Queen of the Sabeans, a nation renowned for its wealth. Such a reference placed in conjunction complementary concerns about life in commercial society. Industry and frugality corresponded to two ideals for the self; fear of debilitation from luxury indicated a need for autonomy, and concern about the anarchy of idleness indicated a desire for a context of fulfillment. Devotion to the public good coordinated these two ideals; it required rational behavior, which was possible only for autonomous men.[5]

The behavior spoken of involved central cultural questions. In addition to earning their subsistence, many colonists were working in order to achieve consumption patterns which conferred status and pleasure and which therefore contributed to self-respect. (The equation of standard of living with comfort is comparatively recent and of limited use in the early American context. After a family attained a certain level of affluence—having a servant might well have been the baseline—increments of wealth did not necessarily correspond with absolute improvements in material well-being; indeed, the medical care, diet, clothing, and household facilities

[4]Cotton Mather, *Bonifacius: An Essay upon the Good,* ed. David Levin (Cambridge, Mass., 1966), p. 9; John Danforth, *The Vile Profanations of Prosperity by the Degenerate among the People of God . . .* (Boston, 1704), p. 35; *A New Standard Bible Dictionary,* ed. Melancthon W. Jacobus, Edward E. Nourse, and Andrew C. Zenos (New York, 1926), p. 793; *The New Westminster Dictionary of the Bible,* ed. Henry Snyder Gehman (Philadelphia, 1970), pp. 859-60. The connection of luxury with effeminacy and of idleness with disorder is also found in the republican tradition; see Daniel Waley, "The Primitivist Element in Machiavelli's Thought," *Journal of the History of Ideas,* 31 (1970): 91-98.

[5]On the relationship of demands for autonomy and the need for inclusion in value changes, see Fred Weinstein and Gerald M. Platt, *The Wish To Be Free: Society, Psyche, and Value Change* (Berkeley, 1969), *passim.*

of the wealthy may have exacted a toll in physical discomfort which people of more middling means avoided.) Hence the attacks on luxury and the insistence on frugality spoke to the crucial matter of the personal motivations which contributed to colonial social development, though they strike confirmed anachronists (for instance, D. H. Lawrence in his remarks on Franklin) as carping trivializations of human wants.[6] The goods and services on which the colonists spent their surplus income—cloth, drink, furniture, carriages, slaves, and entertainment—were tokens of their efforts to achieve identity, dignity, and recogition through the demonstration of their wealth and sophistication, to establish their autonomy from their fellow man and from the most pressing economic demands of life. A study of the historical geography of southeastern Pennsylvania has interpreted these and other patterns of economic behavior as part of a fundamentally "liberal" orientation of the settlers' culture, which placed "individual freedom and material gain over that of public interest"—though I think it is equally significant for the relationship of behavior to values in colonial society that the author cites almost no explicit conceptualization of this outlook.[7] The irony that the identity established through conspicuous consumption depended on others' approval, and that manifestations of independence from economic necessity required unremitting work, did not go unnoticed by colonial social commentators.

The colonists' chief ethical concern was with selfishness, which everyone was capable of and which seemed to flourish in commercial life. In any discussion of economic matters it was assumed that men's individual interests could and should be harmonious. The basis of this assumption was a lingering respect for providential design, combined with an aversion to acceptance of a model of society which took conflict, misery, and injustice not as instances of human failing but for granted as part of nature. This moral disposition toward social harmony was reinforced by the prevailing paradigm of economic change (both individual and society-wide), which construed wealth to be a fixed amount and therefore saw economic development as redistribution; hence gain was possible only at the expense of others. An alternative perspective on the economy suggested that absolute and per capita wealth were increasing, but this was a long-term view; over the short run, it was assumed, one man's gain was usually another's loss.

Views on the relationship between self and society were at the core of considerations about men's livelihoods and appeared in almost every sort of economic discussion, whether about paper money, imbalance of trade,

[6]D. H. Lawrence, *Studies in Classic American Literature*, Doubleday ed. (New York, 1951), chap. 2.

[7]James T. Lemon, *The Best Poor Man's Country: A Geographical Study of Southeastern Pennsylvania* (Baltimore, 1972). For some interesting remarks about slaveholding as conspicuous consumption, see Alan Tully, "Patterns of Slaveholding in Colonial Pennsylvania: Chester and Lancaster Counties, 1729-1758," *Journal of Social History*, 6 (1973): 284-305.

commercial depression, the lack of manufactures, or the myriad of other problems associated with the colonial American economy. While twentieth-century Americans might assume that such matters were susceptible to technical economic analysis, colonial spokesmen did not accept such situations as the unavoidable consequences of economic life itself and interpreted them instead with a view toward the morality of individuals' behavior. They stated explicitly that the issue was one of providing fulfillment within society for a distrusted self; indeed, the theme of distrust often diverted attention from the matter of individual fulfillment, as though in the American environment strictly personal satisfaction was not especially difficult. The impoverishment of language for the analysis of economic action belied the variety and exuberance of behavior which historians associate with the development of commerce and the growth of prosperity in the late colonial period. This impoverishment, particularly in the lack of congruency between values and behavior, is interpreted here as an indication of an intellectual and psychological inability to find accommodation with social change.[8]

In their attempt to find a rational standard by which the social legitimacy of individual economic action could be determined, Americans exhibited several tendencies that had been evident in early modern European ethical thought since at least the sixteenth century. Instead of attempting to sanctify life in a corrupt world through the spiritual transcendence of Christian mystery, as in medieval times, European social thought stressed that behavior itself needed to be changed so that it would be harmonious with the rationally determined needs of society; the imperfections of individual behavior became socially as well as spiritually unacceptable.[9] Combined with changes in European economic life—the diversification and specialization of economic roles, the innovation and growth of financial in-

[8]I must confess that my argument, with its assertion that values can sometimes represent failure at accommodation with and reactions against specific social conditions, still gives a covert priority to "basic" social and economic actions, because they are the objective reality which is ascribed as the stimulus for the peculiar response in values. This backdoor admission of sociological considerations to interpretations in intellectual history is today almost unavoidable. But it might be put forward hypothetically that values not only attest to, but also create, needs which shape action; in the case of attitudes toward work the values entailed a strong need for self-justification by reference to the overarching material demands of society itself. Most of the evidence considered in this study is a manifestation of this need. Neither paradigm necessarily need exclude the applicability of the other in different situations, but the former usually has the status of axiom, the latter of whimsical psychology. The problem, of course, is to find an explanation of why and how values change independently. To look to reason and consciousness is to run counter to our behaviorist dispositions, a condition testified to by our much greater tolerance of an explanational limbo for independent social change—"social change" itself sometimes being called on as a *deus ex machina*.

[9]For a discussion of this point, see J. H. Hexter's introduction to *Utopia*, vol. 4 of *The Yale Edition of the Complete Works of St. Thomas More*, ed. Edward Surtz and J. H. Hexter (New Haven, 1965), pp. cxiv-cxvi; cf. E. J. Hundert, "The Making of *Homo Faber*: John Locke between Ideology and History," *Journal of the History of Ideas*, 33 (1972): 3-23; for a discussion of the medieval situation, see Lester K. Little, "Pride Goes before Avarice: Social Change and the Vices in Latin Christendom," *American Historical Review*, 76 (1971): 16-49.

stitutions, and the increased importance of money in economic life—this shift in ethical concern gave attitudes toward work a special relevance. They became the basic terms for the definition of an individual's relationship with society.

The social impact of the development of commercial life was enormous. Participation in the market changed men's economic orientation from physical subsistence to monetary gain. In a market economy men's livelihoods depended on their success in selling goods, labor, and land, which, insofar as the market was concerned, were commodities and not aspects of social relations. Such changes were in sharp contrast to traditional attitudes toward economic life. It was the traditional view that exchange within a particular community was a social matter involving reciprocity and redistribution; competition, in the sense of one man's gaining at the expense of another, was a violation of this traditional ethic. In response to these changes, men sought to make the traditional values explicit in ways that took the new economic conditions into account. They recognized the individual as an economic entity and then stressed his subordination to communal interests. This "social" valuation of work represented a desire to preserve the social wholeness of men in situations which accentuated their economic capabilities.[10]

In eighteenth-century America the important tension in values applied to work was not that between individualistic and communitarian impulses (for which theoretical accommodation was possible because everyone granted the appropriateness of the regulation of social and economic life); rather, it was the inherent conflict between two types of valuations of work, one social, the other economic. One valuation treated work as a moral problem; the other dealt with it as a topic susceptible to psychological and sociological analysis and therefore distinct from morality.[11] This purely eco-

---

[10]This view derived from readings in economic anthropology, especially the work of Karl Polanyi, *The Great Transformation*, Beacon ed. (Boston, 1957). Max Weber discussed these issues in terms of a distinction between "formal" and "substantive" rationality in economic life; see *The Theory of Social and Economic Organization*, trans. A. M. Henderson and Talcott Parsons, Free Press ed. (New York, 1964), pp. 158-212. For a consideration of the ways in which money is an abstraction of social experience, see Helen Codere, "Money-Exchange Systems and a Theory of Money," *Man*, new ser., 3 (1968): 557-79; cf. Cyril S. Belshaw, *Traditional Exchange and Modern Markets* (Englewood Cliffs, N.J., 1965), pp. 1-10, *passim*. For a qualification of Polanyi's belief that the motive of gain is absent in traditional societies, see S. C. Humphreys, "History, Economics, and Anthropology: The Work of Karl Polanyi," *History and Theory*, 8 (1969): 165-212. A related situation in Antiquity is examined in M. I. Finley, "Aristotle and Economic Analysis," *Past and Present*, 47 (1970): 3-25; cf. Alan Everitt, "The Marketing of Agricultural Produce," *The Agrarian History of England and Wales*, vol. 4, ed. H. P. R. Finberg (Cambridge, 1967), pp. 569-71.

Raymond Firth notes that in "modern Western society" economic and moral standards "often clash or their inconsistencies are unresolved. . . . 'Business is business' and 'love thy neighbour' are normally parallel lines which never attempt to meet, and the State or voluntary organizations have to bridge the gap. In a peasant society business if often keen enough, but since the relationship is often more than a purely economic one, provision for moral obligations can be made within the economic framework itself, which is integrated with the social framework." *Elements of Social Organization*, 2nd ed. (London, 1956), p. 138.

[11]Cf. Alasdair MacIntyre, *A Short History of Ethics* (New York, 1966), pp. 16-17, 126, 166-67.

nomic analysis derived from English mercantilist thought and was used to explain and direct the development of the colonial economy. Because efficient commercial exploitation of material and human resources was its aim, it was inherently amoral in its prescriptions for the dependence of self and society. Certain features of the available economic wisdom, however—its insistence on restricted consumption in order to mobilize employment, and its disposition to see the economic realm as one primarily outside a particular society—deflected from the social valuation of work what would otherwise have been corrosive influences.

The crucial development in attitudes toward work was the tendency to deal with men's livelihoods as economic matters belonging to a separate realm of activity; unlike "trade," the notion of the "economy" as an entity was an undeveloped idea in the eighteenth century. For most of the period the two valuations coexisted in public expression in such a way that work was considered to be a rationalized, but not a strictly economic, topic. This essay traces the interplay of these two valuations in public expression and their implications for American views on the connection between self and society, taking for its starting point the prominence of "the calling" as the basis of social ethics in the early eighteenth century (the history of earlier attitudes toward work being the subject of a classic historiography), and continuing through the secularization of this conception during the Great Awakening and the increased explicitness about life in an extensively commercialized society in the mid-eighteenth century. It concludes with an examination of the relevance of these values to the American Revolution, when public opinion initially displayed an intensification of demands for reform of economic behavior and the subordination of individual interests to public ones, and then after the Revolution resignedly gave greater acceptance to actions justified on grounds of economic necessity alone.

In the questions it poses and the answers it provides, this study differs from the usual forms of modern investigations of attitudes toward work—namely, industrial psychology and the sociology of occupations—even though the colonists themselves were intensely concerned with matters like job motivations and satisfaction, occupational rank and recruitment, work organization, material expectations, and spending habits.[12] The colonists' views on these topics provide much of the material for this study. Similarly, I have avoided any treatment of the role of government in economic regulation, while drawing on colonial writings which dealt with the topic as expressions of values applicable to economic activity. This study is concerned with the rhetoric in which the issues relating to work were discussed. "Rhetoric" here is defined as something quite different from mere grandiloquence. It is the way in which men at a particular time and place communicated most convincingly about a subject by exploiting

---

[12]Theodore Caplow, *The Sociology of Work* (Minneapolis, 1954); Stanley H. Udy, Jr., *Work in Traditional and Modern Society* (Englewood Cliffs, N.J., 1970).

its emotional, as well as its intellectual, significance through references to the common values of a community.[13]

Work was discussed thousands and thousands of times in nearly every conceivable context. And the way in which it was discussed was a coherent one, even though it usually consisted of a sentence here and a paragraph there. Few of the works cited herein were intended to be disquisitions in moral philosophy or economics, though many of them used the learning of these and other disciplines in order to persuade people about particular decisions. I have for the most part, though not without regretful recognition of the costs involved, neglected analysis of the particular context and purpose of specific works. It is apparent that each printed work used here as evidence has its own history—the occasion for its composition and publication, the intention of the author and the resources of persuasion on which he drew, and its relationship with other printed works, both those with which it formed a tradition and those more immediately connected by issues. Individuals, issues, or even events have not been treated either comprehensively or in detail here for the simple reason that most of the ideas and values treated in this study were the objects of affirmation, not dispute. Nearly every type of printed expression set them forth. For this reason, authors have been identified and contexts elaborated only when such information is clearly relevant to the argument; more often, in explanations of the common wisdom on a topic, reference is simply made, with appropriate vagueness, to "men," "people," "spokesmen," "colonists," or "Americans"—though there should be no implication that it would not be of great interest to study the interplay of personal motivation, careers, and public values in individual cases, for these values established the limits of legitimate behavior, while allowing innumerable variations in interpretations and application. It would also be worthwhile to investigate elsewhere whether or not the formal moral statements regarding work could be similar at public and popular levels, while the economic references and rationality of different groups could be quite different. For example, members of various social groups might refer the need for frugality to quite different modes of spending surplus earnings from work; the choices among investment, accumulation, leisure, or display would be a function of the amount of surplus, the livelihood, and the cultural imperatives of the individual. For the least affluent and most numerous segment of the population, surplus income was too scanty and erratic to permit investment or accumulation, and minor display, combined with periodic leisure (drinking and absence from work), was the usual expenditure. At the other end of the social scale, only a few economic roles permitted investment. Thus the bulk of surplus spending went into a combina-

[13]The way in which social psychologists came to interpret "attitude," the orientation of a person to his surroundings, as a conjunction of thought and emotion is traced in Donald Fleming, "Attitude: The History of a Concept," *Perspectives in American History*, 1 (1967): 287-365.

8

tion of accumulation and display, and here there was wide latitude for discretion, sophistication, and the establishment of self-confidence and approbation. The primary concern in the present study, however, is with the bearings of attitudes toward work on the conceptualization of economic life.

The question remains, whose attitudes? Unfortunately, one of the needs of early American history is a theoretical and empirical consideration of this question—namely, what the nature of early American literary culture was and what can be said about the significance of ideas and values that appear in it.[14] We need to know not only what was written, by whom, and why, but also what was read, by whom, and with what effect. Given such a vacuum in our understanding of the sociology of knowledge in colonial America, I am driven to a Pyrrhonist justification for undertaking the study I did instead of a more basic one. Even if we eventually discover a great deal more about American literacy and reading, some of the questions about the intellectual and psychological significance of the content of this literature will remain much the same as they now are. To what extent and how people internalize what they read and hear, and whether or not a diffusion model for ideas and values is workable, are questions that have not been satisfactorily answered. Intellectual historians (understandably) do not advertise the fact, but we lack a workable explanation of the causes and effects of ideas.[15] The benefits of sociological inquiry into literacy and printed communication, though very great, would be negative with regard to questions about the *meaning* of expression for the participants in a literary culture: they would usefully indicate who was *unlikely* to have read what. Nonetheless, it is possible to establish a subjective relationship between behavior and values. In the case of attitudes toward work it is argued that they had the function of providing terms for self-legitimation, and that, therefore, by taking the values and the social criticism couched in their terms as instances of projection, they can provide evidence about the needs of the critic (and his audience) as well as about the character of the behavior itself. Regardless of audience or type of printed matter, there was a remarkable consistency in the expression of certain basic social values at any one time during the colonial period. The elitist character of colonial intellectual life certainly explains much of this consistency, as does American intellectual dependence on Britain, but, until we know more about the diffusion and relevance of literary culture, one should not discount the possibility that an elite's printed expression could represent the values of a society. In the insistence on the priority of social over economic considerations when the two conflict, the values that

[14] For a consideration of the problems involved in the use of literary evidence for the sociology of knowledge, see Robert Darnton, "Reading, Writing, and Publishing in Eighteenth-Century France: A Case Study in the Sociology of Literature," *Daedalus*, 100 (1971): 214-56.

[15] Louis O. Mink, "Change and Causality in the History of Ideas," *Eighteenth-Century Studies*, 2 (1968): 6-25.

were applicable to work during the colonial period resemble the pervasive "moral economy" which E. P. Thompson has examined in late eighteenth-century England, and in the American case, as in the English, adherence to these values cut across class lines.[16] It should at least be noted that the colonial elite often criticized itself in terms which had a populist tone: public spokesmen denounced the decadence of the ruling class as well as the disorderliness of the lower classes.

The values which Americans employed rhetorically regarding work had served the same function in England as in the New World: they represented a yearning for an ideal social order that was an alternative to the one to which they could not accommodate themselves. This ideal, as an obverse projection of their own experience, was characterized by comprehensibility, mutuality, abundant satisfaction of needs, and freedom from distressing wants. These values were necessarily at variance with men's behavior, or there would have been no need to give them as much emphasis as they received. Discussions of the intellectual history of eighteenth-century America sometimes neglect the previous function of these early modern values and instead treat the pervasive lamentations about the decline from earlier virtue as indications of an inability to maintain the values that were appropriate to a static community in a changing one. The values cultivated by nostalgic laments are thus seen as little more than a disturbing residue of ascetic and prescriptive morality from the static society to which they were suited, and the historical interest of the situation lies in the effort to define new values that were more in accord with actual behavior.

But European society had never been static, and there had been a keen awareness of social change for several centuries. One manifestation of this awareness was the explicit conceptualization of aspects of life which might have been taken for granted—Philippe Ariès has shown that this happened with regard to family life; Michele Foucault has investigated the process in linguistic and economic thought; and Max Weber explained the consequences for work.[17] In each of these areas of thought there was an ideal of social stasis—often amounting to an ontological assumption because alterations were taken to be chaotic rather than developmental—which was occasioned by efforts to come to terms with change (personal and family vulnerability; extensive horizontal mobility and speedy, though restricted, vertical mobility; dependence on money for the essentials of life, combined with both acute and chronic inflation), but this ideal was

---

[16]E. P. Thompson, "The Moral Economy of the English Crowd in the Eighteenth Century," *Past and Present*, 50 (1971): 76-136.

[17]Lawrence Stone, "Social Mobility in England, 1500-1700," *ibid.*, 33 (1967): 16-55; Philippe Ariès, *Centuries of Childhood: A Social History of Family Life,* trans., Robert Baldick (New York, 1962); Michele Foucault, *The Order of Things: An Archaeology of the Human Sciences* (London, 1970); Max Weber, *The Protestant Ethic and the Spirit of Capitalism,* trans. Talcott Parsons, Scribner ed. (New York, 1958).

not a reflection of reality. Hence any set of social values which recommended contentment with one's lot, prescribed reciprocity in commercial life, and attributed economic deficiencies to moral traits rather than to structural obstacles could be only an idealization with regard to its applicability and a fabrication in its appeal to a traditional ethic.

If this static society was itself a fabrication, then the values of the jeremiad require some other explanation than simple nostalgic regret. (Some recent historical works also suggest that the conventional contrast between an orderly European society and a volatile and innovative American one may have things turned around.)[18] They represent instead the American phase of a centuries-long response to circumstances for which it was difficult to find intellectual and psychological accommodation and which we identify with modernization: personal responsibility for the achievement of status, fluctuations in prosperity determined by incomprehensible and intangible mechanisms, opportunities for success which entail violation of the acknowledged and familiar order, manipulation of the environment for purposes contrary to customary usage, and the abstraction of personal interaction and individual wants in terms of money.

The adherence to unrealistic values can, of course, tell us as much about the psychological and intellectual history of a society as do the innovations which took place. Values which were publicly asserted show what people wanted to be and how they responded to their failure to live up to their ideal images. In this sense expressed values are directly relevant to behavior, not because they reflect it—which would really tell nothing—but because they are a response to it and therefore tell us about the behavior itself as well as the way in which it was interpreted. Insofar as actions involve purposes, belief gives them meaning, beliefs provide men with a rational understanding and permit them to make a meaningful description of what they have done. Alasdair MacIntyre has argued that values are not the effect of social causation but an expression "of social order and disorder": "to analyze the ideas current in a society is also to discern the limits within which action necessarily moves in that society." When there is a recognized set of standards for the evaluation of behavior, then both conformity with and deviance from the values can be understandable behavior.[19]

Commercialization, not markets per se, was the source of uneasiness regarding work in early America. In most societies there is exchange for the purposes of establishing status, creating obligations, distributing sur-

[18]See Rhys Isaac, "Order and Growth, Authority and Meaning in Colonial New England," *American Historical Review*, 76 (1971): 728-37; on the long-standing commercialization of the English economy, see Everitt, "Marketing of Agricultural Produce," pp. 466-592.
[19]Alasdair MacIntyre, "A Mistake about Causality in Social Science," *Philosophy, Politics, and Society*, ed. Peter Laslett and W. G. Runciman, 2nd ser. (Oxford, 1962), pp. 48-70. See also J. G. A. Pocock, "The History of Political Thought: A Methodological Enquiry," *ibid.*, pp. 183-200; and Quentin Skinner, "Meaning and Understanding in the History of Ideas," *History and Theory*, 8 (1969): esp. 40-53.

plus, and meeting crucial needs; in all societies there is economic life, in the sense that men take risks in the organization of resources in order to maximize satisfaction. Commercialization depends on the degree to which certain prevalent characteristics of exchange—the impersonality of relations between buyers and sellers, the systematization and range of applicability of exchange values, the specialization of roles in buying and selling, the vertical integration of the economy for market exchange, the flexibility of prices as a function of competition, and the use of money— permeate social life and impel it to change.[20] In America, at least as much as in Europe, commerce by the eighteenth century was vital to social life: nearly everyone's livelihood depended on it at some remove or other, and its imperatives shaped choices in most aspects of life—family mobility, career, the extraordinary institution of slavery, and production.

Paradoxically, for a society which was 90 percent rural, subsistence itself was dependent on commerce because of the market in land and the specialization necessary for competitive production. Yet a moralizing tendency in the conceptualization of economic activity continued because of the highly personal nature of commercial transactions. Business organization was usually familially based in order to insure reliability; the extension of credit was commonly from one member of a community to another rather than though institutions; the web of buying and selling was often a seamless one in which the buyer, to insure supply, extended credit to the producer, with the effect that within the community itself economic activity lacked some of the openness of competition necessary for full rationality. The effect of such neighborly integration of economic life was, of course, not a rich sharing of experience but rather an atmosphere of acrimonious charges of wrong-doing, which found salient expression in a persistent litigiousness.[21]

I am convinced that a desire to retain a sense of their social wholeness— and to avoid thinking of themselves as depersonalized economic beings— underlay the colonists' attitudes toward work and indicated both their fear and their respect of themselves as individuals. The strongest evidence, unfortunately negative, for this desire is the difficulty experienced in establishing values which were congruent with the prevailing patterns of work and which would have reduced the stress that accompanied them. Unrestrained, the individual was a source of social disorder; economically isolated, his human qualities were neglected. The colonists' insistence on a moral evaluation of work was in part an effort to maintain this sense of the social wholeness of the individual. Selfishness was a source of guilt

[20]Belshaw, *Traditional Exchange*, pp. 8–9, 109.

[21]James T. Lemon, "Household Consumption in Eighteenth-Century America and Its Relationships to Production and Trade: The Situation among Farmers in Southeastern Pennsylvania," *Agricultural History*, 41 (1967): 59–70; Richard L. Bushman, *From Puritan to Yankee: Character and the Social Order in Connecticut, 1690–1765* (Cambridge, Mass., 1967), pp. 136–37; Sam Bass Warner, Jr., *The Private City: Philadelphia in Three Periods of Its Growth* (Philadelphia, 1968), chap. 1.

and shame, but criticism of it was also an act of human affirmation because it implied that life had a larger meaning than response to the problem of sustenance. Discussions of work indicated a concern that expressions of the self tended to be either passive or destructive and therefore
meaningless. The positive element associated with a sense of guilt was a
sense of responsibility; the colonists refused to concede that behavior was
determined by the attraction which the environment provided for the passions, because such an admission would relieve them of their moral ac-
countability and therefore of their rationality as well.

I

SOCIAL AND ECONOMIC
ATTITUDES TOWARD WORK

A MONG THE SERMONS ADDRESSED TO THE TRUSTEES of the Georgia Company at their annual meetings were several which asked the rhetorical question, *"Are private vices public benefits?"*[1] The question, as everyone in the audience knew, referred to Bernard Mandeville's argument that vices *could* be benefits, which he asserted in his social allegory, *The Fable of the Bees*; and the answer—again, as everyone knew—was an emphatic "no." Mandeville, a physician and man of letters in early eighteenth-century England, delighted in demonstrations of man's capacity for self-deception and employed the egoism of Thomas Hobbes and the skepticism of Pierre Bayle as tools for his social commentary. He argued that self-denial, while laudable in theory, was in practice incompatible with prosperity and that, in any case, what was taken for benevolence was usually a disguise for a deeper selfishness.

Mandeville whipsawed the English reading public with two different but prevalent definitions of legitimate behavior, one social and moral, the other commercial and utilitarian. He wanted to show that it was impossible simultaneously to enjoy the fruits of prosperity and to remain virtuous.

[1]Lewis Bruce, *The Happiness of Man the Glory of God: A Sermon Preached before the Honourable Trustees for Establishing the Colony of Georgia in America, and the Associates of the late Rev. Dr. Bray* . . . (London, 1744), p. 36; Gloucester Ridley, *A Sermon Preached before the Honourable Trustees* . . . (London, 1746), p. 12.

Frugality [wrote Mandeville] is like honesty, a mean starving virtue, that is only fit for small societies of good, peaceable men, who are contented to be poor so they may be easy; but in a large, stirring nation you may have soon enough of it. It is an idle dreaming virtue that employs no hands, and therefore very useless in a trading country, where there are vast numbers that one way or other must be all set to work. Prodigality has a thousand inventions to keep people from sitting still, that frugality would never think of; and as this must consume a prodigious wealth, so avarice again knows innumerable tricks to rake it together, which frugality would scorn to make use of.

As a satire, the *Fable* derived its force from exaggeration, not repudiation, of conventional ethical wisdom. Mandeville accepted his contemporaries' definition of virtue as the subordination of interests of self to those of society. He did not argue that there was another, preferable basis of legitimacy for actions; rather, he maintained that no one could in fact behave legitimately, because everyone acted on the basis of self-interest. This view so shocked the self-esteem of Mandeville's readers that they insisted on misinterpreting his work as a justification of self-interest and a recommendation of vice. Apparently, in order to maintain their self-respect, his readers needed to believe that they kept their selfish instincts under rational control and thereby subordinated themselves to the public good. Mandeville undercut the ethics of strict self-denial which his contemporaries habitually assumed to be the proper standard of behavior.[2] In doing so he disturbed some of their basic ideas about the proper relationship between the self and society.

The issue between Mandeville and his critics about the possibility and consequences of virtue involved more than a philosophical dispute about ethics; implicit in each view were notions about the nature of society and men's actions in it. Mandeville sought to demonstrate that the traditional interpretation of public virtue as self-denial and justice toward others was at odds with a definition of the public good as prosperity. He showed that the values of diligence and contentedness (or industry and frugality) reflected a desire for social stability; their practice could only retard England's growth in wealth and power. Mandeville's model of an acceptable society and the forces which should shape it constituted a break with the orthodox social thought of his time. He denied that society was itself an entity with an articulated moral order to which men should subordinate their actions. He was willing to allow the acquisitive appetites of individuals to determine the nature of trade and economic life generally, regardless of the social consequences. Without the liberation of men's ap-

[2]Bernard Mandeville, *The Fable of the Bees: Or, Private Vices, Public Benefits*, ed. F. B. Kaye, 2 vols. (Oxford, 1924), 1: xlviii, cxviii, 104–5; Paul Fussell, *The Rhetorical World of Augustan Humanism: Ethics and Imagery from Swift to Burke* (New York, 1965), chaps. 1, 5–6. For an explanation of the ways in which the will could be considered a rational appetite, see Norman S. Fiering, "Will and Intellect in the New England Mind," *William and Mary Quarterly*, 3rd ser., 29 (1972): 515–58.

petites, Mandeville asserted, extravagance and luxury would decline and poverty would increase; England could not endure the virtue its inhabitants so badly wanted.[3]

THE SOCIAL MEANING OF GEORGIA

In their opposition to Mandeville's egoism and in their espousals of the project, the Georgia trustees drew on certain strains of thought—popularizations of Christian morality, benevolist ethics, opposition political analysis, and mercantilist economic theory—which comprised the intellectual formulation of eighteenth-century Anglo-American attitudes toward work. Basic among these beliefs was the notion that work was the chief means by which an individual achieved social legitimation. In this case, legitimation refers not to aggressive justifications of new modes of behavior but rather to an establishment of recognized harmony between personal actions and social needs; the implication was that claims on membership in society were in need of justification. Such a social ethic, which appears to be anachronistic and retrospective, was actually a response to social change, chiefly associated with commercial development, and hence was as much a part of the historical situation as the changes themselves.

The legitimation of an individual's work depended on its having certain moral characteristics. The work should be selfless in the sense of being in accord with the public interest and also of being oriented toward only a moderate satisfaction of needs. Yet the relationship of self to society was not one of incapacitating subordination; it was assumed that only in society could real, rational autonomy be had. In ethical thought, the belief in the possibility and desirability of virtue and justice in one's work was in tension with a conviction that man was basically a vicious creature who had difficulty maintaining rational control over his selfish passions. The favorable view of commerce as a mark of civilized achievement and a basis of national strength was at odds with a considerable amount of social criticism which stressed the corrupting influence of wealth, denounced the injustices perpetrated in the name of trade, and recommended a simplification of economic life. Despite such tensions and inconsistencies—which corresponded to ambivalence between denial of a destructive self and fulfillment for a rational one—all these views existed with some sort of rough compatibility in eighteenth-century thought, and taken together they give an idea of the significance and content of Anglo-American valuations of work, with their priority of social and moral considerations over economic ones. The promotion literature for the Georgia project serves as an ideal means by which to study these prevailing attitudes toward work—to see them as responses to particular social developments—because the venture was widely seen as an alternative scheme for orienting work to society.

[3]Mandeville, *Fable*, 1: 25, 36-37, 248-49.

Georgia would make property widely available while limiting its accumulation, would eliminate the extension of credit among citizens, would have everyone become a primary producer, and would have households be the predominant economic unit and institution. The aim was to ensure that commercial ties did not displace social ones.

The immediate objects of Mandeville's satire were the Christian moralists, who urged men to maintain rational control over their passions and equated such control with ascetic self-denial.[4] These seventeenth-century pietists, such as Lewis Bayly, Richard Steel, Richard Allestree, Richard Brathwaite, and Richard Baxter, had a decisive influence on the tradition of English popular religion. They emphasized that all men had the same moral obligations, regardless of social class, and they stressed that these obligations involved a subordination of self-interest to that of the society as a whole. These moralists believed that selfishness was the source of all of man's unhappiness and sins. Every man was cursed by it; it was, Richard Baxter wrote, "the Radical positive sin of the soul, comprehending seminally, or causally all the rest." It was the positive part of man's corruption, "the inordinate Love of Carnal Self"; as such, it complemented the "privative" part of sin, which was ungodliness. Selfishness naturally led to worldliness, which was "a perverting [of] the very drift of a man's life, as employed in seeking a wrong end, and not only of some one faculty or act; it is an habitual sin of the state and course of mind and life, and not only a particular actual sin." The lesson of these teachings was that fulfillment of the self came from its regulation in accordance with rational social needs; individual being was comprehensible only in relation to a general order; material satisfaction was a source of anxiety. To live life according to one's own impulses and in reference to a personal scale of importance was equivalent to "alienating the life from [God's] service, to this present world, and the service of the flesh."[5]

The objective of the pietists was to demonstrate to their readers that the correct answer to the question "What is the vilest creation upon earth?" was "Mine owne self, by reason of my great sins." The intent of such statements was to undermine men's self-confidence so that they could not set their own standards of behavior. Left to itself, the self was a dangerous thing. Work was the chief way to discipline it. Baxter thought that physical as well as spiritual corruption resulted from idleness.

For want of bodily labour a multitude of the idle gentry, and rich people, and young people that are slothful, do heap up in the secret receptacles of the body a dunghill of unconcocted, excrementitious filth, and vitiate all the mass of humours which should be the fuel and oil of life, and die by thousands of untimely deaths,

[4]Philip Harth, "The Satiric Purpose of *The Fable of the Bees*," *Eighteenth-Century Studies*, 2 (1969): 333–34.

[5]Richard Baxter, *A Christian Directory: Or a Summ of Practical Theology, and Cases of Conscience . . . ,* 4 pts. (London, 1673), pp. 116, 225 (the pagination of pts. 1-3 is continuous).

(of fevers, palsies, convulsions, apoplexies, dropsies, consumptions, gout, &c.) more miserably than if thieves had murdered them by the highway, because it is their own doing, and by their sloth they kill themselves.

The body was thought to possess its own stores of energy; the healthful and natural thing for a man to do was, through labor, to keep "the mass of blood and other nutritious humours in their proper temperament, fit for motion, circulation, and nutrition," and to assist in "the preparation, alteration, and expulsion of all the excrementitious matter." This view of the body's metabolism revealed a fear and dislike of consumption, which was associated with a poisonous passivity; these feelings were iterated in the belief that, "next to abstinence, labour is the chief preserver of health."[6] The pietists spoke most directly to the subject of consumption, to the situation in which men found themselves when economically successful, and they warned that a self worthy of respect was in danger of submergence by frivolous leisure or expenditure.

A second school of English moral thought, the benevolists, as represented by Anthony Ashley Cooper, third earl of Shaftesbury, offered an alternative to such thoroughgoing criticism of selfishness. Benevolism had been prominent in English ethical thought since at least the late seventeenth century, when Latitudinarian divines had expressed most of its basic doctrines, partly as a negative response to Hobbes' egoism. Though benevolists countered such cynical psychologizing with a benign hypothesis, they gave the motivational game away by setting aside the classical issue of the respective responsibilities of the will and the reason. The benevolists articulated an ethic which presented self-love as a motivation of work and social relations generally and held that virtue, considered as a matter of public duty, was harmonious with a rational self-interest. The benevolists believed that man was a social creature who naturally desired a peaceful relationship with his fellow men. People derived pleasure from doing good for others, and there was no conflict between this good and the true self-interest of the individual.[7]

Rather than argue that self-interest was ipso facto legitimate, however, the benevolists sought to show that there was such a thing as a legitimate self-interest; they did not deny that there was such a thing as selfishness or that it was evil. There were selfish as well as benevolent passions. Shaftesbury's description of the vice of selfishness did not differ very much

[6]Lewis Bayly, *The Practice of Piety: Directing a Christian How to Walke That He May Please God* . . . , 27th ed. (Edinburgh, 1630), p. 280; Baxter, *Christian Directory*, p. 448.

[7]Overton H. Taylor, "Tawney's Religion and Capitalism, and Eighteenth-Century Liberalism," *Quarterly Journal of Economics*, 41 (1927): 718-31; Henry W. Sams, "Self-Love and the Doctrine of Work," *Journal of the History of Ideas*, 4 (1943): 320-32; C. A. Moore, "Whig Panegyric Verse, 1700-1760: A Phase of Sentimentalism," *Publications of the Modern Language Association*, 41 (1926): 374; R. S. Crane, "Suggestions toward a Geneology of the 'Man of Feeling,' " *ELH: A Journal of English Literary History*, 1 (1934): 206; *idem*, review of William E. Alderman, "Shaftesbury and the Doctrine of Benevolence in the Eighteenth Century," *Philological Quarterly*, 11 (1932): 203-5.

from that of the Christian moralists, but he substituted a genuine holism for their unfulfillable ideal of harmony. He objected to the notion that "the Interest of the *private Nature* is directly opposite to that of *the common one*," because such a view would assume that "there is much Disorder and Untowardness [in men's constitutions] . . . unlike to what we observe elsewhere in Nature." By arguing from a principle of design—the presumption that man's nature could not be the only chaotic element in an orderly universe—the benevolists were able to reconcile self- and social interests by showing that expressions of the first contributed to the second. It was possible, however, for self-love to become perverted in such a way that more attention was paid to one's own interest than to that of others; such a "habit" introduced "a certain Narrowness of Spirit." According to Shaftesbury, the fullest satisfaction of self-interest was almost inadvertent. "All social Love, Friendship, Gratitude, or whatever else is of this generous kind, does by its nature take place of the self-interesting Passions, draws us out of ourselves and makes us disregardful of our own Convenience and Safety."[8] In matters of practice rather than theory, however, few of Shaftesbury's contemporaries could share his optimism; for them benevolence was less a description of man's nature than a standard of behavior which was very difficult to meet. According to this pessimistic version of benevolism, virtue was indeed the only basis of true happiness, but there were doubts about the existence of a natural harmony between instinct and reason; this discord of men's higher and lower capacities was most likely to occur in economic life. Thus the ethical concern of someone of benevolist leanings bore a resemblance to that of a pietist, with reason replacing conscience as the agency of control.

Benevolism was synonymous with a high degree of ethical abstraction; but in cases of application, such as the trustees' plan for Georgia, it is evident that the benevolists retained an uncertainty about the favorable disposition of the self. Despite their presumption of a harmony between self and society, they wanted the former to be autonomous yet regulated in the interests of the latter. Most of the philosophers of benevolist ethics were reluctant to show how benevolism operated in society itself, yet in practice benevolism was a markedly interventionary movement. This ambivalence of reliance and caution regarding the self is evident in the thought of Adam Smith, the benevolist philosopher who was most concrete

[8]Edmund Burke, *A Philosophical Enquiry into the Origin of Our Ideas of the Sublime and Beautiful*, ed. J. T. Boulton (New York, 1958), p. xxxix; Oliver Wendell Elsbree, "Samuel Hopkins and His Doctrine of Benevolence," *New England Quarterly*, 8 (1935): 540–41; Anthony Ashley Cooper, "An Inquiry concerning Virtue and Merit," *Characteristics of Men, Manners, Opinions, Times*, 6th ed., rev. (London, 1737–38), pp. 80, 58, 79; Agnes Marie Sibley, *Alexander Pope's Prestige in America, 1725–1835* (New York, 1949), pp. 26–38, 49; C. A. Moore, "Shaftesbury and the Ethical Poets in England, 1700–1760," *Publications of the Modern Language Association*, 31 (1916): 302–7; Alexander Pope, *Epistles to Several Persons (Moral Essays)*, ed. F. W. Bateson (New Haven, 1951), pp. xxxix, xl; *idem, An Essay on Man*, ed. Maynard Mack (New Haven, 1951), pp. xxvi–xli.

in his ethical references. He simultaneously endowed acquisitiveness with positive social functions for the creation and distribution of wealth and worried that in their drive for others' recognition men lost their own self-respect. Like the pietists, Smith identified happiness with the tranquility of restrained wants.

Power and riches appear then [when a man considers his real happiness] to be, what they are, enormous and operose machines, contrived to produce a few trifling conveniences to the body. . . . They keep off the summer shower, not the winter storm, but leave him always as much, and sometimes more exposed than before, to anxiety, to fear, and to sorrow; to diseases, to danger, and to death. . . . But we rarely view it in this abstract and philosophical light. . . . And it is well that nature imposes upon us in this manner. It is this deception which rouses and keeps in continual motion the industry of mankind.[9]

Smith's social analysis amounted to a highly tempered version of Mandeville's cynicism combined with a dilute, nearly inexplicit, advocacy of rational self-fulfillment. His thought was a lineal descendant of benevolism, but it also showed how that theory could resolve into a benign view of the relationship of the self to society; pessimism about the self could be mitigated by optimism about the result of its interaction with others.

Seen in this intellectual context of concern for the integrity of the self, the economic restrictions placed on the Georgia settlers had social as well as commercial significance. The trustees sought to prevent the isolation of man as an economic being;[10] they regarded the economic organization of the Georgia settlers as necessary for the protection of their virtue against expressions of their material self-interest. In part, the supporters of the Georgia project conceived of the new colony as a practical refutation of Mandeville's ethics and social analysis. Georgia would demonstrate that men were capable of virtue and that the results of its exercise were socially beneficial. To accomplish this purpose, strict limitations would be placed on commercial and economic expressions of men's self-interest. A market in land would be virtually prohibited, and a market in labor discouraged. The only commercial relations would be established in overseas trade; the Georgia Company would exercise a monopoly of domestic commerce. Undesirable institutions associated with the commercial development of the other colonies, such as slavery and lawyers, would be prohibited. The chief form of group participation would be military service, which was required

[9]Adam Smith, "The Theory of Moral Sentiments," *The Works of Adam Smith*, 5 vols. (London, 1811-12), 1: 312-19; M. L. Myers, "Philosophical Anticipations of Laissez-Faire," *History of Political Economy*, 4 (1972): 163-75. See also Ralph Anspach, "The Implications of the Theory of Moral Sentiments for Adam Smith's Economic Thought," *ibid.*, pp. 176-206; cf. William D. Grampp, "Adam Smith and the Economic Man," *Journal of Political Economy*, 56 (1948): 315-36.

[10]Karl Polanyi, *The Great Transformation*, Beacon ed. (Boston, 1965), examines the development in the late eighteenth century of the idea that men are economic rather than social beings.

of all adult male inhabitants. (These views were, of course, partly an expression of the social position of the trustees, most of whom were of considerable prominence, especially in the church and in politics; the trustees were quite deliberately prescribing behavior for their social inferiors. But in making these prescriptions they were projecting onto their subordinates concerns which they had about themselves as well, for they as carefully regulated their own self-interest in the Georgia Company as that of the actual colonists.)

The story of the Georgia project as one of the great philanthropic enterprises of Augustan England has been treated in numerous accounts.[11] These histories of Georgia may differ slightly with one another in the amount of stress placed on each element, but they generally agree that three types of motivation were behind the creation of the colony—strategic, commercial, and philanthropic. Less familiar is the social vision which gave a moral coherence to the way in which military, commercial, and philanthropic elements of the project were discussed. The Georgia project represented a critical examination of social conditions in Britain and America and drew on widely current notions about the characteristics of a good society and of proper behavior, especially work, in such a society. It should be noted parenthetically that, while the trustees' primary concern lay with the social problems of England, they were well aware that the same conditions were present in the American colonies in an incipient form, and that hence any reform efforts would require more care than simple transmigration of the Atlantic.

The pamphlets in which the trustees and those who were sympathetic to their aims discussed the new colony were unabashedly polemical and rhetorically shrewd; they spoke to those concerns, aspirations, and discontents which the authors thought would produce a positive response to the Georgia project. The aptness of their appeal was demonstrated by the support it won; numerous subscriptions, much bad poetry, sympathetic sermons, and parliamentary grants all assisted and encouraged the trustees with their plan.[12] The trustees' rhetorical enterprise was an extraordinary

[11] For a discussion of eighteenth-century English philanthropy as a mixture of pious, benevolent, and utilitarian motives, see David Owen, *English Philanthropy, 1660-1960* (Cambridge, Mass., 1964), pp. 11-15. On the history of the Georgia project, see E. Merton Coulter, *A Short History of Georgia* (Chapel Hill, 1933); Albert B. Saye, *New Viewpoints in Georgia History* (Athens, Ga., 1943); Trevor Richard Reese, *Colonial Georgia: A Study in British Imperial Policy in the Eighteenth Century* (Athens, Ga., 1963); Amos A. Ettinger, *James Edward Oglethorpe, Imperial Idealist* (Oxford, 1936); and W. W. Abbot, *The Royal Governors of Georgia, 1754-75* (Chapel Hill, 1959).

[12] On the popular appeal of the Georgia project, see Saye, *New Viewpoints*, pp. 13-14, 37-39; Ettinger, *Oglethorpe*, chaps. 4-5; Coulter, *Short History*, pp. 20-22. Favorable public opinion of the project was essential for the trustees' success in obtaining parliamentary grants for the colony: though forty-four of the seventy trustees were members of Parliament, their ability to secure these grants depended less on their power as a bloc than on the popularity of the Georgia project with the political nation. The government provided 90 percent of Georgia's financial support while it was a private colony; the total grant was £136,000,

success, considering Parliament's reluctance to spend money on the colonies and a widespread suspicion of projects and projectors generally in the aftermath of the South Sea Bubble. That the colony itself was a failure does not render the values behind it any the less significant for being impractical. On the contrary, Georgia demonstrates some of the functions of utopian fantasies in societies that undergo rapid and ill-understood social change—namely, to provide a critical understanding of the situation and to hold out the possibility of a re-establishment of self-esteem. What makes Georgia especially interesting is the actual attempt to translate such a hypothetical alternative into a reality.

The founders of Georgia intended the new colony to be a concrete expression of the prevailing work ethic. They combined respect for productive labor with an anxiety about its personal and social consequences: the individual could be corrupted by excessive consumption, and society could be fragmented if commercial relations became the basic ones among men. The ethic was marked by an obsessive distrust of unrestrained selfishness and an affirmation of community obligations. Thus a bias against domestic commercial relations could be combined with mercantilist standards of economic utility because members of the community could express their rationality in productive work while having their acquisitive urges channeled to meet the crucial needs of society as a whole. The appeal of the project for men's imaginations lay in the opportunity it presented to experiment with reforms that were desired for England as well as the colonies, but that were also recognized as difficult or impossible to implement in England. As Daniel Boorstin has written, the trustees "were less interested in what was possible in America than in what had been impossible in Europe."[13]

Because of the failure of the initial philanthropic plan, historians have usually assumed that the trustees' purposes were unrealistic and that the real significance of the Georgia experience lay in its demonstration that the prescriptive, closed system of European values was incompatible with the openness and individualism that characterized American behavior and values. It may be worthwhile, however, to determine just what these English values were and why men held them, especially because—as will be shown in the following chapters—Americans espoused the same values. In America, as in England, these patently impractical values were less signifi-

---

which was greater than the support given to any other colony for nonmilitary uses. The trustees were too "heterogenous to make possible the existence of a bloc of Georgia votes, unless loyalty to Georgia came before loyalty of party." Arthur A. Luce, *The Life of George Berkeley, Bishop of Cloyne* (New York, 1949), pp. 103, 138; Richard S. Dunn. "The Trustees of Georgia and the House of Commons, 1732-1752," *William and Mary Quarterly*, 3rd ser., 11 (1954); 551-65.

[13]Boorstin has contrasted "security and dependence," which be believes were the most valued features of eighteenth-century English society, with "the flavor of American life [which] was compounded of risk, spontaneity, independence. initiative. drift, mobility and opportunity." *The Americans: The Colonial Experience* (New York, 1958), p. 84.

cant as guides to behavior than as terms for understanding social changes for which it was difficult to find intellectual and psychological accommodation. These attitudes toward work could serve the same function in the New World as in England: to represent men's yearning for an ideal social order that was an alternative to the one in which they found themselves.

In justifying their philanthropy, the supporters of the Georgia project indicated what they believed to be the proper motivation for all work—namely, a desire to harmonize the pursuit of self-interest with the public good. The trustees allowed themselves no economic interest in the Georgia Company; they contrasted themselves and their "diffusive Spirit of Benevolence" with the founders of other colonies, whose interests were simply those of personal gain. For the Georgia trustees, most of whom found themselves on the fringes of power, the Georgia Company represented a chance to affirm their self-evaluation as exceptions to the prevailing corruption in English politics and society. In a pamphlet which may have been written by James Oglethorpe himself, the trustees were praised in a fashion which revealed both their moral arrogance and their concern that they too might succumb to temptation and neglect their duties in favor of self-indulgence. "[The Trustees] have, for the benefit of mankind, given up that ease and indolence to which they were entitled by their fortunes and the too prevalent custom of their native country. They, in some degree, imitate their Redeemer in sympathizing with the miserable, and in laboring to relieve them." One purpose of the Georgia project was to demonstrate that "charity and humanity" could still find expression in a society where irrational selfishness reigned.[14] In view of the many regulations needed to ensure the Georgians' virtue (and their own), however, it was clear that the trustees had little faith in men's capacity for public-spirited self-restraint. In acting as reformers the trustees sought to give witness to their own virtue, but their self-distrust was evident in their prescriptions for others. Devotion to the public interest was one means to allay this anxiety.

In explaining the nature and function of benevolence in their sermons, the preachers to the Georgia trustees sought to demonstrate that for reasons of both necessity and morality man was a social creature. Concern about selfishness was the negative component of an affirmation of, and a longing for, community solidarity, and thus in economic matters constituted an ethical qualification to what would otherwise have been the strictly economic ethic of "possessive individualism." For example, one sermon contains what appears to be a remarkably forthright justification of such individualism. "Every man considered in his *natural Capacity* has certain Powers distinct from the rest of his Fellow Creatures, which

[14][James Edward Oglethorpe?], "A New and Accurate Account of the Provinces of South Carolina and Georgia" [1733], *Collections of the Georgia Historical Society*, 1 (1890): 45. The trustees were quite taken with their own saintliness, to say the least; one preacher said that their effort to provide employment for the poor was "a God-like Employment." James King, *A Sermon Preached before the Honourable Trustees* . . . (London, 1743), 10.

he should use for the Advancement and Happiness of himself: There is an unalterable Property derived from the Labour of his own Hands, which, without Consent, no other Man has a Right to enjoy, much less to violate." But the minister went on to qualify this decidedly Lockean position on property rights with the assertion that it would be unthinkable for God to give such powers, "or this Thirst after Happiness, unless there were Opportunities also of using them *properly*." And to use them properly meant to act in conformity with the public good; there was, said the minister, "an obligation, antecedent to all human Laws, of extending these natural Powers for the Protection and Benefit of each other."[15]

Of course, the trustees took their own society to be something quite different from a realm of cooperation and benevolence. Their perception of England's social ills resembled the social criticism which Isaac Kramnick has identified with Henry St. John, first viscount Bolingbroke, and his circle of opposition polemicists. The complaints of these writers derived in part from political frustration, and they attributed their problems to economic changes which were undermining their social pre-eminence. For them the financial revolution of the early eighteenth century had been a disaster. Aristocrats, lesser gentry, and small traders found themselves threatened by a new economic order which was "inscrutable and dangerous." They lamented the changes whereby money had become the basis of social relations, replacing public virtue, honor, family, and friendship.

Though the occasion for their worries was economic change, the terms in which Bolingbroke and his associates expressed these social anxieties and made their political appeal were moral rather than strictly economic. They saw the selfishness of man as the chief social danger, and this trait appeared to have freest rein in commercial life; they associated vice with selfishness, selfishness with luxury, and considered luxury to be the natural outcome of trade. In its negative references, its criticism of selfishness, luxury, and the evils of life in a market economy, this variety of social thought was most indicative of attitudes toward work. Political analysis by the Commonwealth men, the radicals in English politics, shared much of this pessimistic outlook on society with that of the Tories of Bolingbroke's circle; the influence of their republicanism was evident in the land policy for Georgia, which sought to preserve the hardy independence of an armed citizenry by providing land for every household and by preventing domestic ties of economic dependence. But their view of external commerce was less denunciatory; they believed that in its early stages trade could increase the power of a nation. The moral thrust of both styles of social criticism was to encourage men to desire a return to a mythical, simpler past in

[15]Bruce, *The Happiness of Man*, p. 18. John M. Dunn has argued that even Locke viewed property as a type of social obligation; see *The Political Thought of John Locke: An Historical Account of the Argument of the "Two Treatises of Government"* (London, 1969), pp. 196, 218, 248; cf. C. B. McPherson, *The Political Theory of Possessive Individualism* (New York, 1962).

which men worked for the good of the community. These "primitivist" notions had wide currency in eighteenth-century England, and the opposition writers were simply the most persistent proponents of the view.[16]

Because it was based on an ethics of repudiation and was colored by historical pessimism, this social analysis was not adaptable to the reform of existing conditions in England. Alternatives to the present situation had to be located externally and often involved a revival of a supposed Golden Age. Such a connection between efforts at reform through colonization and the ideas of writers who were sympathetic to Bolingbroke can be traced through the career and writings of George Berkeley during the 1720s. While in England, Berkeley became an intimate of the circle, meeting frequently with Swift, Arbuthnot, Steele, Gay, and Pope (but not with Bolingbroke himself, who may have seemed too dangerously Tory for the moderate Berkeley). For them as well as for Berkeley, the South Sea Bubble epitomized all that was wrong with English society and had a profoundly disillusioning effect. The Bubble, Berkeley thought, was a crucial example of the way in which English society tolerated the sacrifice of public interests to private interests, and he responded to the situation with "An Essay towards Preventing the Ruin of Great Britain." He attributed this ruin to England's commercial development, which had fostered luxury and allowed financial ingenuity to become a substitute for honest work.[17]

The case of Berkeley demonstrates that even the most acute contributors to Anglo-American social thought were unable to come to terms with prosperity, an inability which derived in large part from a reluctance to accept, and a lack of understanding for, the social changes that were taking place. The source of this resistance may have been a traditional fear of the consequences of the economic activities of individuals. The question for Berkeley which loomed out of his perception of England's disordered social condition pointed to the essential issue of the individual's relationship with society at large. What if it were true not only that England's prosperity *depended* on the liberation of self-interest, on extravagance, competition, exploitation, and the decline of traditional virtues (an analysis to which Berkeley subscribed and which was the basis for his predictions of ruin for an ostensibly prosperous Britain), but also that this prosperity would *con-*

---

[16]Isaac Kramnick, *Bolingbroke and His Circle: The Politics of Nostalgia in the Age of Walpole* (Cambridge, Mass., 1968), pp. 39, 246-47; Lois Whitney, *Primitivism and the Idea of Progress in English Popular Literature of the Eighteenth Century* (Baltimore, 1934), p. 50; Daniel Waley, "The Primitivist Element in Machiavelli's Thought," *Journal of the History of Ideas*, 31 (1970): 95; Oscar Handlin and Mary Handlin, "James Burgh and American Revolutionary Theory," *Proceedings of the Massachusetts Historical Society*, 73 (1963): 46; Alan Dugald McKillop, "The Background of Thomson's 'Liberty,' " *Rice Institute Pamphlet*, 38, no. 2 (1951): 7; Raymond D. Havens, "Primitivism and the Idea of Progress in Thomson," *Studies in Philology*, 29 (1932): 45-48.

[17]George Berkeley, "An Essay towards Preventing the Ruin of Great Britain," *The Works of George Berkeley, Bishop of Cloyne*, ed. A. A. Luce and T. E. Jessop, 9 vols. (Toronto, 1948-57), 6: 71, 74-75, 77, 85. Kramnick discusses this pamphlet and its relevance to the Bubble, but he does not identify it as Berkeley's; *Bolingbroke*, pp. 69-70.

tinue to increase indefinitely and hence that progress rather than decline was the pattern for the history of civilization, and confidence rather than distrust was the appropriate attitude toward the unrestrained self. (Such an anti-Christian assertion of the sufficiency of the world had of course been made by Mandeville, and it was Berkeley who composed the most effective denunciation of the *Fable of the Bees* in Augustan literature, in the second dialogue of *Alciphron*, which he wrote at Newport while awaiting the outcome of his Bermuda project.)

Berkeley could not accept developments in his own society and hoped instead for a revival overseas of the Golden Age. In his only serious poetic effort and the most famous of his words, he wrote:

Westward the Course of Empire takes its Way;
The First four Acts already past,
The fifth shall close the Drama with the Day;
Time's noblest Offspring is the last.

Berkeley's own contribution to this progeny would be rather modest; he planned to establish a school for missionaries at Bermuda with recruits drawn from among the American Indians and colonists. For Berkeley, Bermuda was a model of the reformed society envisaged for America, and as such represented a social alternative to the evils of England and America. Bermuda had ample natural produce but little trade, and the Bermudans themselves were noted for their "innocence and Simplicity of Manners." Berkeley ascribed to Bermuda the same social advantages which would later be identified with Georgia; in each case the society was idealized because of the simplicity of its economy, its lack of commerce, and the contentment of its inhabitants.[18] When Berkeley's plans failed to materialize, it seemed only natural to his supporters that they transfer their interest to the Georgia project.[19]

As was the case with Berkeley and Bermuda, the stimulus for the Georgia project came from the trustees' awareness of social disorder in England. This perception is evident in a poem about Georgia which played on English primitivist anxieties in order to show that the country's very prosperity and commercial development were signs of impending decline:

Wealth without End, from such Exploits as These,
Crown'd our large Commerce, and extended Sway,
And hence, dissolv'd in soft luxurious Ease,
Our ancient Virtue vanish'd soon away.

[18]"Verses by the Author on the Prospect of Planting Arts and Learning in America" and "A Proposal for the Better Supplying of Churches in Our Foreign Plantations, and for Converting the Savage Americans to Christianity," *Works of George Berkeley*, 6: 373 and 7: 345, 349, 352; R. C. Cochrane, "Bishop Berkeley and the Progress of the Arts and Learning: Notes on a Literary Convention," *Huntington Library Quarterly*, 17 (1954): 229–49.

[19]Percival to Berkeley, 23 December 1730; and Oglethorpe to Berkeley, May 1731, *Berkeley and Percival: The Correspondence of George Berkeley . . . and Sir John Percival . . .* , ed. Benjamin Rand (Cambridge, 1914), pp. 270, 275–76, 283–84.

The state of English economic and social life indicated a diminution of the inhabitants' virtue. Too many people in England were "forced to seek a livelihood from vice and wickedness." London was "the Refuge and Asylum of luxurious Vices," and the people had become less industrious. One pamphleteer asked his readers to "consider the crowds employed in the retail trade, and mechanicks, starving and eating up one another: the swarms of servants retreating into ale-houses . . . to the nusance and debauchery of every neighbourhood." Faced with such social disorder, advocates of the Georgia project drew on classical history for examples of states which had encouraged the orderliness and virtue of their societies through the establishment of colonies. The Romans, it was pointed out, had used colonies to achieve both economic and moral improvements: "They consider'd such Expedients as these, as *necessary* to *improve* their *Revenues*, and *enrich* their *Government*, to keep a Spirit of *Industry* among the People, and to *extirpate all* such *Vices* as were *dangerous* to the Common-wealth; *such* as *Theft, Rapine, Effeminacy, Idleness, Luxury*, and the *like*." The Georgia project had the same goals; a "new kingdom" would be created there "out of the refuse of our own people."[20]

As these remarks about unemployment indicated, the need to use resources efficiently had moral as well as economic connotations. The promotion of the Georgia project revealed the peculiar ambivalence toward commerce which was common in the Augustan period. On the one hand it was inevitably the agent of corruption because the accumulation of wealth enabled people to indulge their irrationality in luxury. But in its early stages commerce was an expression of rationality and a criterion of civilization. There were natural as well as social forms of luxury; one involved the waste characteristic of underdevelopment, the other that of overdevelopment. Thus the vacancy of Georgia was "a great reproach to the industry and wisdom of men, who were appointed to cultivate the earth." Georgia, one poet asserted, was

A wide waste Land, beneath the Southern Skies!
Where kindley Suns for Ages roll'd in vain,
Nor e'er the Vintage saw, or ripining Grain;
Where all things into wild Luxuriance ran,
And burden'd Nature asked the Aid of Man.[21]

The juxtaposition of the unused potential of Georgia and the idleness prevalent in an overdeveloped England showed the imperative need to put men's industry to fuller use.

Unemployment offended the mercantilist sensibilities of the directors of the Georgia project; they felt a need to be useful themselves and to enable

---

[20][Samuel Wesley], *Georgia: A Poem* . . . (London, 1736), p. 14; George Watts, *A Sermon Preached before the Trustees* . . . (London, 1736), p. 14; Bruce, *The Happiness of Man*, p. 28; Ridley, *A Sermon*, pp. 5, 11; Robert Warren, *Industry and Diligence in Our Callings Earnestly Recommended* . . . (London, 1737), p. 11.

[21]Watts, *A Sermon*, pp. 7, 23; [Wesley], *Georgia*, p. 6.

others to enjoy productive work. "Any poor," wrote Benjamin Martyn, secretary of the trustees, "must lie a dead weight on the public, and as every wise government, like the bees, should not suffer any drones in the state, these poor should be situated in such places, where they might be easy themselves, and useful to the commonwealth." The trustees disputed the notion that population was a simple measure of a nation's wealth, an idea they attributed to a "misapplication of Sir William Petty's Political Arithmetic, and Sir William Temple's Observations on the united Netherlands."[22] The trustees were particularly interested in a special type of unemployment; they sought to find work for relations of the gentry and for tradesmen who lacked employment because of circumstances which characterized a market economy, such as periodic unemployment, overproduction, a surplus of unskilled and clerical workers, speculation and trade depression.

The founders of Georgia were struck by the uncertainty and risk in making a living in such a highly developed market economy as England's. The prosperity of England had apparently encouraged too many people to participate in the country's commercial life. More people were hoping to work as middlemen, public officials, shopkeepers, and tradesmen than could possibly earn livings in these occupations. One writer urged potential contributors to the Georgia project to consider "the multitude of unfortunate people in the kingdom of reputable families, and of liberal or at least easy education: some undone by accidents in commerce, some by stocks and bubbles. . . . What various misfortunes may reduce the rich, the industrious, to the danger of a prison, to a moral certainty to starving!" This pamphleteer did not anticipate that gentlemanly disdain for manual labor would be very strong; in a society where commercial life penetrated to all levels, anyone could be forced by unfortunate circumstances to take whatever work he could get. A serious problem for these tenuous members of the middle class was that they were unsuited and untrained for most work. The parasitic occupations that they were likely to try, such as keeping public houses, were already overcrowded. Only in Georgia, with its great fertility and abundance of free land, could "the better sort of the indigent" prosper.[23]

The trustees' rhetoric was ostensibly aimed at sympathy for the poor, but, in fact, by the "poor" they chiefly meant those who had sought success in the competitive market economy of England and had failed. This recruitment scheme for Georgia demonstrates the limitations of the trustees' philanthropy, which hinged on their repudiation of English social conditions and was thus shaped by just that framework of eighteenth-century commercial life which they sought to reform. Because of their preoccupa-

[22][Benjamin Martyn], "Reasons for Establishing the Colony of Georgia, with Regard to the Trade of Great Britain" [1733], *Collections of the Georgia Historical Society*, 1 (1890): 204; [Oglethorpe?], "A New and Accurate Account," p. 59.
[23][Oglethorpe?], "A New and Accurate Account," pp. 56–58.

tion with the problems of work in commercial society, the trustees were unable to visualize any radical reorientation for the organization of work; instead, they could resort to reform only through simplification of existing arrangements and through externally imposed controls on the expression of self-interest. They sought to restore men's autonomy, but their chief means for doing so was to isolate them on small farms.

Part of the attractiveness of Georgia lay in the possibility to re-establish there a proper balance between productive and commercial functions, a balance which had been upset in England as its trade expanded. The trustees' goal was an economic life simplified in terms of its commercial relations, the variety of its roles; and the range of its rewards. The idealized version of the colony described a society in which people who were largely self-sufficient could also contribute to the wealth of the mother country by supplying her with cheap materials; but, within Georgia, commercial relations would be remarkably absent. A model of the economic and social promise of the new colony is evident in a pamphlet which urged the "man of benevolence" to

think himself in a visit to Georgia. Let him see those, who are now a prey to all the calamities of want . . . living under a sober and orderly government, settled in towns, which are arising at distances along navigable rivers . . . the whole face of the country changed by agriculture, and plenty in every part of it. Let him see the people all in employment of various kinds, women and children feeding and nursing the silk worms, winding off the silk, or gathering the olives; the men ploughing and planting their lands, tending their cattle, or felling the forest.[24]

Besides its anticommercial implications, the most noticeable feature of this idealized vision of Georgia was its faith in the sufficiency of labor outside a commercial context. It was assumed that if impoverished men had an opportunity to work they could support themselves and their families in a decent prosperity. There was no hint that manual labor was demeaning; on the contrary, the virtue of a man who worked his own farm was unquestioned.

The trustees projected upon Georgia their vision of a properly oriented society, a vision which was based on a negative image of the behavior and institutions they disapproved of in English and colonial society. Like Berkeley with Bermuda, they believed that the Georgia project was an effort "in a literal Sense to begin the World again." They sought to pre-

---

[24][Martyn], "Reasons for Establishing the Colony of Georgia," p. 231. A. W. Coats has shown that there was strong criticism in England at this time of the charity school movement because it failed to enable the poor to lead productive lives. This criticism corresponded to a sympathetic attitude toward the poor and a desire to raise their standard of living; though socially conservative, this attitude represented a change from previous, harsher views that the amelioration of a laborer's lot only resulted in his diminished industry. "Changing Attitudes to Labour in the Mid-Eighteenth Century," *Economic History Review*, 2nd ser., 11 (1958): 35–51; *idem*, "Economic Thought and Poor Law Policy in the Eighteenth Century," *ibid.*, 13 (1960): 39–51.

vent in Georgia a repetition of the history of the other American colonies, "where Worldly Interest overruled their Obligations to Duty, and the sacred Precepts of Christianity give Way to some imagin'd Conveniences of Trade." The restrictions on commerce, combined with their "industry and contentment," would permit the Georgians to prosper without submitting themselves to unchecked avarice. The settlers would engage in honest toil like "the free-born *Romans*," and the agrarian law would ensure that they "enjoy[ed] themselves, in a virtuous frugality." The prospective inhabitants were fortunate that a precise balance of opportunity and challenge would enable them to gain a "comfortable subsistence" without "the Pressures of Poverty and the Surfeits of Abundance."[25]

In order to conduct their social experiment the trustees needed to have authority over the structure and management of the colony, for they recognized that social disorder in the American colonies was at least as great as that in England. They saw human selfishness, in the form of an endless acquisitive urge, as the chief obstacle in the way of their success. They therefore carefully contrived institutions which would limit its expression because they believed that covetousness was the cause of the social failure of the other colonies, just as it had been in England. The elaborateness and precision of their scheme revealed on the one hand the clarity of their notion of what a proper society was—or rather what it was not, because most of the institutions were restrictive rather than attractive—and on the other hand their conviction that clear restraints on men's instinctual nature were needed if the envisaged society were to succeed. The chief restrictions involved the prohibition of slavery, the limitation of the inheritance of land to male heirs, the prohibition of the sale of land, and the limitation of individual landholdings to 500 acres. The aim of these regulations was a society in which men's work met approved ethical, social, and economic standards. The colony was to consist of small, owner-worked farms; there was to be no servant class. The goal was a simple and stable society made up of contented citizens. The planners of Georgia assumed that among the destitute were many industrious men who were poor simply because of misfortune; they also assumed that these men would find sufficient happiness in being their own masters to be willing to remain in the roles prescribed for them by the trustees. The trustees' aim was to put the immigrants "in a Christian, moral, and industrious way of life, and [to instruct] them how to labour to gain a comfortable subsistence for themselves and [their] families."[26]

[25] John Burton, *The Duty and Reward of Propagating Principles of Religion and Virtue . . .* (London, 1733), pp. 25, 30; Philip Bearcroft, *A Sermon Preached before the Honourable Trustees . . .* (London, 1738), p. 8; William Best, *The Merit and Reward of a Good Intention* (London, 1742), p. 22; Samuel Smith, *A Sermon Preach'd before the Trustees . . .* (London, 1733), p. 23.
[26] John W. Reps, "Town Planning in Colonial Georgia," *Town Planning Review*, 30 (1960): 273–85; Vernon W. Crane, "The Philanthropists and the Genesis of Georgia," *American His-*

For all their sublime confidence in the possibility of individual fulfillment, the trustees displayed the pessimism of philanthropy for society at
large by assuming community and commerce to be incompatible. Georgia
was to be a monument to cooperation and charity. In order to preserve
these values, it was necessary to prevent certain practices which were typical of market activity, such as free pricing and competition. In an effort
to restrict domestic trade, the trustees set up a wholesale warehouse, and
they sought to limit consumption through the establishment of several retail stores with regulated prices. In addition to the effort to maintain a
company monopoly over domestic commerce, the trustees also empowered
their agents in the colony to limit competition among tradesmen; in several
cases forges were pulled down and the shops of iron merchants were closed
because there were already people in the colony who performed these
functions. An early report about Savannah from the company's commis-
sioner described the results of these regulations in terms based more on
desire than on fact: "The Blessing of God seems to have gone along with
this Undertaking; for here we see industry honoured, and Justice strictly
executed, and Luxury and Idleness banished from this happy place, where
Plenty and Brotherly Love seem to make their Abode."[27]

Though the Georgia publicists frequently cited brotherly love and a
sense of community as merits of the new colony, the only workable index
of these characteristics was the absence of domestic commercial life. Aside
from the militia—which was the locus of public virtue—there were few explicit discussions of the consequences of community membership. As
J. G. A. Pocock has shown in his investigations of the "neo-Harrington-
ian" element in Anglo-American political thought, the desire to foster
public spirit, to encourage individual identification with the community,
and to recover a lost shared experience required that man be autonomous
in the sense of being free of dependence on the will of others.[28] In the right
conditions individualism and devotion to community were complementary.
Georgia was intended to be just such a community of autonomous men,
and the Harringtonian and Machiavellian element in the Georgia plan
was clearly evident in the land policy, which facilitated individual ownership of land in order to enhance the military virtues of the inhabitants and

---

torical Review, 27 (1921): 63–69; Geraldine Merony, "The London Entrepôt Merchants
and the Georgia Colony," William and Mary Quarterly, 3rd ser., 25 (1968): 230–44; Oglethorpe to Berkeley, May 1731, Berkeley and Percival, p. 277.

[27] Jonathan Brownfield to Trustees, 6 March 1736, The Colonial Records of the State of
Georgia, ed. Allen D. Chandler, 26 vols. (Atlanta, 1904–16), 21: 139; [Thomas Stephens],
"A Brief Account of the Causes That Have Retarded the Progress of the Colony of Georgia
in America" [1743], Collections of the Georgia Historical Society, 2 (1892): 103, 130; "An
Extract of the Journals of Mr. Commissary Von Reck . . . and of the Reverend Mr. Bolzius . . ."
[1734], Tracts and Other Papers, Relating Principally to the Origin, Settlement. and Progress
of the Colonies in North America . . . , 4 vols. (Washington, D.C., 1836–47), 4: 10.

[28] J. G. A. Pocock, "Machiavelli, Harrington, and English Political Ideologies in the
Eighteenth Century," William and Mary Quarterly, 3rd ser., 22 (1965): 549–83; idem, "Civic
Humanism and Its Role in Anglo-American Thought," Il Pensiero Politico, 1 (1968): 172–89.

which also imposed an agrarian law in the form of limits on total holdings, sale, and inheritance. But the consequence of this policy in Georgia was a perversion of neo-Harringtonianism. In its usual guise this doctrine made the health of the polity dependent on the social structure, but in the case of Georgia the social values of agrarian republicanism became ends in themselves, and the trustees' lack of confidence in the colonists resulted in a complete absence of representative institutions in the model society.

Yet the supporters of the project saw their expectations confirmed by the happiness of the settlers, "who meant to abide in the Colony, and not to run away [and who] were well contented without the permission to sell their property." In particular, the Salzburghers, who were displaced Austrian Protestant peasants, were an idealization of the desired Georgia settlers; they worked on independent farms without servants, yet they cooperated in pursuit of their mutual interests. With their ability to "live together in the utmost Harmony and Happiness," the Salzburghers were supposedly "an amiable Copy of the first Ages of the World."[29]

Americans sometimes shared this fantasy about the felicity of the new colony. In South Carolina, the colony taken by the Georgia trustees as the prime example of what a colony ought not be because it depended on exploitation within the community and thrived on extravagant display and consumption, there were several expressions of admiration for Oglethorpe and his project. Unlike South Carolina, Georgia was the result of careful planning, philanthropy, and parliamentary approval, so it was believed that the work of people there could only be in the public interest. William Byrd of Westover was impressed by the sound attitudes toward work found in Georgia, which he attributed to the absence of slavery there. Slaves, he wrote in a letter to Egmont, "blow up the pride and ruin the industry of our white people, who seeing a rank of poor creatures below them detest work for fear it should make them look like slaves."[30]

The crucial regulation for the restraint of selfishness, as Byrd understood, was the prohibition of slavery. Slavery involved all the social dangers which the Georgia project sought to avoid—a disrespect for manual labor, a concentration of wealth in a few hands, an economic dependence of some men on others, and of course a fundamental commercialization of social relations. The introduction of slavery would result not only in the corruption of the colonists and a deviation from the blueprint for Georgia's society but also in the repudiation of the basic principle of the colony, that independent men could gain a decent living by their own labor. Besides their distaste for doing the same work as Negroes, the small farmers would

[29]Egmont's comment in Patrick Tailfer et al., A True and Historical Narrative of the Colony of Georgia . . . with Comments by the Earl of Egmont [1741], ed. Clarence L. Ver Steeg (Athens, Ga., 1960), p. 104; Jonathan Martin Bolzius to Harman Verelst, 14 March 1739, Colonial Records of Georgia, vol. 22, pt. 2, pp. 120-21; Thomas Francklin, A Sermon Preached before the Honourable Trustees . . . (London, 1750), p. 11.

[30]South Carolina Gazette (Charleston), 24 March 1733 and 21 December 1734; William Byrd to Lord Egmont, 12 July 1736, American Historical Review, 1 (1895-96): 88-90.

cease to work because their envy of rich planters would make them want to become masters themselves; social status would come to be measured by a man's ability to get others to work for him. The prohibition of slavery was the most important of the various measures designed to control the function of market mechanisms, in this case to protect the laborers of the colony from competition. Georgia had been founded in order to relieve the excess of people involved in commercial life; the Georgia plan sought to demonstrate that, once in Georgia, those who had previously been unemployed could be happy doing manual labor on a farm. The result of competition between whites and blacks for work could only be a social structure which the Georgia planners sought to avoid. "The colony would soon be too like its neighbours, void of white inhabitants, filled with blacks, and reduced to be the precarious property of a few, equally exposed to domestick treachery, and foreign invasion."[31]

Despite the trustees' precautions, the pressures of commercial life generally and the profit of slave labor specifically proved to be irresistable. Experience testified that the trustees had overestimated the desire of the colonists for the moral benefits which Georgia offered. The colonists' aspirations for wealth and the status to be attained by spending, combined with commercial imperatives for a profitable staple crop, prevented the success of the simple community of farmers planned for the new colony. Georgia's history as a philanthropic venture provides an example of the difficulty of applying an anticommercial and community-oriented attitude toward work as a policy for the guidance of actual institutions, a difficulty which stemmed from the reform's basis on the negation of existing ways of life. Such reform was inherently moral and hence personal in its orientation, rather than rely on the manipulation of institutions to redirect behavior, it expected transformations of character to bring about social change. The historical conditions against which the ethic was in part a reaction made it a difficult one to put into consistent practice. Many men had unlimited economic aspirations, and even those with more finite goals had to take part in market activities because the competition of other men and general economic uncertainty presented them with a simple choice between a constant striving for success or eventual ruin.

[31]"Journal of the Trustees for Establishing the Colony of Georgia in America," *Colonial Records of Georgia*, 1: 507; William Stevens to Benjamin Martyn, 1 December 1742, *ibid.*, 23: 446-47; John Dobell to Trustees, 30 November 1742, *ibid.*, 24: 435-36; Tailfer *et al.*, *True and Historical Narrative*, p. 113; Benjamin Martyn, "An Impartial Inquiry into the State and Utility of the Province of Georgia" [1741], *Collections of the Georgia Historical Society*, 1 (1890): 172; Francis Moore, "A Voyage to Georgia Begun in the Year 1735" [1744], *ibid.*, pp. 96-97; There was also a conviction among some of the supporters of the Georgia project that slavery was wrong, but apparently they thought that moral objections alone were not sufficient to justify its exclusion from the colony. "Let avarice defend it as it will, there is an honest Reluctance in humanity against buying and selling, and regarding those of our own species as our wealth and possessions." T. Rundle, *A Sermon Preached at St. George's Church . . . to Recommend the Charity for Establishing the New Colony of Georgia* (London, 1734), p. 13.

The criticism implicit in the social valuation of work persisted in England and America during the eighteenth century, but the definition of the fundamental problem as a moral one which encompassed the relationship of the self to society deflected analysis from the social locus to the shortcomings of individuals. The radical view would be a moral indifference (rather than a glorification of self-interest) which would substitute a psychological account of work and its meaning for an ethical one. First, however, men had to lose some of their fear of the social danger posed by the unrestrained individual and to gain some confidence that individual selfishness could be channeled in socially useful ways. Until well into the eighteenth century, mercantilist economic thought was the most likely place in which to find such tough-minded realism.

THE MERCANTILIST NOTION OF USEFULNESS: ISOLATION OF THE ECONOMIC IMPULSE

In order to develop his central paradox in *The Fable of the Bees*, Mandeville used an empirical, morally neutral definition of public benefits and contrasted it with an overly scrupulous definition of vice. Mandeville concerned himself with the economic results and not the morality of men's actions, and he came to the conclusion that selfishness was both unavoidable and the basis of prosperity.[32] He was aware that his contemporaries admired commerce and desired the material benefits it conferred; they also subscribed to an empirical, utilitarian, and morally indifferent method for the evaluation of the economic consequences of men's behavior. This evaluation involved an isolation of the economic realm because it defined the desirability of actions by productive efficiency and measured them in monetary values. Indeed, by its nature as an analysis of the production and distribution of material welfare, economic thought denied itself the possibility of moral evaluation. The chief body of thought which incorporated these habits of mind was mercantilist economic theory. The intellectual radicalism of the mercantilists derived from this willingness to ignore perforce the habitual moralism that characterized most contemporary social criticism.

Most of the mercantilists were not theorists; their writings spoke to specific and partisan issues and their advocacy was grounded in facts and experience, not in general principles. Most had difficulty dealing with causal relations largely because they did not conceive of all economic behavior as having a uniform character and therefore as responding to the same laws. For example, there was a general inability to see the same process of exchange taking place in such apparently different contexts as marketing and production. Nonetheless, it has been persuasively argued by William Letwin that precisely because economic arguments corresponded

---

[32]Nathan Rosenberg, "Mandeville and Laissez-Faire," *Journal of the History of Ideas*, 24 (1963): 183–96.

to personal interests and special pleading it was necessary to find an impersonal form of argument in which to put them forth so that they would seem to be derived from indisputably true principles. "The needs of rhetoric brought forth the method of economic theory."[33]

British mercantilist writers of the seventeenth and eighteenth centuries treated the public good as a quantitative matter. By dealing exclusively with matters of commercial prosperity, they explicitly considered men's economic utility to be a measure of their worth to society. The moral thought of the period had also considered contributions to the public welfare in utilitarian terms, but it treated utility as a moral and social, as well as an economic, matter.[34] Thus mercantilist thought had a twofold importance for Anglo-American views on work: it supplied terms for the assessment of economic life and it had the intellectual potential to provide a perspective on work which was at variance with the moral tradition.

Throughout Europe from the sixteenth to the eighteenth century, an individual's social utility, defined in various ways but usually concerned at least in part with material prosperity, became a qualification for his membership in society. The insane, the idle, and all others who did not measure up to the rational standard of social utility in a particular society were either excluded from that society, confined within it, or coerced into becoming useful. This utility was an active principle: it was no longer sufficient for a gentleman to possess admirable qualities; he had to exercise them. Livelihoods generally came to be categorized as productive and unproductive in relation to their contributions to the wealth of society. A corollary of the mercantilist treatment of social roles was the belief that society and the actions of men in it had no fixed order but were instead susceptible to rational manipulation for desired ends. To determine how to achieve their version of order, mercantilist theorists undertook an empirical investigation of the elements of economic behavior.[35] The basic problem for these early political economists was individual productivity, and they sought to determine who was useful and who was not. (They were themselves very active in public affairs, though not necessarily in commerce; most of them had experience as members of trading companies or as administrative officials, and several of the most prominent were trained on

[33]William Letwin, *The Origins of Scientific Economics: English Economic Thought, 1660–1776* (London, 1963), pp. 43–49, 97. The term "mercantilist" is used generically here to refer to contributors to economic discussions before Adam Smith. The question of whether or not there was one comprehensive economic theory of "mercantilism" (and even more dubiously, whether there was one such policy in government) cannot be treated here, though it should be noted that historians on both sides of the question refer to much the same group of writers. The particular concern here is with the phenomenon of economic theory at this time.

[34]Leslie Stephen, *History of English Thought in the Eighteenth Century*, Harbinger Books ed., 2 vols. (New York, 1962), 2: 68–109.

[35]Michel Foucault, *Madness and Civilization: A History of Insanity in the Age of Reason*, trans. Richard Howard (New York, 1965), pp. 44–64; Elie Halévy, *The Growth of Philosophic Radicalism*, trans. Mary Morris (London, 1952), pp. 3–34.

the Continent as physicians. One thinks of the similar educational background of Mandeville.)

Charles Davenant, revenue officer and pamphleteer, typified some of the political economists' thinking on the usefulness of work. He employed the analogy of the body and the state, long familiar in political discourse, in a significantly new way. The analogy was usually a means to encourage both subordination and service appropriate to one's station.[36] For Davenant, however, the most important thing about a body was that it *used resources*, which needed to be properly distributed if the organism was to survive. The idle threatened the whole society because they consumed more goods than they produced. If they were to work, he asked, "to what pitch of Wealth and Greatness might we not be brought if one Limb were not suffer'd to draw away the Nourishment of the other: and if all the members of the Body Politick were render'd useful to it." Davenant had statistics to show that "the industry of not half the People maintains in some degree the other part." In order to improve conditions in such a poorly organized society, "it must be distinguished who by their Arts, Labour or Industry are increasing, and who by their Expense, Poverty, or Sloth, are decreasing the Kingdom's Wealth."[37]

Sir William Petty, medical student at Leyden, friend of Hobbes, and adviser to the Restoration Stuarts, was the foremost representative of this effort to measure the nation's wealth and the usefulness of its citizens in quantitative terms, and it is worthwhile to examine his analysis at length in order to learn the terms and the implications of the new conception of social roles. Petty's aim was to determine "the precise Truth in what condition *the common Interest* stands," and this interest was something amoral and measurable. He recognized the novelty of his approach. "The Method I take to do this is not yet very usual; for instead of using only comparative and superlative Words, and intellectual Arguments, I have taken the course (as a Specimen of the Political Arithmetic I have long aimed at) to express myself in Terms of Number, Weight, or Measure; to use only Arguments of Sense, and to consider only such Causes, as have visible Foundations in Nature." One of Petty's central arguments in the *Political Arithmetic* involved a proof that in England there existed a surplus of labor and potential employment sufficient to earn £2 million per year in excess of the present amount, which increase could be used for military purposes. To do so, he first calculated the "expense," or the lowest acceptable cost of living, taking the annual budget of a laborer as his index of individual consumption. Having determined the minimum income necessary for national subsistence, he then established its theoretical maximum. On the basis of trade statistics from Norwich, he thought that it was

[36]W. H. Greenleaf, *Order, Empiricism, and Politics: Two Traditions of English Political Thought, 1500–1700* (New York, 1964), chaps. 2, 12.

[37]Charles Davenant, *An Essay upon the Probable Methods of Making a People Gainers in the Balance of Trade . . .* (London, 1699), pp. 13, 53.

possible for this labor force to produce £10 worth of goods apiece, and thus provide a profit of £25 million over their basic expenses. Nothing like such a national profit existed, and so Petty sought to discover whether or not there was additional employment which was not being made available to English workers. There was, of course, and it was being lost to foreigners. In order to compute the amount lost in wages and profit, it was necessary to determine "[1] How much money is paid, by the King of England's Subjects, to Foreigners for Freights of Shipping. [2] How much the Hollanders gain by their Fishing Trade, practised upon our Seas. . . . [3] What the value is of all the Commodities Imported into, and spent in England; which might by diligence be produced, and Manufactured here."[38] The total amount lost, Petty computed, was £5 million. The accuracy of such calculations was less significant than the new attitudes toward work which they represented. The mercantilists themselves were not necessarily morally or socially insensitive men. On the contrary, aside from considerations about the power of England relative to other nations, they were most interested in the reduction of unemployment. But their intellectual method, the terms in which they treated social problems, was insensitive to moral considerations and to traditional institutions.

For men concerned enough with the use of resources to want such measurements in the first place, the discrepancy between potential and actual wealth was the source of anxiety about the soundness of their society and a stimulus to reform the nation's economy. This reform would be shaped by the same principles that were implicit in Petty's discussion: full employment as the token of economic health, the restriction of consumption (especially of foreign goods) for the mass of the population, and the impossibility of increasing wealth without additional exportation of production. Whichever of the various indicators of national wealth—the importation of precious metals, or the balance of trade, or the technological capability of a nation, or the number of laborers—was employed, the problem in need of a means of assessment was the production of goods for commercial advantage. Subsequent political economists have made the mercantilists' theory of value a byword for confusion. Money and capital were frequently indistinguishable in their writings, as were output and productivity, because profit was conceived in relation to the net spending on labor rather than to returns in productivity. They equated prosperity with the amount of spending needed to maintain full employment and slighted problems of capital accumulation and investment. The extent of employment, rather than comparative advantages in the allocation of capital, was taken as the measure of productive efficiency. When in the late seventeenth century the balance of trade receded as a theoretical problem

[38]William Petty, *Political Arithmetick: Or a Discourse concerning, the Extent and Value of Lands, People, Buildings* (London, 1690), preface and pp. 104-5, 108. On the idea of foreign paid incomes, see E. A. J. Johnson, *Predecessors of Adam Smith: The Growth of British Economic Thought*, Kelley ed. (New York, 1960), chap. 15.

and concern for the commercial importance of employment increased, the mercantilists continued to concentrate on the increase of foreign rather than domestic trade because it was thought to be an easier and more effective means to increase spending and hence employment. Unlike domestic trade, foreign commerce was conceived to have a productive as well as a distributive function because it was believed that labor itself was exported and thus was paid for overseas.[39] Obviously, without considerations of capital utilization the desirability of a favorable balance of labor was at least as wrongheaded as a balance of trade, for increased costs, not increased income and consumption, were the aim of the doctrine. But for present purposes these ideas are less significant as economic fallacies than as indicators of a peculiar attitude toward work whose historical importance lies in the effort to assess the utility of work in monetary terms.

With such a theory of value the economic utility of goods and services (for the national economy, which was the locus of economic analysis), other than money itself, derived from their ability to secure commercial advantages, which would be accomplished only in foreign trade.[40] John Bellers, a Quaker philanthropist who contributed frequently to discussions of economic and social issues, stated the conventional wisdom about the difference between domestic and foreign commerce. "Foreign manufactures is the most profitable Labour, we can imploy our present Idle Poor upon, excepting Husbandry and the Fishery: for whatever home Manufactures we imploy them upon, we do but take that work from some

[39]William D. Grampp, "The Liberal Elements in English Mercantilism," *Quarterly Journal of Economics*, 66 (1952): 468, 474; Johnson, *Predecessors*, pp. 15, 275; Stephen, *History of English Thought*, 2: 253-54; Jacob Viner, *Studies in the Theory of International Trade* (New York, 1937), pp. 31, 55; Charles Wilson, "The Other Face of Mercantilism," *Transactions of the Royal Historical Society*, 5th ser., 9 (1959): 84-85.

[40]There was an association, but not an equivalency, between treasure in the form of precious metals and the notion of wealth. Treasure was necessary for correcting deficits in the international balance of payments. and therefore the importance of treasure in relation to the nation's total wealth depended on the amount of the imbalance and on the ease of transferring payments. Thus, while treasure was the final term in the measurement of wealth, it was small in amount in comparison with total costs and profits. For an explanation of the uses and needs of treasure in the conduct of foreign trade in the mercantilist period, see Charles Wilson, "Treasure and Trade Balances: The Mercantilist Problem," *Economic History Review*, 2nd ser., 2 (1949): 152-61; K. N. Chaudhuri, "Treasure and Trade Balances: The East India Company's Export Trade," *ibid.*, 21 (1968): 480-502; Eli Heckscher, "Multilateralism, Baltic Trade, and the Mercantilists," *ibid.*, 3 (1950): 219-28. Wilson argued that, until late in the eighteenth century, payments were basically bilateral, and that therefore bullion reserves were important, regardless of the total balance of payments, though he problem was somewhat alleviated by Dutch willingness to invest in England after 1660. Chaudhuri showed that a multilateral trade and payments system existed in Europe between 1550 and 1720, but that treasure remained essential for settling balances. Heckscher argued that multilateralism was highly prevalent, that governments were unable to regulate international payments, and that the balance of trade with the Baltic (which Wilson had thought to be the great drain of bullion) was much less unfavorable than that with India—all with the implication that the mercantilists considered the balance of payments by treasure to be of more importance and a greater problem than it was in fact.

other Labourers in the Nation that will want it." Strictly domestic exchange did not increase the total wealth of a nation, but it did serve to distribute the profits of trade to the lower classes. "Merchants, Artificers, Farmers of Land . . . are the three sorts of people which by their study and Labour do principally, if not only, bring in Wealth to a Nation from abroad: other kinds of People, *viz. Nobility, Gentry, Lawyers, Physicians, Scholars* of all sorts, and *shopkeepers,* do onely [*sic*] hand it from one to another at home." There was recognition of course that capital improvements could increase the national wealth, but it was characteristic of mercantilist thought to consider such improvements as a means of simultaneously increasing employment and expanding exports or reducing imports; efficiency in existent industries was less significant.[41]

Taking for granted the importance of wealth for the commonwealth, and having demonstrated that individual contributions to the wealth of the nation could be evaluated, the mercantilists were in a position to argue that participation in foreign trade was the most useful activity for a citizen. Such participation was possible for many more citizens than just the overseas merchant. Producers of foodstuffs and laborers in manufacturing were essential to foreign trade, the one providing the food surplus which allowed the other to produce goods for export. Thomas Mun, a prominent member of the East India Company, gave classic formulation to this principle of the importance of the balance of trade in his frequently reprinted book, *England's Treasure by Foreign Trade.* "The ordinary means to increase our wealth and treasure is by *Foreign Trade,* wherein we must ever observe this rule, to sell more to strangers yearly than we consume of theirs in value." Mun distinguished two types of wealth in a kingdom, "natural" and "artificial." Natural wealth derived from what could be spared "from our own use and necessities" and thus exported. In order for natural resources to be employed most usefully, the consumption of domestic as well as imported production had to be kept to a minimum. Artificial wealth depended on "manufactures and industrious trading with foreign commodities."[42] Because artificial wealth depended on technological developments and the conditions of trade, its potential for contribution to economic growth was greater than was the case with the supply of natural production; human resources were thought to be more amenable to rational manipulation than physical ones.

The mercantilists valued both natural production and the creation of value through commercial advantage, but they held the latter source of

[41]A. Ruth Fry, ed., *John Bellers, 1654-1725, Quaker, Economist, and Social Reformer: His Writings Reprinted* . . . (London, 1935), p. 65; Josiah Child, *Brief Observations concerning Trade and Interest of Money* (London, 1668), p. 16; Eli F. Heckscher, *Mercantilism,* trans. Mendel Shapiro, 2 vols. (London, 1935), 2: 193; N. J. Pauling, "The Employment Problem in Pre-Classical English Economic Thought," *Economic Record,* 27 (1951): 60.

[42]Thomas Mun, "England's Treasure by Foreign Trade" [1664], in *Early English Tracts on Commerce,* ed. J. R. McCulloch (originally pub. 1856; Cambridge, 1954), pp. 125-33.

wealth in higher esteem. In his *Political Arithmetic*, Petty ranked the different types of work by their creation of wealth. "There is much more to be gained by Manufacture than Husbandry, and by Merchandize than Manufacture." Natural production was devoted to the production of food and raw materials, and profits from them went only to a few hands, but "the people which live by the Arts are far more in number than they are who are masters of the fruits." The producers of artificial wealth composed "the greatest strength and riches both of King and Kingdom: for where the people are many, and the arts good, there the traffique must be great, and the Country rich." The role of the merchant was to convert the production of farmers and artisans into wealth through foreign trade. The experience of Holland had demonstrated that natural production was of minimal importance in the increase of a nation's riches; in fact, too much natural richness could diminish a people's need for industry. Few mercantilist writers doubted that Holland offered the example to England of the best means to become rich, which was by foreign trade. "Nor has *Holland*," wrote William Temple, several times a diplomat in the country and author of *Observations upon the United Provinces of the Netherlands*, a basic source of conventional economic wisdom in the eighteenth century, "grown rich by any Native Commodities, but by force of Industry; By improvement and manufacture of all Foreign growths; By being the general Magazine of *Europe*, and furnishing all parts with whatever the Market wants or invites; And by their Sea-Men, being, as they have properly been call'd, the common Carriers of the World."[43] It would be difficult to exaggerate the persuasiveness of this image of a society's economic health for Americans, who had extraordinary natural abundance but who were also impelled by commercial necessity and models of civilization to develop foreign trade and to attempt manufactures.

The mercantilists' fascination with Holland's commercial success was an example of their preoccupation with the problem of putting the resources of a nation to their fullest use; it was axiomatic with them that the most important resource in a country was its labor force. Commercial skill was relatively more important than labor, but without the employment of labor such skill was useless. References to the laboring population as the basis of a country's strength can be found in the works of almost every writer on economic matters. For William Temple "the Time of Labouring or industrious Men [was] the greatest Native Commodity of any Country." Nicholas Barbon, one of the chief rebuilders of London after the fire of 1666, believed that "the people are the riches and strength of the country." John Bellers thought that "regularly laboring people are the kingdom's greatest treasure and strength." The mercantilists needed a prin-

[43]Petty, *Political Arithmetick*, p. 12; Mun, "England's Treasure," p. 133; Malachy Postlethwayt, *The Universal Dictionary of Trade and Commerce*, 4th ed., 2 vols. (London, 1774), 1: ix; William Temple, *Observations upon the United Provinces of the Netherlands* [1673], ed. G. N. Clark (Cambridge, 1932), p. 129.

ciple of service to replace, or at least to substitute for, aristocratic notions of public virtue, and they found it in the definition of usefulness as the increase of national wealth. The mercantilist writers were at pains to show that men in commerce served the public: "the Merchant is worthily called the *Steward of the Kingdoms Stock* . . . that so the private gain may ever accompany the publick good." In fact, if their definition of usefulness were accepted, then it was clear that merchants were the most estimable subjects of the kingdom. Merchants and their colleagues in economic life, the "artificers" and farmers, were the "most profitable Engines of the Kingdom."[44]

The respect for labor, however, was explicitly amoral.[45] The mercantilists used the notion of economic man as a term for the analysis of economic behavior, but they did not confer legitimacy on self-interest, though they were at pains to establish the legitimacy of trade itself. In contrast to the more anticommercial and community-oriented work ethic represented by the trustees' Georgia plan, the mercantilists simply assumed that selfishness in man was ineradicable. Selfishness was not a justification for actions, but it was taken into account as a constant impulse which could be directed for ends whose desirability was economic though not necessarily moral. The mercantilists had very little confidence in conscience or a sense of duty as sufficient guides for the subordination of work to the public good. Rather, they thought that self-interest in the form of a desire for material gain was the main motive in men's economic behavior. With their strictly economic analysis of the national interest, the mercantilists assumed that "private gain is the Compass men generally sail by." They believed that, "where the good of the Publique and private mens go not together, the Publique is seldom greatly advanced."[46] To adopt this approach was to renounce the merits of self-denial, but the desired result remained unchanged: the activities of the individual were to be subordinated to the public interest through manipulation of his self-interest. In this regard the mercantilists were more elitist than the casuists. They believed that only a few men could sufficiently detach themselves from their self-interests to enable them to regulate men's work in a way that served the national interest; the rest of the population was to be deluded into serving the nation by pursuing their own inclinations. As interpreted by the later mercantilists, the public good differed from what would be the liberal view because it did not equal the sum of individual interests as autonomously expressed. It was equivalent to the structure imposed on individual inter-

[44]Child, *Brief Observations*, pp. 13, 16; Temple, *Observations*, p. 93; Mun, "England's Treasure," p. 122. These and similar views are quoted in Edgar S. Furniss, *The Position of the Laborer in a System of Nationalism: A Study in the Labor Theories in the English Mercantilists* (Boston, 1920), pp. 22–23; cf. E. J. Hundert, "The Making of *Homo Faber*: John Locke between Ideology and History," *Journal of the History of Ideas*, 33 (1972): 3–23.

[45]Heckscher, *Mercantilism*, 2: 285–96; Johnson, *Predecessors*, p. 14.

[46][Thomas Culpepper], "A Tract against Usurie, Presented to the High Court of Parliament" [1621], reprinted in Child, *Brief Observations*, pp. 29, 24.

ests, and thereby ignored the traditional moral dimension of the public good, which tested the legitimacy of men's motivations against interests which transcended individual wants.

The mercantilists recognized self-interest in order to discipline it. Economic conditions were to be shaped in such a way that men would avoid useless work because it was unrewarding and do without luxuries because they were too expensive. The mercantilist belief in the need for state regulation derived from traditional beliefs about the selfishness and irrationality of human nature. The occasional criticism of the wisdom of such a policy of regulation usually depended on the extension of the distrust of selfishness to the policy-makers as well as to the citizens at large. It was sometimes argued that any trade policy must necessarily favor some special interests. Reasonable as such fears may have been, the desire for economic regulation, at least of foreign trade, prevailed.[47]

The mercantilists sought to demonstrate that the regulation of selfishness depended on a careful control over the impact of prosperity on a society. There was a danger that if material rewards were too readily accessible then men would cease to work after their basic needs were met. Sir Josiah Child, head of the East India Company, thought that the laboring population had little economic rationality and followed self-interest in the most brutish, subsistence-oriented way. "They [the poor] live better in the dearest countries for provisions, than in the cheapest, and better in a dear year than in a cheap, (especially in relation to the Publick Good) for that in a cheap year they will not work above two days in a week; their humor being such, that they will not provide for a hard time; but just work so much and no more, as may maintain them in that mean condition to which they have been accustomed." William Temple thought that the experience of the Dutch had shown that the situation was not quite so hopeless. If internal conditions were unfavorable in just the right way, men might develop habits of industry and frugality. "I conceive [he wrote] the true original and ground of Trade, to be, great multitude of people crowded into small compass of Land, whereby all things necessary to life become dear, and all Men, who have possessions, are induced to Parsimony; but those who have none, are forced to industry and labour, or else to want. Bodies that are vigorous, fall to labour; Such as are not, supply that defect by some sort of Inventions or Ingenuity. These Customs arise first from Necessity, but encrease by Imitation, and grow in time to be habitual in a Country." For the maximization of productivity men needed both the carrot of gain and the stick of necessity. Economic individualism on the part of laborers was to be condoned, not because it had any sort of moral justification, but because it produced, in the proper conditions, the desired economic results for the nation. Nor was individualism favored because of its efficiency as a means of satisfying personal needs; on the contrary, satisfaction had to

[47]Viner, *Studies*, pp. 91–103, 109.

be rather difficult if beneficial results were to be had. To demonstrate this point, Temple described Ireland, "Where, by the largeness and plenty of the Soil, and scarcity of People, all things necessary to Life are so cheap, that an industrious Man, by two days labour, may gain enough to feed him the rest of the week; Which I take to be a very plain ground of the laziness attributed to the People: For Men naturally prefer Ease before Labour, and will not take pains, if they can live idle; though, when, by necessity, they have been inured to it, they cannot leave it, being grown a custom necessary to their Health, and to their very Entertainment: Nor perhaps is the change harder, from constant Ease to Labour, than from constant labour to ease."[48]

The mercantilists' scheme of rewards was simple in theory but difficult to apply in practice. They saw that men's avarice, combined with the possibility of satisfying it, was the motive force in the economy; but the same satisfaction whose prospect stimulated men to engage in commerce in the first place could also lead to the ruin of the system if it was excessive. Temple gave a typical mercantilist argument against the belief that luxury stimulated trade: "It may be so to that which impoverishes, but is not to that which enriches a Country; and is indeed less prejudicial, if it lie in Native, than in Foreign Wares. But the Custom, or Humour, of Luxury and Expence, cannot stop at certain Bounds: What begins in Native will proceed in Foreign Commodities; And though the Example arise among idle Persons, yet the Imitation will run into all Degrees; even of those Men by whose Industry the Nation subsists." Because they assumed human nature to be selfish and irrational, the mercantilists faced a theoretical and practical dilemma. Their system depended on men's willingness and ability to try to satisfy unlimited material wants, and only the prospect of this satisfaction motivated men in their work. Yet anything more than a moderate satisfaction of these wants could have undesirable effects both for the individual and for society.[49] And the chief quality absent from selfishness was rational moderation.

Views on the wastefulness of consumption were closely tied with those on the productive capacity of commerce. It is a point so obvious as sometimes to be neglected that the mercantilists and other writers on economic matters in the late seventeenth and early eighteenth centuries considered

[48]Child, *Brief Observations*, p. 11; Temple, *Observations*, pp. 129-30; cf. David Bertelson, *The Lazy South* (New York, 1967), pp. 3-11.

[49]Temple, *Observations*, p. 143. "The very aim of increased wealth, pursued by mercantilists with such ardour, necessarily led to effects which, in their view, would cancel this result, for wealth was considered the mother of all idleness. . . . The conclusion at which they arrived was therefore this: wealth for the nation, but wealth from which the majority of the people must be excluded." Heckscher, *Mercantilism*, 2: 166. David Hume, while arguing against Mandeville's views, also questioned the mercantilist assumptions about motivation and the need for restrictions on the satisfaction of needs. He believed that a desire for work was a part of human nature which required prosperous conditions for expression. "Essays: Moral, Political, and Literary," *The Philosophical Works of David Hume*, 4 vols. (Boston, 1854), 3: 296.

economic activity primarily in relation to foreign trade. Wealth was produced by taking more than by making, and trade was a means by which
to take from foreigners. The domestic economy—commercial relations
which began and ended within the society—was neglected as a topic of economic concern for the mercantilists because it was not the chief sphere for
the creation of wealth. The domestic economy was the realm in which men
satisfied their basic material necessities and in which the wealth gained
through foreign trade was distributed.[50] The primary economic importance
of employment and consumption lay in the effect they had on the balance
of foreign trade; the greater the employment in the manufacture of goods
for export the better, and the lower the consumption of foreign goods the
better.

As they gained more confidence in the steadiness of laborers' work
habits, the mercantilists recognized the possibility that the satisfaction
of more than the minimal needs of the mass of the population might act
as a stimulus for production, both as an incentive for increased earnings
and as an expanded market. But there were three important points in this
qualification of the faith in frugality: first, large expenditures were thought
to be best restricted to the upper classes, who, in consuming domestically
produced luxuries, provided employment for the poor; second, the production
of goods for export was preferable to such make-work; third, it was rarely
put forth unabashedly. Luxury was still viewed as destructive of prosperity
in the long run. Thomas Mun, in a discussion of the "excesses and evils"
which "decay not our trade nor Treasure," argued that "the pomp of Buildings, Apparel, and the like, in the Nobility, Gentry and other able persons,
cannot impoverish the Kingdome." It was essential to mercantilist economics, however, that these works "be done with . . . our Materials, and by
our own People." If this situation prevailed, then the consumption of
luxuries "will maintain the poor with the purse of the rich, which is the
best distribution of the Commonwealth." Consumption of this type did not
create wealth; it distributed it roughly according to men's needs. There
were always more desirable forms of employment which could provide
workers with wages and the nation with wealth. This view, with only in-
significant qualifications, remained the prevailing economic wisdom until
at least the middle of the eighteenth century. By then a rise in the standard
of living for the mass of the population was conceived to be not only possible but also an indication of national economic well-being. "Great Luxury
is inseparable from such a Situation [when a state 'enjoys all the Strength
and Vigor it is susceptible of'] . . . ; it extends to every Class of People,
because they are all happy: but that Luxury, which is the Effect of the
public Ease, and proceeds from an Encrease of Labor, need never be
feared; foreign Rivalship is sure to Prevent it's rising to too great a Height,

---

[50]Postlethwayt, *Universal Dictionary*, 1: i.

which would otherwise soon put a fatal Stop to such Prosperity."[51] In America, however, the suspicion of consumption was, if anything, stronger and longer lasting than in Britain because the colonies were dependent on imports for all but their basic necessities and some rudimentary comforts.

Domestic consumption, especially of luxuries, was a continual source of anxiety for these men for whom the creation of wealth was the basic measure of utility. To consume needlessly was the height of inefficiency. To Mun's eyes the English appeared "too much affected to Pride, monstrous Fashions, and Riot, above all other Nations"; they were "a people not only *vicious* and *excessive*, wasteful of the means we have, but also improvident & careless of much other wealth that shamefully we lose." This shame and the fear accompanying it would last well into the period of England's commercial prosperity. Luxury, it was felt, led to a "general leprosie of our Piping, Potting, Feasting, Fashions, and misspending of our time in Idleness and Pleasure," which would lead to the downfall of England because it would make its people "effeminate in our bodies, weak in our knowledge, poor in our Treasure, declined in our Valour, unfortunate in our Enterprises, and contemned [*sic*] by our Enemies."[52] Charles Davenant, though a prominent writer on commercial topics, had reservations about all trade because it resulted eventually in a people's corruption. "Trade," he wrote, "[is] without a doubt . . . a pernicious thing; it brings in that Wealth which introduces Luxury; it gives a rise to Fraud and Avarice, and extinguishes Virtue and Simplicity of Manners; it depraves a People, and makes way for that Corruption which never fails to end in Slavery, Foreign or Domestick. *Licurgus*, in the most perfect Model of Government that was ever frame'd, did banish it from his Commonwealth." Yet trade was "a necessary Evil" because of the threat posed by other countries. Without trade "We shall be continually expos'd to Insults and Invasions without such a Naval Force, as is not to be naturally but where there is an extended Traffick. However, if Trade cannot be made subservient to the Nation's Safety, it ought to be no more encouraged here than it was in *Sparta*; And it can never tend to make us safe, unless it be so managed as to make us increase in Shipping and in the Breed of Seamen."[53] This republican ambivalence between the expediency of an expanding trade and the virtuous isolation of self-sufficiency would be a persistent theme as Americans came to think of the various provinces as economic entities.

In contrast to Davenant, with his second thoughts on the social effects of trade, a few writers in the early eighteenth century argued from a com-

[51]Mun, "England's Treasure," p. 180; Malachy Postlethwayt, *Great Britain's True System* (London, 1757), p. 237; Hume, "Essays," 3: 302, 306; Pauling, "Employment Problem," p. 57; Coats, "Economic Thought," p. 44; E. A. J. Johnson, "Unemployment and Consumption: The Mercantilist View," *Quarterly Journal of Economics*, 46 (1932): 698–719; Jean Starobinski, *The Invention of Liberty, 1700–1789* (Geneva, 1964), pp. 22, 39.
[52]Mun, "England's Treasure," pp. 192–93.
[53]Davenant, *An Essay*, pp. 154–55.

monsensical and morally indifferent point of view that economic life provided men with what they wanted and therefore should be accepted as a fact of life instead of as a source of guilt. Their view remained unorthodox for many years; nonetheless, it is important to examine their opinions because they show that mercantilist economic analysis made a vocabulary and an intellectual framework available for a new understanding of men's livelihoods which could have replaced the established one if men had been so inclined. They praised the economic benefits of luxury, encouraged selfishness, and glorified man's nature as an economic creature.

In 1691 Dudley North, a wealthy merchant and member of the Turkey Company, published *Discourses upon Trade*, a work which was subsequently much admired by liberal historians of mercantilism but which North himself consented to have suppressed. (It is also likely that the maxims on free trade which gave the work its nineteenth-century fame were written by North's brother, Roger.) North's theoretical position was an anomalous one; he was a free-trade mercantilist. He was not in the least troubled by men's propensity to consume luxuries. "The main spur to Trade, or rather to Industry and Ingenuity, [he wrote,] is the exorbitant Appetites of Men, which they will take pains to gratifie, and so be disposed to work, when nothing else will incline them to it; for did Men content themselves with bare Necessaries, we should have a poor World." He did not believe that luxuries should be available only to the rich. On the contrary, avarice and jealousy provided a spur to economic activity for men at all levels of society. "The meaner sort seeing their fellows become rich, and great, are spurr'd up to imitate their Industry. A Tradesman sees his Neighbour keep a Coach, presently all his Endeavours is at work to do the like, and many times is beggered by it; however the extraordinary Application he made, to support his Vanity, was beneficial to the Publick, tho' not enough to answer his false Measures as to himself."

North expressed none of the ambivalence toward material success shown by his contemporaries because he had an abounding confidence in the process of trade itself. Unlike most of the mercantilists, who thought that trade had to be carefully regulated if it was to result in the increase of the nation's wealth, North assumed that "the Increase of Trade is to be esteem'd the only cause that Wealth and Money increase." Because the process of trade, whether foreign or domestic, itself brought wealth, it was in the interest of everyone to trade. "A Nation in the World, as to Trade, is in all respects like a City in a Kingdom, or Family in a City." Mercantilists assumed that most profits derived ultimately from foreign trade and believed that regulations were necessary in order to encourage such trade. North inverted these propositions and argued that only natural trade—by which he meant unregulated trade—could secure profits, which it could do in any economic exchange. "To force men to deal in any prescribed manner, may profit such as happen to serve them; but the public gains not, because it is taking from one subject to give to another." He assumed that men engaged in trade in order to maximize wealth, and so "there can be

46

no trade unprofitable to the Publick; for if any prove so, men leave it off; and wherever the Traders thrive, the Publick, of which they are a part, thrives also.''[54]

Mandeville also had confidence in the benign effects which resulted from the boundlessness of men's economic appetites. He showed that frugality was detrimental to prosperity because it was an impediment to production. Like any good mercantilist, he wanted the productive capacity of the country to be put to its uttermost use. He urged that the economic man, which traditional morality had warned lurked within every individual, be unleashed. "Diligence and industry [he wrote] are often used promiscuously, to signify the same thing, but there is a great difference between them. A poor wretch may want neither diligence nor ingenuity, be a saving, painstaking man, and yet without striving to mend his circumstances remain contented with the station he lives in; but industry implies besides the other qualities a thirst after gain, and an indefatigable desire of meliorating our condition." Mandeville even denied the traditional polarity of industry and laziness. Contentment was, he thought, more like laziness than industry and was even contrary to industry. Without men's acquisitiveness, society would be a miserable place. Money, he was saying, was indeed the motive of most men's actions, and as such it sustained society.

> The root of evil, avarice,
> That damn'd ill-natur'd baneful vice,
> Was slave to prodigality,
> That noble sin; whilst luxury
> Employ'd a million of the poor,
> And odious pride a million more:
> Envy itself, and vanity,
> Were ministers of industry;
> Their darling folly, fickleness
> In diet, furniture and dress,
> That strange ridic'lous vice, was made
> The very wheel that turn'd the trade.

Without the liberation of men's appetites, extravagance and luxury would decline and poverty would increase: "In splendour, they that would revive A Golden Age, must be as free, For acorns, as for honesty."[55]

In *The Complete English Tradesman* Daniel Defoe dealt explicitly and benignly with the actions of economic man within his own society. Defoe's work was a manual of conduct for tradesmen. The desired conduct was economic success, and a tradesman was a retailer or wholesaler of goods whose trade was within England. The tradesman was explicitly distinguished from the artisan, who sold his own goods, and the "merchant,"

[54]Dudley North, "Discourses upon Trade," in *Early English Tracts on Commerce*, ed. J. R. McCulloch (originally pub. 1856; Cambridge, 1954), pp. 513, 528–29; Letwin, *Origins of Scientific Economics*, 251–72.
[55]Mandeville, *Fable*, 1: 25, 36–37, 248–49.

who dealt in overseas trade. Defoe was therefore assuming the legitimacy and existence of internal market relations. In doing so, he unconsciously made clear why men had been so reluctant to give this realm of activities an autonomous economic importance. For Defoe simply took for granted that where moral or social scruples were an obstacle to economic success they were best ignored.

Defoe considered the arena of trade to be exempt from the ordinary standards and patterns of behavior.

> Custom indeed has driven us beyond the limits of our morals in many things, which trade makes necessary, and which we cannot now avoid; so that if we must pretend to go back to the literal sense of the command, if our yea must be yea, and our nay nay; if no man must go beyond, or defraud his neighbour, if our conversation must be without covetousness, and the like, then it is impossible for tradesmen to be Christians, and we must unhinge all business, act upon new principles in trade, and go by new rules: in short, we must shut up shop, and leave off trade, and so in many things we must leave off living.

Defoe showed that it was impossible to live consistently both as a Christian and as a tradesman, and yet he praised the latter role. He was aware of the toll that devotion to economic life took from a man, but he believed the price to be worthwhile. Partnerships were to be avoided: if the partner were capable he would eventually get rid of you, and if bad he would ruin you. Thus the tradesman had to be on guard against friend and competitor alike; Defoe described this situation as a fact of life, without regret for the emotional cost involved.

His tradesman was allowed little self-respect. "He must be a *complete hypocrite*," Defoe warned, "if he will be a *complete tradesman*." Nothing should "turn away either the body or the mind of a tradesman from the one needful thing which his calling makes necessary, and that necessity makes his duty; I mean, the application of both his hands and head to his business." The tradesman was allowed certain sharp practices, such as asking a higher price than was really acceptable or putting off creditors by promising to pay at a later date. Such deceptions were not immoral because, as anyone of sense should have realized, "promises ought to be taken as they were made, namely, with a contingent dependence upon the circumstances of trade."[56]

These writings of North, Mandeville, and Defoe indicated a way in which mercantilist thought could have profoundly influenced American valuations of work, not necessarily by endowing self-interest with any special moral claims, but rather by allowing economic considerations of legitimacy to become primary ones, and thereby removing altogether the traditional problems of morality and justice in work which were social as well as economic in nature. The moral imperative of commitment to the

[56]Daniel Defoe, *The Complete English Tradesman, in Familiar Letters* . . . (London, 1727), pp. 4, 234, 213, 94, 97, 231.

community and the complementary belief in the danger of selfishness prevented Americans from using mercantilist theory in this way. Instead, the mercantilists provided Americans with an empirical understanding of their economy and its health. As will be seen in a later chapter, Americans adopted mercantilist principles even though they were themselves incorporated in the mercantile system of Britain and therefore had a conflicting interest in the balance of trade. Americans sought to make their economies meet mercantilist standards: they tried to accumulate specie by exporting a greater value of native production than they spent in importing foreign goods, especially luxuries; they wanted full employment because it was a sign of efficiency; and they encouraged technological developments in manufacturing. Most important of all, Americans used the mercantilists' model of economic man as a means to understand their own economic behavior. They viewed commerce as a basic requirement of civilization, and they assumed that self-interest was the chief motivation in economic activity. What they did not do was to give this economic man social legitimacy; taken separately, economic justifications of actions which infringed on the interests of others were not respectable. It was assumed that legitimate economic interests were harmonious with those of others; in this context mercantilist analysis could be used in conjunction with other considerations of the public good. Because industry and frugality were basic principles in both moral and economic thought, Americans were able to apply moral imperatives to situations which the mercantilists had considered in morally neutral terms.

II

THE LEGACY OF THE CALLING

THE TRADITION OF CHRISTIAN SOCIAL THOUGHT represented by the pietists transmitted to America the attitude toward work which subordinated economic considerations to social ones. During the seventeenth century, manuals of piety gained a popularity in England and America among Anglicans and dissenters alike which they retained well into the eighteenth century; if a household in eighteenth-century America contained any book besides the Bible, it was likely to be one of these works of moral guidance.[1]

The popularity of the pietists depended on their ability to articulate anxieties occasioned by acquisitiveness and to provide a means for greater self-understanding and self-control in circumstances of unaccustomed prosperity. They taught that the self, left to its own course in economic activity, was a danger to itself and society.[2] The notions that one's social

---

[1]On this tradition, see R. H. Tawney, *Religion and the Rise of Capitalism*, Mentor ed. (New York, 1947), *passim*; W. Lee Ustick, "Changing Ideals of Aristocratic Character and Conduct in Seventeenth Century England," *Modern Philology*, 30 (1932-33): 147-66. For examples of its transmission to America, see Louis B. Wright, *The First Gentlemen of Virginia: Intellectual Qualities of the Early Colonial Ruling Class* (San Marino, Calif., 1940), pp. 15, 133, 275; Stephen B. Weeks, *Libraries and Literature in North Carolina in the 18th Century* (Washington, D.C., 1895); Helen R. Watson, "The Books They Left: Some 'Liberies' in Edgecombe County, 1733-1783," *North Carolina Historical Review*, 48 (1971): 245-57; cf. Caleb Smith, *Diligence in the Work of God, and Activity during Life* (New York, 1758), p. 19.

[2]Richard Baxter, *A Christian Directory: Or a Summ of Practical Theology, and Cases of Conscience . . .* , 4 pts. (London, 1673), p. 262 (the pagination of pts. 1-3 is continuous);

role was a matter of obligation to and dependence on others and that the proper self-conception was that of a servant of God, with their displacement of personal responsibility for the establishment of purposes, were symptomatic of a distrust of self or at least of an inability to define a workable reliance on oneself as a guide for behavior. Yet the idea of stewardship also held out the possibility of a Christian form of self-fulfillment. By thinking of himself as a steward, a man could make the most of himself, in accordance with his human nature and his individual potential. If the worldly context of work was itself sanctified, the terms of legitimation could be largely utilitarian. Hence pietists often stated the service owed to God in terms of the efficient use of time and energy and saw nothing ironic in the use of commercial metaphors for Christian stewardship. "Think how much work is *behind*, how slow thou hast wrought in the time which is *past*; & what a reckoning thou shouldst make, if thy Master should call thee this day to thine accounts. Be therefore careful henceforth, to make the *most* advantage of thy *short* time that remains, as a man would of an *old* lease, that were near expiring: and when thou disposest to recreat thy self remember how *small* a time is alloted for thy life." God had interwoven man's "Interest so with his Duty, that the discharge of it is his only means of being happy even in this world." Though He valued no role intrinsically, God blessed all good stewards equally: "there is no condition of life so low or poor, but may be *sanctified*, and *fruitful*, and *comfortable* to us."[3]

Though literally a matter of property, in fact the doctrine of stewardship applied especially to work and the way it resulted in the production of goods and the accumulation of wealth. The pietistic moralists believed that commercial life gave men the most dangerous, as well as the most likely, occasion for selfishness, and they relied on men's consciences to restrain them from uncharitable behavior. Because they viewed work as an obligation to the community and thought of the social order as one of divine ordination, they assumed that every calling could "be followed with Truth and with a good Conscience"; to argue that necessity required otherwise was tacitly to "make the holy God to be the Author of Sin. . . . Cursed is that Trade that cannot be followed without Sin." It was just for one to work diligently and seek to prosper; there was an "honest increase and provision, which is the end of our labour; and therefore ['it is no sin, but a duty'] to choose a gainful calling rather than another, that we may be able to do good, and relieve the poor."

It is a truism that all economic theories involve social and moral norms, but twentieth-century theorists, operating with preoccupations of economic growth, can envisage trade-offs between economic gains and

---

Jeremy Taylor, *The Rule and Exercises of Holy Living* . . . , 17th ed. (London, 1695); Richard Allestree, *The Gentleman's Calling* (London, 1660), p. 3.

[3]Lewis Bayly, *The Practice of Piety: Directing a Christian How to Walke That He May Please God* . . . , 27th ed. (Edinburgh, 1630), pp. 310-11; Allestree, *Gentleman's Calling*, pp. 2, 96; Baxter, *Christian Directory*, p. 627.

losses of justice. Such a comparison was theoretically impossible for most early modern proto-economists (and a fortiori so for nontheorists commenting on economic matters), even those few who occasionally conceived of economic development as something sustained and extensive. Christian moralists treated work more as a social matter than as an economic one; considerations of justice and sustenance had priority over those of productive efficiency and commercial advantage. The purpose of exchange was to enable men in their separate callings to provide one another with what they could not provide for themselves. The rule of such market mechanisms as supply and demand and competitive pricing was subordinate to the necessity of others. For each item or service there was a just price which depended on what one would be willing to pay to another in similar circumstances: "an upright Conscience must be the Clerk of the Market." It was therefore unjust to profit from another's need or ignorance. Economic life depended on honesty: "You must not live upon cheating and thievery to prevent your ruin: and what can it be less to get another man's money against his will, if you hide your case, which if he knew he would not lend it you." When the situation demanded it, prices were to be reduced sufficiently for a poor person to acquire what he needed.

The Christian moralists were unable to isolate economic problems from social and moral ones. This view was peculiarly suited to an economy in which extensive development was unthinkable, one in which the literate urged economic rationality on the population at large in order that subsistence itself be maintained. They warned against competition, which deprived some men of their work; even intrinsic superiority was not a justification for such competition, "for if you *should* do it *better*, the disorder will do more harm than you did *good* by bettering his work." The Christian moralists' distrust of highly developed commercial life and their assumption that economic relations were imbedded in social ones were evident in the way Baxter applied the Christian standard of utility to men's various callings.

The callings most useful to the publick good, are the Magistrates, the Pastors, and Teachers of the Church, Schoolmasters, Physicians, Lawyers, etc. Husbandmen, (Plowmen, Graziers, and Shepherds): and next to them are Marriners, Clothiers, Booksellers, Taylors, and such other that are employed about things most necessary to mankind: And some Callings are employed about matters of so little use (as Tobacco-sellers, Lace-sellers, Feather-makers, Periwig-makers, and many more such) that he may choose better, should be loth to take up with one of these, though possibly in it self it may be lawful. It is a great satisfaction to an honest mind, to spend his life in doing the greatest *good* he can; and a prison and constant calamity to be tyed to spend ones life in doing little good at all to others, though he should grow rich by it himself.

The range in the types of work which such an analysis found useful was much wider socially, though narrower economically, than the mercantilists' strictly commercial distinction between productive and unproductive labor. These moralists wanted to foster a Christian social order and sought to relieve men of "that *Anxiety*, which torments carnal Men; who have perhaps the greatest part of their Estate floating upon the Sea, and therefore can scarce eat, or drink, or sleep by reason of their unworthy fears."[4]

For all their ability to articulate worldly men's anxieties and thus hold out some promise of relief, the pietists did not address the matter of economic life itself; rather, they spoke of the wrongdoings which an individual was likely to commit in that life. The psychological issue involved the self's relationship with society, and the usual resolution was to condemn self-expression. Related to this shunting of responsibility for a man's way of life onto the individual was the conceptual problem that economic life per se was largely lacking in recognition while the moral consequences of economic malfeasance were only too immediately apparent in the community. The pietists viewed the individual as a danger to himself and to others, yet they also relied on the individual as the primary means of achieving discipline over himself. They sought to instill their audience with a conviction of the need to perform work for valued purposes. But in fact there were few specific directions for the conduct of their work; the moral potential of doctrines like stewardship and the calling lay in their usefulness as instruments for condemning undesirable activities. The individual at work was valued as highly as anyone else in society, and he was allowed to follow his instincts in choosing his work. These instincts were disciplined, however, by inculcation of the belief that happiness derived solely from the pursuit of self-interest was evil.

The doctrine of the calling was the most explicit and precise formulation of these pietistic social attitudes. "The God of Calvinism," wrote Max Weber, the foremost student of the concept of the calling, "demanded of his believers not single good works, but a life of good works combined into a unified system."[5] A man's calling had two related orientations, one religious and one social: by his Christian conversion he was called to join the elect, and by his vocation he was called to honor God on earth. The significance of the calling for men's attitudes toward work lay in its imposition of a definite obligation and a positive moral value to daily labor. For English Protestants this idea about their vocations was "arguably the most important concept in their ideology." The concept of the calling involved a belief that the being of all men was defined by temporal and spiritual conditions imposed by God and peculiar to each individual.[6] The calling gave men a recognition of their selfhood; it encouraged them to take an objec-

---

[4]Richard Steele, *The Tradesman's Calling* . . . (London, 1684), pp. 17–18, 108, 145; Baxter, *Christian Directory*, pp. 449, 628, and pt. 4, pp. 120–21, 125, 132. See also Elizabeth Fox Genovese, "The Many Faces of Moral Economy: A Contribution to a Debate," *Past and Present*, 58 (1973): 161–68.

[5]Max Weber, *The Protestant Ethic and the Spirit of Capitalism*, trans. Talcott Parsons, Scribner ed. (New York, 1958), p. 117.

[6]Charles H. George and Katherine George, *The Protestant Mind and the English Reformation, 1570–1640* (Princeton, N.J., 1961), p. 169. For the believer in the calling, the fulfillment of daily tasks

tive view of themselves. Because it attributed this selfhood to an omnipotent God, it also instilled in men a conviction of the insufficiency of their own autonomy.

Until about 1730, far longer than was the case in England, a belief in the calling was the chief element in the American colonists' attitudes toward work. Expression of the doctrine was frequent in New England, but less so elsewhere, notably in the South, where printed communication was scanty before the 1730s; yet the prevalence in Southern libraries of Anglican pietistic handbooks, in which the recommended attitude toward work was very similar to the teachings of the calling, hints of a familiarity there with the ideas involved. In any case, from Pennsylvania northward there is abundant evidence to suggest that the calling was used by Congregationalists, Anglicans, and Quakers to define and to criticize men's work.[7] For the first three decades of the eighteenth century, it was the most important element of the European ethical heritage transmitted to America.

As a principle of social organization, the calling can be understood only in a Christian context. To a religious man like William Perkins, who was the major teacher of theology at Cambridge in the late sixteenth century and gave the doctrine its classic form, the secular notion of a personal vocation was meaningless except in relation to the general calling of Christian life. The general calling consisted of a sense of being in God's grace and of a commitment to the Christian way of life. This commitment was put into practice in the personal calling: "That we may the better join both our callings together, we must consider the main end of our lives, and that is, to serve God in serving of men in the works of our callings." It was, said Perkins, heathenish to think "that the particular condition and state of man in this life comes by chance, or by the bare will and pleasure of man himself." God intended each man's calling to be a contribution to the public good. For an action to be a "good work," "three things [were] required: first, it must be done in obedience: secondly, in faith: thirdly, it must be directed to the glory of God."[8]

A century after Perkins wrote his treatise on the calling, his doctrine was still largely intact in American thought. Nathaniel Henchman, preaching at the funeral of a member of the Massachusetts Council, explained the central importance of the calling for a "holy and useful life" in terms that

---

assumes a peculiarly objective and impersonal character, that of service in the interest of the rational organization of our social environment. For the wonderfully purposeful organization and arrangement of this cosmos is, according both to the revelation of the Bible and to natural intuition, evidently designed by God to serve the utility of the human race. This makes labor in the service of impersonal social usefulness appear to promote the glory of God and hence to be willed by Him.

Weber, *Protestant Ethic*, p. 109.

[7] Timothy Hall Breen, "The Non-Existent Controversy: Puritan and Anglican Attitudes on Work and Wealth, 1600–1640," *Church History*, 35 (1966): 273–87.

[8] William Perkins, "A Treatise of the Vocations," *The Works of . . . William Perkins* (Cambridge, 1605), pp. 903, 911, 913.

Perkins would easily have understood "All Men considered in relation to God are in the Quality of Servants; and his power over them is as universal as the *Potters* is over his *Clay*. . . . the Almighty requires that all be confined to some particular state of life, for the accomplishing the grand end, for which he exerted his power in creating: Every man hath (or ought to have) a particular calling as a Rational Creature, *wherein he is to abide*, and at the same time to follow his general calling as a Christian." After 1700, however, the relationship between the general and the personal calling became less precise as recognition of personal autonomy displaced the previous stress on divine omnipotence. (Note that both Henchman's metaphor and Mather's, which follows, portray the relationship of general to personal calling as one of power.) This confusion was apparent in Cotton Mather's mysterious metaphor for a *Christian at His Two Callings*. A Christian was, said Mather, "A Man in a Boat, Rowing for Heaven; the *House* which our Heavenly Father hath intended for us. If he mind but one of his *Callings*, be it which it will, he pulls the *Oar*, but on *one side* of the Boat, and will make but a poor dispatch to the Shoar of Eternal Blessedness."[9] For Mather the two callings were obviously related, but he gave an autonomous force to the man in the boat, though traditionally such power and direction had come from God.

The social ethics of the calling were oriented toward an economy which was static and local, one in which there was a mutuality of benefits in exchange and a division of social responsibilities in such a way that the division of labor was not a strictly economic principle, one in which social and economic roles were interwoven. Such a paradigm of the economy was implicit in schemes of social organization based on the calling, an ethical never-never land derived more from dissatisfaction and aspiration than from congruence with reality. Selfishness prevailed in village life as well as in expanding commercial societies, and in America, as in England, the sheer scale and extent of economic change—opportunities for the exercise of self-interest, population growth and mobility, local changes in production and productivity, increases in disposable incomes, and the proliferation of commercial exchange, especially in its monetary aspects, throughout the economy—eventually made the calling unworkable even as an ideal. Social considerations about work were eroded by the predominance of situations which required economic valuations of action.

Yet, as the concept of the calling lost its religious integrity and the general and personal callings were separated, men continued to think that morality and work were closely connected. The feeling remained that "Persons may be Diligent about their Business, without being real Chris-

---

[9]Nathaniel Henchman, *A Holy and Useful Life, Ending in Happy and Joyful Death . . .* (Boston, 1721), p. 7; Cotton Mather, *A Christian at His Calling . . .* (Boston, 1701), pp. 37–38; Robert S. Michaelson, "Changes in the Puritan Concept of Calling or Vocation," *New England Quarterly*, 26 (1953): 315–36.

tians, but they cannot be Real Christians, that have no Care about their Business."[10] By the 1730s the colonists often discussed work without reference to God's providential order. Despite this recognition of man's self-sufficiency, however, the moral legacy of the calling still inclined men to believe that work was basically an ethical matter by which men fulfilled certain duties to themselves and society. Two of the most important themes that made up this legacy were views about economic success and related views about the relationship between man's active nature and his social obligations.

MAN'S ACTIVE NATURE AND HIS
SOCIAL RESPONSIBILITIES: INDUSTRY

As part of the conception of the calling, Americans inherited two assumptions about human nature from their English Protestant intellectual background which shaped their attitudes toward work. They viewed man as a naturally active being, and they believed that he depended on others for his survival.

To the colonists, life seemed to be synonymous with exertion. In urging industry and diligence Benjamin Colman, minister of the socially prominent Brattle Street Church in Boston, wrote: *"All Nature is Industrious and every Creature about us diligent in their proper Work. Diligence is the Universal Example."* But no sooner was the self's need for expression mentioned than the concern that it act in an orderly context was voiced. If men looked "thro' the whole *Creation*," they would see that their callings were part of a grand scheme in which "every *part* of it has a Work and Service assign'd it, to which it diligently keeps." Out of the whole creation only men were "an *Exception* from and a *Contradiction* unto the other Works of God, if we are *Negligent* in the Duty which He has prescribed to us."[11]

An examination of man's faculties demonstrated that he was no exception to the active principle in the scheme of creation. His rational nature indicated "that man was made, and continues, a Creature capable of Action, and Design." Activity was the essence of his soul; in order to live "a Rational Life" he had to "Exert the powers and faculties of [his] Rational Nature." The body alone was "stupid and inactive"; by "the law of creation" its powers were "subjected to the Empire of the Soul, and fitted to be her instruments in the prosecution of her designs." The quality of being human depended on man's use of his rational faculty to direct his life in accordance with the divine will. To be human was not merely to act but to act correctly—that is, according to God's will. Man had the privileges and the responsibilities of a special place in creation. "To what purpose

[10]Nathaniel Clap, *The Duty of All Christians Urged, in a Discourse on 1 Cor. XV, 58 . . .* (New London, Conn., 720), p. 26.
[11]Benjamin Colman, *A Sermon at the Lecture in Boston after the Funerals . . .* (Boston, 1717), p. 14.

else," asked Ebenezer Pemberton, "can we suppose men ennobled with such exalted powers? . . . can we suppose God thus to furnish him for no *Design*, or no valuable one, *proportionable* to those powers? to imagine this would be an absurd reflection upon Divine Wisdom and Goodness." Constant activity was a condition of human life, not a punishment for sin. Adam's happiness before the Fall lay in his being "ever Employ'd in doing Good." In order for Adam, even in his innocence, to live in the Garden he had to "dress" it. "*Adam* and his *Head* and *Heart* and *Hands* all fram'd for Work and fill'd with it. His *Mind* was made for *Contemplation*, which is *Intellectual* work; his Heart was fram'd for *Moral* and *Divine* Services, and his Hands for *Secular* and *Worldly* business."

Man's final, as well as his earliest, condition was an active one. Heaven lacked any appeal as a place for relief from earthly travails. There would be plenty of work needed after death. It was "a carnal conceit" to think "that in the heavenly World all Work and Service for God will be at an End: as if the happiness of Heaven consisted only in Enjoyment, and a stupid Indolence." It might be pleasant for men to see "the future happiness be Set forth under the Notion of *Rest*; yet it is not a Rest from Work and Service suited to their Exalted State." And what better way to organize the jobs than in a system of callings; in heaven there were probably "distinct Stations, and differing Posts, of Honour and Service, to which they are assigned according to their Improvement in Grace, and the Services they performed in the State of Trial on Earth."[12]

Not only was man active; he was also disciplined. His nature was plainly intended "for an exact and regular, constant Course of Action," just as "the *Wheels* of a *Clock* or *Watch* when set in order and wound up, are manifestly designed by the *Artificer* for *Motion*." In contrast to the regularity and exactness of a clock, however, some images of man's activity also revealed that human energy was a restless, almost manic force with a self-destructive potential. The images were often those of war or ordeals. The life of a Christian was "compared to a *Race*, a *Warfare*; *Watching*, *Running*, *Fighting*; all which imply Activity, Earnestness, Speed, &c. and we are bid to *Labour* and *Strive*, and *gird up the loins of our minds*." This race called "for the utmost striving of the whole Man, unfainting Resolute Perseverance, and unwearied patience."[13]

Despite their almost uncontrollable energy, men were "poor, weak, dependent creatures, who, taken singly, can neither guard against numberless dangers that continually surround [them], nor procure many of the simplest and most common necessaries or comforts of life, without some

<hr />

[12]Ebenezer Pemberton, *A Christian Fix'd at His Post* . . . (Boston, 1704), pp. 6–7; Benjamin Colman, *A Holy and Useful Life Recommended from the Happy End of It* . . . (Boston, 1715), p. 6; *idem*, *A Sermon at the Lecture*, p. 4; Ebenezer Pemberton, *A True Servant of His Generation Characterized, and His Promised State of Refreshment Assigned* . . . (Boston, 1712), pp. 21–22.

[13]Colman, *A Sermon at the Lecture*, pp. 12–13; Henchman, *A Holy and Useful Life*, p. 8.

assistance from others." This second assumption about human nature, that man was a social being who required the assistance of others to survive, was the complement to the idea that man was an active creature. In order to aid men's survival and to demonstrate their dependence on Him, God endowed men with a social nature. God had created men for specialized tasks in order "to make us depend, more or less, one upon another . . . and thus hath he laid the foundation of justice and equity between man and man, by making each in his several station, condusive to the preservation and benefit of the whole, and, in return, to receive protection and assistance from others."[14] This principle of reciprocal dependency provided a moral guide for the direction of man's energies. It was contrary to nature for man to "Subsist by himself, independent one of another . . . [and] therefore he that is of a Publick Spirit, & doth Act accordingly, doth well accord to the Divine Intention, and so is of a right Worthy Spirit." If he wanted to secure his true self-interest, a man should apply his peculiar talents in a way which was useful to the society as a whole. This subordination of personal interests to public interests was equitable because "We expect *Benefits* from *Humane Society*. It is but equal, that *Humane Society* should Receive Benefits from *Us*." The benefits were those of specialization and protection. Society could provide men with goods and services that were beyond their capacities as individuals to provide. "It is best that some should imploy themselves in labours of the Hand, & others in the labours of the Minds, that some should Till the Ground, and others go down to the Sea in Ships, to fetch from distant Lands the Commodities of Life, which our own Country doth not afford, that some should Study and Practice for the health of the *Body*, & others give themselves wholly to the Service of *Souls*, that some should study the Art of Ruling & be improv'd in Government, and others give diligence in Mechanical Trades."[15] As was the case with pietistic social teachings generally, the doctrine of the calling related an economic principle—the division of labor—to the functioning of society as a whole and hence to moral obligations.

Acceptance of a calling was a commitment to self-subordination, for a calling made one a servant to God's will and to the needs of society. At the basis of Christianity lies the value of self-sacrifice, the radical inversion of worldly concerns. In its most extreme form the rhetoric urging this value seemed perversely wasteful, as, for example, when Cotton Mather described "the serviceable man" as one who "commonly ventures the *loss* of all other things; he spends his Time, Saps his Estate, exposes his Esteem, and runs the risque of his very *Life*" in order that "the People of God may fare the better for him." For all men a "Calling is such an honest

<hr />

[14]Thomas Bacon, *Sermons Addressed to Masters and Servants, and Published in the Year 1743* . . . (Winchester, Va., 1813?), p. 1.

[15]Mather, *A Christian at His Calling*, p. 37; Samuel Whittelsey, *A Publick Spirit Described & Recommended* . . . (New London, Conn., 1731), p. 23.

and lawful exercise, as renders us useful in the world," and the measure of one's usefulness was his contribution to society.[16]

Such utilitarian considerations were more moral than economic. Men were stewards of the resources of time and possessions which God gave them, and He expected a strict accounting of their proper use. People had to be *"Blessings in the World"* if they were to be *"blessed* after it." If, instead of fulfilling their duties, men relied on God to answer all their needs, they were seeking destruction. *"Reliance* on God is vain and *provoking* without a diligent use of Means. If a *drone* pretend to *trust* in Providence he does but *tempt* God."[17] To challenge the sufficiency of God's beneficence was the epitome of pride.

Idleness, like selfishness and discontent with one's lot, was a vice found among all classes. It involved a neglect of "Duty and lawful Employment . . . for Man is by Nature such an active Creature, that he cannot be wholly Idle; if he be not employed in what is good and commendable, he will be employed in Vice and Sin." Unlike the hibernating animals, man could not be inactive for long; he "will ordinarily be *doing something,* either innocent and good, or bad and criminal, except when he is asleep." The intentional idleness of an able-bodied man was, of course, intolerable. Cotton Mather stated that the idle poor had no claims on society. *"We should let them Starve;* and as for those that when they Get, will melt and wast our Money in Drunkenness, 'tis a Sin to supply those Monsters with what may be Fuel for such a Beastly Vice. Let never any thing but a *Nought,* stand for them, in the *Books of Accounts."* The idle rich might not have trembled at the thought of such a threat, but other possibilities might have given them pause. "If Persons live upon the Labours of others, and spend their Time in Idleness, without any Imployment, for the Benefit of others, they cannot be numbred [*sic*] among Christians. Yea, if Persons Labour, to get great Estates with this design, chiefly, that they and theirs may live in Idleness, They cannot be Acknowledged for Christians."[18] Unlike the able-bodied poor, the idle rich might easily have maintained their claims of membership in society, but at a later time they would have had to pay for their parasitic past.

If social disorder resulted from the moral failings of individuals, then social order prevailed when men fulfilled their responsibilities with moral

[16]Cotton Mather, *The Serviceable Man* . . . (Boston, 1690), p. 14; *The Poor Orphans Legacy: Being a Short Collection of Godly Counsels and Exhortations to a Young Arising Generation* . . . (Philadelphia, 1734), p. 29; Pemberton, *A True Servant,* p. 14; *The Pious Man's Directions: Showing How to Walk with God All His Days* (Boston, 1729), p. 18.

[17]Ernest Troeltsch. *The Social Teaching of the Christian Churches,* trans. Olive Wyon (New York, 1931), p. 646; Cotton Mather, *Honesta Parsimonia: Or, Time Spent as It Should be* . . . (Boston, 1721), p. 4; Pemberton, *A Christian Fixed at His Post,* p. 25; Colman, *A Sermon at the Lecture,* pp. 6–7, 17.

[18]*The Poor Orphans Legacy,* p. 29; Jonathan Mayhew, *Christian Sobriety: Being Eight Sermons on Titus II.6* . . . (Boston, 1763), p. 157; Cotton Mather, "The True Way of Thriving," *Durable Riches: Two Brief Discourses, Occasioned by the Impoverishing Blast of Heaven* . . . (Boston, 1695), p. 20; Nathaniel Clap, *The Duty of All Christians,* p. 8.

uprightness as defined by the calling. Yet, in taking the calling as a guide for social organization, it was necessary to assume what occasioned anxious doubt, namely, the possibility of a natural harmony of men's callings. For example, Increase Mather thought that Massachusetts' balance of payments problem was the result of the moral failings of individual men, not the inevitable result of the colony's political and economic dependence on England. A lack of money, he thought, "brought a deadness on Trade, and incommoded publick Interests. And is not this Evil owing to a private self-seeking spirit: Are there not those among us, who if they can themselves grow rich by sending all the money in the Country away, that's all that they care for."[19] For this ethic of subordination of private interest to public interest to be effective, men had to believe that the basic structure of society was sound and that it was in fact possible to fulfill the roles as set out in the ethic. When behavior violated the ethic the initial response was to evaluate social disorder as individual failure rather than as an inherent conflict between the ideals and the situation in which men found themselves.

THE RESPONSE TO SUCCESS: FRUGALITY

The ethics of the calling condemned the enjoyment of material success, partly because it involved a submission to temptations of the flesh and partly because it distracted men from the duties of their vocations. Weber suggested that this ascetic rationality was the most significant characteristic of the influence of the Protestant ethic on the development of a peculiarly modern psychology. He equated this rationality with a systematic, uniform approach to problems, one which disregarded traditional standards and sought to minimize irrational and instinctual influences on action. Weber was aware that English Protestant thought condemned an excessive concern with wealth; without the combination of asceticism with the obligation to fulfill a particular calling, men would not have participated ceaselessly in their vocations. Weber sought to establish the way in which this "worldly asceticism" could have led paradoxically to a need for worldly success, and he assumed he had found the key in the spiritual uncertainty and anguish of men who held the Protestant belief in the predestination of souls. According to Weber, most Protestants could not be satisfied with Calvin's teaching that states of grace were unknowable. "For them the *certitudo salutis* in the sense of the recognizability of the state of grace necessarily became of absolutely dominant importance . . . in order to attain that self-confidence intense worldly activity is recommended as the most suitable means."[20] Though this was an ingenious, and for many of Weber's readers a plausible, account of Protestant psychology,

[19]Increase Mather, *The Excellency of a Publick Spirit Discoursed* . . . (Boston, 1702), p. 26.
[20]Weber, *The Protestant Ethic*, pp. 110-12; cf. Stuart Bruchey, *The Roots of American Economic Growth, 1607-1861* (New York, 1965), pp. 42-43.

there is reason to doubt that it is applicable to the Anglo-American religious situation. The history of evangelical movements in early America would suggest that it was not the unknowability of salvation which troubled sensitive spirits but rather a sense of personal denial of what was ostensibly a marked and clear conviction. The phenomenon of revivalism itself indicates that spiritual anxiety tended to have acute and transitory manifestations. There is no demonstrated correlation between individuals with high anxiety about their state of grace and those with compulsions for enterprise combined with an indefinite postponement of gratification, and it is at least as plausible as Weber's hypothesis that nagging uncertainty would have an incapacitating effect. Autobiographical evidence of the colonial period shows that the strongest psychological effect of a concern about predestination was a need for order, not economic success.[21]

Because they viewed the world as a place of wickedness in which men constantly had to restrain their sinful natures, Protestant adherents to the notion of the calling were uneasy with anything more than moderate economic success. There was general agreement that a rich man had great difficulty living as a Christian: "The Temptations which Prosperity plonges a Man into, are infinitely harder to vanquish than those to which Adversity exposes us." Prosperity inclined men toward pride. The pursuit of wealth tempted men to place an autonomous importance on life on earth, and the doctrine of the calling had held that life on earth was important only if it agreed with the providential scheme of things. Wealth was frequently portrayed as a force destructive of men's autonomy and identity. It corrupted from within like a disease: "every outward Blessing carries a mortal Poison with it, which usually infects the Possessor." And it tempted from without like a seductress: 'our worldly Possessions tend to *Encrease* our *Lusts*; our Pride, Ambition, Luxury, and the like; and so more subject the Soul under the Government of the world." John Barnard argued that material success "bars the Happiness of the future World, and evidently destroys the well-being of the Soul. . . . For 'tis next to impossible, that a Rich man should not set his Heart upon these things; and contented with his present Portion, take no thought of securing a Portion in the Kingdom of God." Cotton Mather expressed the same extreme suspi-

---

[21]Michael Walzer, "Puritanism as a Revolutionary Ideology," *History and Theory*, 3 (1963): 84; Georgia Harkness, *John Calvin: The Man and His Ethics* (New York, 1931), p. 189; Jerold C. Brauer, "Reflections on the Nature of English Puritanism," *Church History*, 23 (1954): 102–3. Weber was aware that there were different kinds of success, but he was inclined to equate a legitimization of gain with an encouragement of it. "It is true that the usefulness of a calling, and thus its favour in the sight of God, is measured primarily in moral terms, and thus in terms of the importance of the goods produced in it for the community. But a further, and, above all, in practice the most important criterion is found in private profitableness." English Protestants' distrust of worldly success was stronger than Weber took it to be. "In conformity with the Old Testament and in analogy to the ethical valuation of good works, asceticism looked upon the pursuit of wealth as an end in itself as highly reprehensible; but the attainment of it as a fruit of labour in a calling was a sign of God's blessing." *The Protestant Ethic*, pp. 126, 162, 172, 267n.

cion of wealth when, after a serious fire in Boston, he warned against giving any importance to material possessions. "To labor insatiably for these things, is you see, to *Labour in the Fire*; perhaps for it; it is to *weary your selves for very Vanity. O Uncertain Riches! O Deceitful Riches! What Fool will Trust in you!*" The recommended attitude toward prosperity was humility combined with an awareness of its temptations.[22]

Acceptance of a calling as a guide to activity implied a willingness or a need to live with a constant sense of purpose. But what were the boundaries for executing this duty, and how was one to know when it had been fulfilled? In practice, the accumulation of riches might have provided such a guide, but in theory this convenient means of measurement was denied. Indeed, a frequent theme in discussions of wealth was the suggestion that happiness and self-possession depended less on the attainment of some material goal, which was always receding, than on the maintenance of restrained desires. There was no direct proportion between riches and grace. A dependence on providence, however, meant that one had to be grateful to God for whatever prosperity one had. Colonial expressions of belief in the calling often demonstrated a reluctance to assert men's self-sufficiency. An English work, a portion of Richard Lucas's popular devotional manual which was reprinted in Boston as "Rules Relating to Success in Trade," showed that a desire for increased wealth amounted to a denial of the notion of man's dependence on God:

What need would there be of shifts and equivocations, of fraud and circumvention, if a man had faith enough to believe, that God's blessing upon his industry were the only way to grow truly rich; I mean, to get, if not so much as he would, yet as much as would be good for him? what temptation would men lie under to bondage and drudgery, or to perplexity and anxiety, if he could contain his desires within those narrow bounds which nature and his station have prescribed him? what fears could disquiet the mind, which were formed into an intire resignation to, and dependence upon God?[23]

Contentment with one's material lot was the soundest attitude for mental and spiritual health.

God rewarded faithful societies, not individuals, with prosperity. In order to keep the activities of individuals subordinated to the public good, it was necessary that men, in their private callings, be prevented from basing an assurance of their state of grace on the degree of their material success. Timothy Cutler, whose religious career would carry him from the rectorship at Yale to an Anglican ministry in Boston, thought that it was obvious "that a Good Man hath not Outward Prosperity Promised to him,

---

[22]Nathaniel Walter, *The Character of a Christian Hero* . . . (Boston, 1746), p. 9; John Barnard, *The Hazzard and the Unprofitableness of Losing a Soul for the Sake of Gaining the World* (Boston, 1712), pp. 15, 17; Cotton Mather, *Advice from Taberah: A Sermon Preached after the Terrible Fire* . . . (Boston, 1711), p. 25; *The Pious Man's Directions*, p. 21.

[23]Richard Lucas, *Rules Relating to Success in Trade . . . Taken from His Enquiry after Happiness* (Boston, 1760), p. 20.

as a certain Reward of the greatest Piety and Vertue; and there is no need of it: for as he is an Immortable Being he may Receive his Happiness in another World." Everyday experience showed that "the Providences of God as to Particular Persons, are many times very promiscuously Administered. 'Tis observable, that Wicked Men are sometimes suffer'd to Flourish & Prosper, while the Righteous are afflicted." But societies existed only on earth, and so they required a different system of rewards and punishments. "The next world being no place for National Rewards, God usually indulges Religious Nations with much Outward Prosperity." Conversely, "Sometimes God testifies his displeasure against a sinful People, *by withholding or removing his blessings from them.*" The handiest terms for evaluating a society's prosperity, and hence its virtue, were mercantile ones. "A Nation is then said to be prosperous, when the Subjects of it are numerous and increasing, when its Limits are sufficient to contain and Support them; when it has a flourishing Trade, the Ballance of which is greatly in it's Favour."[24] Such crass economic measures of virtue were not suitable to individuals.

The outlook on material success which was inherent in the conception of the calling—a mixture of certainty and uncertainty because wealth was not a sign of grace, yet God willed the distribution of the world's goods— was manifest in the case of the unsuccessful, the poor. The poor were defined by the fact of their need, not by the process which caused it. Poverty was assumed to be part of the order of things, not necessarily a personal or social flaw, and therefore the responsibility of the community for the welfare of the poor was unquestioned. Though the exponents of the Protestant ethic are sometimes thought to have had a harsh attitude toward the poor, in fact they accepted a traditional Christian responsibility toward the weak and the impoverished. Providence tested men as well as favored them, and it was possible that "persons may sometimes come to *pinching poverty*; yet not for any particular, remarkable Sin or fault of their own." Sermons repeatedly assured the poor that they were not necessarily without grace.[25]

[24]"The Puritans conceived of public welfare as something entirely apart from the welfare of each of the individuals who collectively comprised the public. Rather the term indicated a positive pattern of virtue determined by God's unalterable and eternal law and ratified by a covenant between God and society." Stephen Foster, "The Puritan Social Ethic: Class and Calling in the First Hundred Years of Settlement in New England" (Ph.D. diss., Yale University, 1966), p. 43. See also Timothy Cutler, *The Firm Union of a People Represented . . .* (New London, Conn., 1717), p. 28; Samuel Whitman, *Practical Godliness the Way to Prosperity . . .* (New London, Conn., 1714), pp. 7–8; Nathan Bunkham, *The Just Expectations of God, from a People When His Judgments Are upon Them for Their Sins . . .* (Boston, 1741), p. 38; Henry Caner, *Joyfulness and Consideration: Or, the Duties of Prosperity and Adversity . . .* (Boston, 1761), p. 13.

[25]Benjamin Wadsworth, *Vicious Courses, Procuring Poverty . . .* (Boston, 1719), pp. 4–5; Cotton Mather, *The Fisher-mans Calling . . .* (Boston, 1712), p. 3; *idem, Some Seasonable Advice unto the poor . . .* (Boston, 1726), p. 9. David J. Rothman, *The Discovery of the Asylum: Social Order and Disorder in the New Republic* (Boston, 1971), chap. 1.

Though the community's respect and responsibility for the poor were repeatedly recommended, there were hints that these feelings were forced and also contrary to the inclinations of many citizens. This conflict of sentiment is evident in a pamphlet which urged leniency toward poor debtors. "Success therefore (so wise we are) seems to be the established Criterion to judge Men's Conduct and Characters by.—*But the Race is not to the Swift, nor the Battle to the Strong, nor Bread to the Wise, nor Riches to Men of Understanding*; and therefore to judge a Man's Principles or Conduct, to be Good or Bad, merely from his Success and Prosperity, or his Misfortunes and Adversity, is a very weak (if not a malicious) Conclusion and Judgment." As a group the poor had a traditional place in Christian society; poverty simply was not a sign of divine disfavor. As individuals, however, some of the poor were suspected of sin. Men tended to be dominated by particular vices, and there were several which led directly to poverty. "*Sloth* and *Idleness*, *Lust* and *Whoredom* are such Sins as in their nature, bring the Subjects of them to *Poverty*, and their Bodies and Names under *disagreeable Circumstances*."[26] Economic and moral conditions were related, but only in imprecise ways that varied from individual to individual.

If it was difficult for a rich man to live without sin and possible that a man was poor because of his sin, then how could a man be successful without failing in his calling? The answer involved something other than economic success, and though simple in theory it was difficult to apply in specific cases: man's success in fulfilling his calling was measured by his contribution to the well-being of the society as a whole. The ideals of stewardship and service provided guides for the proper consideration of success, and fulfillment of them required rational calculation in the Weberian sense. Stewardship required an individual to aim "at an *Eminence* of Service to the utmost of [his] Ability, and to *Shine* before others in the *Sphere* that Providence has set [him] in. It implies a *Publick Appearance* and an *Extensive Usefulness*." This kind of usefulness could involve mercantilist standards of utility, but it also comprehended noneconomic matters. Riches, of course, were "not sufficient in themselves to constitute a People Happy; yet they are considerable Blessings, which are Promised by God, and are in their Place and Order to be sought, and valued by men."

Commentators on colonial social conditions continued to believe that selfishness was dangerous to social order, and devotion to the wealth of the community seemed to them to be one means of restraining the destruc-

---

[26] *The Ill Policy and Inhumanity of Imprisoning Insolvent Debtors* . . . (Newport, R.I., 1754), p. 5; John Barnard, *Sin Testify'd against by Heaven and Earth: A Sermon Preached* . . . *after the Great and Terrible Earthquake* . . . (Boston, 1727), p. 11. "Abject poverty, the inability to maintain oneself on one's own income, the New Englanders feared as much as any men, but a very moderate financial competence punctuated by periodic reverses had a curious attraction for them." Foster, "The Puritan Social Ethic," p. 257.

tive force for the purposes of a stable and prosperous social order. The ceaseless nature of this effort to increase the community's wealth, "to promote *Trade* and *Merchandize, Husbandry,* and *Plenty* in a Land; to Endeavour as much as in them lies," may have been a means for men "to serve their Generation," but it also indicated a loss of confidence in the old social order, an order based on religious ideals.[27]

THE GREAT AWAKENING AND
THE CRITIQUE OF THE CALLING

The Great Awakening had the ironic effect of providing a religious context for the secularization of the social ethics of the calling. What was largely missing from the social ethic of the antagonistic parties in the revival was an awareness of an omnipotent God who ordered the world by His will. This notion had been part of the conception of the calling in its earlier formulation. By the middle of the eighteenth century, however, the calling had a more secular relevance to social organization.

In the Great Awakening the evangelical clergy attacked what they believed to be the inappropriate spiritual significance still attributed to the personal calling. Critics of the Awakening found themselves obliged to justify the notion of a personal calling, and they did so mostly on grounds of practical morality. Each side tended to concern itself with one of the callings to the exclusion of the other—the evangelicals with men's spiritual callings as Christians, and the nonevangelicals with the social nature of men's personal callings. Neither side was very successful in maintaining an integrated view of the two callings. Yet in their different ways they quarreled over the meaning of the calling for the same reason; both sides sought to preserve and to improve communal relations. Each side articulated its peculiar version of the idea that benevolence, a general concern with the welfare of others based on the identity of interests shared by members of a society, was essential for a proper life. In recommending this virtue they drew on ideas and values that were associated with the calling, but the way in which they employed these terms amounted to a less precise social ethic than the calling itself and a closer approximation to English benevolist thought.[28] Apparently, the emphasis on the public good and the denial of unrestrained economic individualism, two characteristics of a social philosophy based on the calling, continued to be valued by men even after their religious importance was lessened. As the religious sanctions weakened, social sanctions became all the more necessary. Changes in intellectual and economic life—the development of more empirical social thought and the increase in the variety and flexibility of economic roles—had made the calling's particular combination of values

[27]Colman, *A Holy and Useful Life,* p. 7; Pemberton, *A True Servant,* p. 5; Mather, *Durable Riches,* p. 8.
[28]Perry Miller, *Jonathan Edwards* (New York, 1949), pp. 244-45, 293.

unworkable, but men retained a desire for values which could maintain social order and their self-respect. Such a process would suggest that an awareness of certain social and personal evils was enough by itself to encourage the retention of a moral code applicable to work and that the sources of guilt were not strictly religious.

The evangelical clergy was skeptical of the notion that simple fulfillment of a social role which contributed to an objective public good like the prosperity of the community had a religious value. The mentality that accepted the notion of the calling had always contained a readiness to see the world as a place of potential evil where true happiness was impossible. But through the device of "weaned affections," by which men fulfilled their duties on earth in order to glorify God, Protestant social ethics provided for a transcendence of the corruption of the world and made work a positive obligation. This view of work implicitly sanctioned the particular economic and social arrangements of a society and legitimized men's ordinary activity in it. Now that sanction was questioned.[29] The Great Awakening saw the erosion of a social frame of reference for the criticism of economic activity. Views on commerce began to be aligned for and against it, rather than maintaining the previous stress on its subordination to moral questions. The hierarchical arrangement of values began to transform into a polarity. The tendency to forsake economic life, or at least to voice the proposition, was a development of the late colonial period; it was not part of a traditional legacy of values to be set aside in circumstances of unaccustomed commercial exuberance.

The preachers in the Great Awakening attacked the spiritual and social abuses which had occurred when men lacked a proper understanding of the notion of the calling. Their attack on conditions in society was so extensive in scope that nearly all economic activity was thrown into a questionable light, and the notion that the social order had a divine sanction lost tacit acceptance. For example, in an election sermon in Boston, Samuel Wigglesworth claimed to be criticizing only man's excess in earthly pursuits, but he gave little advice on how to pursue one's calling in a religious manner. *"The Powerful Love of the World, and Exorbitant Reach after Riches,* which is become the reigning Temper in Persons of all Ranks in our Land, is alone enough to awaken our concerns for abandon'd, slighted and forgotten Religion." Wealth, which had previously been a source of anxiety, now seemed to be an outright condemnation of its possessor. Gilbert Tennent, the leader of the revival in the middle colonies, contrasted those people with the "riches of Christ" with

---

[29]For an account of the psychological connections between the revival and economic expansion (with its attendant disruption of the social order) which presents the conflict as one between ambition and traditional authority, see Richard L. Bushman, *From Puritan to Yankee: Character and the Social Order in Connecticut, 1690–1765* (Cambridge, Mass., 1967); cf. Alan Heimert, *Religion and the American Mind from the Great Awakening to the Revolution* (Cambridge, Mass., 1966), pp. 55–56.

"another Generation, of as mean and sordid Wretches, in whose grovling Bosoms, beates nothing that is great or generous; who imagine Happiness is to be had in temporal Wealth and Riches . . . don't ye see the contrary with your Eyes, that the most grow in Wickedness, in Proportion to the Increase of their Wealth." Jonathan Edwards saw moral dangers in all economic life. "The circumstances of the affairs and business of the male sex does in some respects expose them to many more temptations than those of the female. Their business leads them more into the world, to be concerned more extensively with the affairs and business of the world, when they have more worldly objects in their view to tempt them." At the millenium, Edwards envisaged, commerce would be a means for men to communicate their love throughout the world, but in the meantime "wicked debauched men" used trade as a means "to favor men's covetousness and pride."[30] A generation earlier adherents of the calling had thought that the benefits of commerce could be more immediate.

For the evangelical clergy the great sin was selfishness. Previously, selfishness was usually thought to be evident simply as a deviation from accepted standards of behavior, but for the evangelicals it could be characteristic of any action because it involved men's attitudes toward others and not just their actions. Selfishness was most to be feared when it was least evident; hence the evangelicals especially distrusted situations which seemed to encourage men's Pharisaism by conferring tacit merit on a mere conformity to objective standards of behavior. "However full of love persons may seem to be to their neighbours," Edward's theological disciple, Joseph Bellamy, warned, "if all arises merely from self-love, or is for self-ends, nothing is genuine; and that whether things worldly, or things religious, occasion their love." Tennent, like many of the other evangelicals, was transfixed by the destructive power of selfishness.

It is the most egregious, enormous, and blasphemous villany! pregnant with numerous and crimson iniquities, and the fatal source of all that train of evils and calamities, that have innundated this lower world, and made it groan and travel, since the apostacy of our first parents, even 'till now; an evil that makes this dark globe a Bedlam, a Hospital, a Bochim, an Acaldama: An evil that tears in pieces all the sinews of society, all the strong and tender tyes of nature, honour, justice, grace and gratitude! An evil which is the grand makebain in the church and state; the sworn enemy to order and harmony, to peace, unity, and love![31]

[30]Samuel Wigglesworth, *An Essay for Reviving Religion* . . . (Boston, 1733), p. 25; Gilbert Tennent, "The Unsearchable Riches of Christ" [1739], and Jonathan Edwards, "A History of the Work of Redemption" [1777], sermons published in *The Great Awakening: Documents Illustrating the Crisis and Its Consequences*, ed. Alan Heimert and Perry Miller (New York, 1967), pp. 16, 30; Perry Miller, "Jonathan Edwards' Sociology of the Great Awakening," *New England Quarterly*, 21 (1948): 67; idem, "Jonathan Edwards and the Great Awakening," *Errand into the Wilderness* (Cambridge, Mass., 1956), p. 165.

[31]Joseph Bellamy, "True Religion Delineated" [1750], in *The Great Awakening*, ed. Heimert and Miller, p. 558; John Odlin, *Doing Righteousness: An Evidence of Our Being Righteous* . . . (Boston, 1742), p. 14; Gilbert Tennent, Introduction to *Self Disclaimed and Christ Exalted* . . . , by David Bostwick (Philadelphia, 1758), p. viii.

Such a sin was worth avoiding, but the evangelical preachers thought that the corruption of the calling as a guide to Christian life had prevented men from becoming aware of their situation. Too often, or so it seemed to men of tender conscience, the sin of security complemented that of selfishness. It was stupid as well as dangerous, Tennent warned, to "keep Driving, Driving, to Duty, Duty, under this Notion, That it will recommend natural Men to the Favour of God, or entitle them to the Promises of Grace and Salvation: And thus those blind Guides fix a deluded World upon the false Foundation of their own Righteousness, and so exclude them from the dear Redeemer." The recognition that the personal calling, when divorced from the spiritual calling, was a "blind force" led men to seek a new formulation for the criteria of legitimate activity. What troubled the sensitive spirits of the time was the numbing effect of what should have been alarming developments. "We see a poor secure World going on boldly in the Paths of Destruction and Death, not withstanding all the Terrors of the Law of God, notwithstanding all the faithful Warnings of the Ministers of Christ, and all the shocking Dispensations of Providence. What an astonishing Thought is this. Can rational Creatures cast themselves down the dreadful Precipice with their Eyes open!"

The discussion of the sin of security seems to give some substance, if only by giving it recognition as an object of attack, to the thesis, advanced in different ways by R. H. Tawney and Max Weber, that belief in the notion of the calling led eventually to a rough equation of worldly success with spiritual election. But the audiences of preachers like Edwards had such confidence badly shaken, and perhaps reversed, when they heard that "men's worldly possessions and worldly honour with which they are so taken very commonly prove their undoing; setting their hearts so much upon them occasions them to neglect God, and so they have their portion in this life, and when they have enjoyed all that comfort that they have to enjoy in those things, they have ruined their soul's salvation, there remains nothing else for them." Edwards claimed to have reason to believe that the seeds of uneasiness were already planted in the hearts of the secure.

Instead of your seasons becoming more convenient, have not you found on the contrary that they have grown more and more inconvenient? Do not you find now that you are much more incumbered with the business and concerns of the world than when you were young, your heart more charged with those things, and less and less at liberty, and less and less disposed to mind the affairs of your soul? . . . Is it not now high time to set about the work, without any more putting off? When you have been pursuing a shadow thirty or forty years together without overtaking it, is it not then time to give over?[32]

---

[32]Gilbert Tennent, *The Danger of an Unconverted Ministry* . . . (Philadelphia, 1740), p. 10; Jonathan Dickinson, "The Witness of the Spirit" [1740], in *The Great Awakening*, ed. Heimert and Miller, p. 101; Miller, "Jonathan Edwards' Sociology," pp. 73, 64–65; Heimert, *Religion and the American Mind*, pp. 52–55.

Having lost confidence in the calling's ability to integrate social and spiritual life, the evangelical preachers nevertheless continued to urge self-subordination as the basis of religious and social life. This idea was of course inherent in the calling's initial formulation. Subordination had previously been an impersonal matter, based on differences in power and involving the fulfillment of social duties in order to glorify God, but the evangelicals made self-subordination a matter of affection. The evangelicals lacked confidence in the belief that the social order was an expression of God's will. For them society was a shapeless thing; they cared about society in the sense of valuing the ties among men, but in their view the most significant of these ties were emotional. The functional and institutional aspects of social and economic relations were less important to them. Decent social arrangements were, they thought, impossible without brotherly love.

For the evangelicals, service, the means for the expression of one's acceptance of a calling, became an attitude of mind rather than an actual activity. In part this change stemmed from their heightened conviction of the evil of the world and a distrust of any doctrine which seemed to give work an autonomous spiritual importance. In a funeral sermon, Samuel Davies, the leading Presbyterian minister in Virginia in the 1750s, contended that "the melancholy occasion of this day may convince you that success in trade, and a plentiful estate, procured and kept by industry and good management, is neither a security against death, nor a comfort in it." Previous colonial funeral sermons had not encouraged the hope that success was a comfort after death, but neither had they disparaged the industry of a respected man. The evangelicals believed that successful Americans were unable to maintain weaned affections, and, in an effort to preserve the spiritual ties of Christian love among men, the preachers warned against the confusion of the moral with the economic importance of work. This spiritual gain, however, came at the expense of the previous hierarchical integration of economic and moral questions, in which matters of justice were viewed as having the prevailing weight. The result was the disparagement of the importance of work as an expression of the rational nature with which God had endowed man. The criteria for right action had become subjective; what counted was how one felt while acting, not how one acted. The line between this form of brotherly love and the benevolism of the nonevangelical clergy was often unclear, especially after the height of the Great Awakening had passed. But for the nonevangelicals brotherly love, or charity as they usually labeled it, was an instrumental virtue as well as an emotional tie. The evangelicals were less concerned with such concrete expression of their faith. Their indifference to the role of work in a holy life was evident in their version of Edenic innocence. "That the state of innocence was a state of ease and spontaneous plenty, we may infer also from the fatherly care of the Creator, in planting a garden in Eden, richly furnished with every tree pleasant to the eye, or good for food, and placing the man there to look after it, not for his toil, but for his pleasure, and to live upon the divine bounty, spontaneously springing out of the earth."[33] Previous descriptions of Eden and heaven, it will be remembered, showed them to be anything but places of "ease and spontaneous plenty."

The evangelicals often tacitly recognized the extent of individualism in their society in their confused efforts to encourage a public spirit. During the Great Awakening and continuing in its aftermath, preachers gave sermons on the need for brotherly love and the need for a subordination of self to society. Membership in a society was still considered to be important, but the old conviction that only ruin could come from independence was shaken. Independent men were prospering only too well. Instead of relying on the prescription of roles as a guide for behavior, men needed instruction in proper social attitudes if the community was to be preserved. "Mutual *Love* is the *Band* and *Cement*; which unless it be preserv'd and express'd, *Society* becomes a *Snare* and *Torment* . . . by the Neglect of its Exercise, and much more by its Contrary, [men] will be tempted, against the *Law* of *Nature*, to seek a *single* and independent State, in order to secure their *Ease* and *Safety*."[34] In an effort to convince their followers of the spiritual insufficiency of "a single and independent state," the evangelicals stressed men's religious obligations rather than their social ones. Though much of the stimulus for the intensity of the evangelicals' religious views may have come from their dissatisfaction with the way in which men in their society worked, they did not try to reform men's actual work. The evangelicals continued to recommend the attitudes that had been associated with the calling—they urged individuals to be content with their lot and to see their own happiness in relation to that of others—but they ceased to stress the obligation for work itself. Thus Gilbert Tennent could recommend responsible social behavior in the traditional terms of men's dual callings while actually minimizing the importance of a personal calling for a Christian life. "Now the Business we have to do is two-fold, namely, of our *general* and *particular* Calling. The former concerns us as Christians, the latter as Members of a Community; as such we should have some Office Civil or Religious, which may profit Mankind; the Duties of which we should conscientiously perform. It is a base Thing to live like a Drone upon the Fruits of others Labours, without doing any Thing for our Sup-

[33]Samuel Davies, "Indifference to Life Urged from Its Shortness and Vanity" [1759] and "The Primitive and Present State of Man Compared" [1758], *Sermons on Important Subjects*, 3 vols. (New York, 1841), 1: 435 and 3: 301; William Balch, *A Publick Spirit, as Express'd in Praying for the Peace and Seeking the Good of Jerusalem* . . . (Boston, 1749), p. 19; Jonathan Ashley, *The Great Duty of Charity* . . . (Boston, 1742).

[34]Gilbert Tennent, *Brotherly Love Recommended, by the Argument of the Love of Christ* . . . (Philadelphia, 1748), p. 3; see also Samuel Cooper, *A Sermon Preached in Boston, New England, before the Society for Encouraging Industry and Employing the Poor* (Boston, 1753).

port, while we have a Capacity!"[35] Such a sharp division between general and personal callings had the ironic effect of giving an autonomous value to secular pursuits, though Tennent's sermon was an attack on men's preoccupation with earthly things. The viability of the calling was undermined when social and economic necessities gained priority as guides to activity.

Faced with what seemed to be a repudiation of the traditional social ethic, the nonevangelical clergy defended the secular importance of the calling. Belief in one's calling was too complicated a matter, they thought, to be sustained by a commitment to "mutual love," a vague notion that lacked the power to compel personal endeavor which the idea of executing God's will had had in the classic formulation of the calling. The calling had been a persuasive model for men's work because it had enabled men to achieve a sense of religious dignity in their daily activities. The nonevangelical clergy wanted to maintain the belief that in fulfilling their roles in society men were sustaining an order ordained by God. A generation before the Awakening, Timothy Cutler had explained that social order was best preserved by an awe of God and not by a reliance on human goodness.

The Favour of God, the Serenity of Conscience, the Mighty Rewards we Expect from our Maker, are too Spiritual Things for a Carnal Mind to See and Relish, Death, and the Final Judgement, and the Miserys of Hell are things too far off (though God knows, near enough) to express Fear on our Minds. And thus by keeping the Outward Actions of Men in due Bounds and Channels, the Good of Humane Society is Secured; besides what Advantage the Practice of what is Good, and Avoiding of what is Evil may be to the Mortifying of Corrupt Principles within us.[36]

As expressed by the nonevangelical clergy, the importance of the personal calling became nearly so great that the notion of glorifying God by fulfilling one's social role was nearly lost sight of. John Barnard, urging men to good works, practically equated service for other men to that for God. "Good works specially denote, our being, some Way or other, useful and beneficial to those about us, and so they are comprehensive of our doing good to the Souls of Men, and endeavouring to promote their spir-

---

[35]Gilbert Tennent, *The Necessity of Studying to be Quiet and Doing Our Business . . .* (Philadelphia, 1744), pp. 19-20. Alan Heimert views this stripped-down version of the values of the calling as an innovation which "divested Americans of this quasi-feudal intellectual heritage by defining virtue not as a variety of deportments that differed from class to class and calling to calling but as a 'temper' essentially the same for all men, regardless of station." The concept of the calling had, of course, recommended the same "temper" for all men in their work. Heimert is probably right, though, in saying that the lessened stress on personal callings played an important part in adapting men's values to life in a more open society. *Religion and the American Mind*, pp. 55-56.

[36]Cutler, *The Firm Union*, p. 161; Increase Mather, *Ichabod: Or, a Discourse, Shewing What Cause There Is to Fear That the Glory of the Lord is Departing from New England . . .* (Boston, 1729), p. 78.

itual and eternal Interests, and our doing good to the Bodies of Men, or promoting their temporal Interest." The spokesmen for this more secular interpretation of the calling thought that the revivalists lacked a clear idea of the limits which human nature imposed on religious life on earth. In an effort to dispel the more sublime visions of rampant brotherly love, they made some outright justifications, hitherto rare, of self-love as a guide to conduct. These justifications of self-interest were not individualistic, however, but rather an incorporation of current ideas about the ethical merits of benevolence with the rigorist ethic associated with the calling. The result was a strongly corporatist social scheme which relied on benevolist ethics for the maintenance of justice and order. In his recommendation of support for the Boston Society for Encouraging Industry and Employing the Poor, the Reverend Samuel Cooper, while legitimizing rational self-love, pointed out that men depended on one another for physical survival, and that this interdependence was a means for their fulfillment. "The Author of Nature has plainly framed and fitted us for one another; and our mutual Wants, Weaknesses and Dependencies, do oblige us to unite together, and embrace and support each other by a mutual Charity. . . . Universal Charity may very well be compared to the great Law of Gravitation, by which all Particles of Nature mutually operate upon, and attract each other."

Both sides drew on the benevolist theory of ethics. The "Liberals" emphasized the doctrine's teachings about the possibility of harmony between self-love and public virtue, and the evangelicals contrasted benevolence with a type of selfishness that was evil because it lacked the pleasures of brotherly love. Noah Hobart, in a discussion of the obligations of a member to his community, pointed out that industrious and frugal men served themselves as they served the public. "Whatever any man gains by honest Labour, is just so much gained to the Society of which he is a Member." In an election sermon about the relationship between religion and prosperity, James Lockwood showed a similar haphazard approach to relations which the notion of the calling had previously dealt with more comprehensively. "'Tis the appointed Way, for Persons to thrive in the World, and acquire Wealth & Riches. . . . Now, the Wealth of particular Members, is the Riches & strength of the Community: and where Idleness and its natural Consequents are generally avoided; and Industry & Frugality are the Character of a People; such a community is, so far, in a prosperous and flourishing State." John Thomson, a leader of the antirevivalists, found self-love to be a way to achieve both earthly and religious happiness. "Self-love is so incorporated with our rational Constitution, that its simply impossible for us to denounce it, it is supposed in all the Promises and Threatnings of the Word, of both Law and Gospel, it is supposed in our Happiness which is joined together with the Glory of God, as Mans chief End, in our Catechism, and therefore it must be acknowledged to be, tho' not the Sole and Adequate, yet the partial and inadequate Foundation, *i.e.* Motive of our Obedience."[37] The conditions of right living had become more secular, and the importance of spiritual states and conscience was slighted, perhaps because the revivalists had preempted these aspects of the calling and promised extravagant and unrealizable things from them.

The nonevangelical clergy could come to terms with the practical necessities and arrangements of the world more easily than the evangelical preachers did. Though they appeared to be less anxious than the evangelicals about the inherent spiritual problems involved in a Christian life, the nonevangelical clergymen were much more concerned with the practice of religious ideals in society. Charles Chauncey, who strongly criticized the social disorder associated with the Great Awakening, spoke about charity in terms that reveal little suspicion of the world's activities and that portray justice and love as matters of practice and not just feeling. At a funeral Chauncey described the deceased as "an active spirit, diligent in business; [who] did not pursue it to the neglect of the one thing needful. His share of this world's goods, the fruit of his own labour, under the divine blessing, was very considerable; but he did not keep it to himself. He 'honoured the Lord with his substance'; chearfully embracing the opportunities providence put into his hands of relieving the necessities of the poor. He was 'rich in good works, ready to distribute, willing to communicate.'" The nonevangelical clergymen believed that everyone was "obliged to discountenance the bad Things, prevailing in the Land," but this obligation applied to men in their callings. They asked: "Can there be Order, where Men transgress the Limits of their Station, and intermeddle in the Business of others? So far from it, that the only effectual Method, under God, for the Redress of *general Fails*, is, for *every one* to be faithful, in doing what is *proper* for him in his *own Place*: And even *all* may *properly* bear a Part, in *rectifying the Disorders* of this Kind, at this Day."[38]

The most immediate disorders resulted from the revival itself, and it was on the question of the proper relationship between piety and livelihood that the nonevangelical clergy showed its commitment to preserve a

---

[37] John Barnard, *A Zeal for Good Works Excited and Directed* . . . (Boston, 1742), p. 16; Cooper, *Sermon Preached in Boston*, pp. 12–13; Noah Hobart, *Civil Government the Foundation of Social Happiness* . . . (New London, Conn., 1751), p. 19; James Lockwood, *Religion the Highest Interest of a Civil Community, and the Surest Means of Its Prosperity* . . . (New London, Conn., 1754), p. 31; John Thomson, "The Government of the Church of Christ" [1741], in *The Great Awakening*, ed. Heimert and Miller, p. 116. Heimert simplifies and exaggerates the approval which the "Liberals" gave to self-interest. For them there was not a "seeming impossibility" in the reconciliation of "an essential individualism" and "a conservative desire to preserve the ancient landmarks of the social order," because they accepted the notion that the order depended on a commitment to the public good and a restraint on selfishness. *Religion and the American Mind*, pp. 251–52; cf. Bushman, *From Puritan to Yankee*, pp. 278–80.

[38] Charles Chauncey, *Charity to the Distressed Members of Christ Accepted as Done to Himself, and Rewarded, at the Judgment-Day* . . . (Boston, 1757), p. 30; *idem, Seasonable Thoughts on the State of Religion in New England* . . . (Boston, 1743), p. 366.

specific social order. The revivals, with their insistence that brotherly love precede and inform any act of charity or duty, were often too much of a good thing. "There are Duties to be attended, as well as *religious Meetings*; But han't [*sic*] the Zeal of People to attend the *latter*, been so great, as to leave little Room for the *observable* Practise of the former?" The critics of the Great Awakening always returned to the question of how men were acting in their specific social roles. Had not the revival diverted men, Chauncey asked, from what should be "their Care about those Laws of God, which regard their Conduct, in the *several Relations* and *Capacities of Life*? Have they been, in any Proportion zealous to be better *Husbands* and *Wives*, better *Masters* and *Servants*?"[39]

It has been rightly said of these "liberal" preachers that they were defensive of the status quo in society and that they relied on authority as a means of maintaining social order. They believed that the public good was still something definable and that men benefited most as individuals when they worked in harmony with others. Conversely, the hints of antisocial attitudes on the part of the evangelicals opened the way for new social attitudes with regard to the flexibility of roles and the pursuit of individual interests. In the middle of the eighteenth century, however, the most significant characteristics of evangelical social thought were its indifference to traditional problems, its lack of concern for social institutions, and its distrust of explicit guidelines for behavior.

As the excitement of the Awakening died down, the evangelicals began once more to pay attention to men's actual behavior and assigned it more importance in a Christian life than they had previously. Joseph Bellamy, writing about Christian prosperity in the millenium, showed that the calling, though an insufficient guide for present life, was still seen as an ideal way for ordering humanity. "While everyone improves his time well, and is diligent in his calling, according to the rules of our holy religion, and all luxury, intemperance, and extravagance are banished from the nations of the earth, it is certain that this globe will be able to sustain with food and raiment, a number of inhabitants immensely greater than ever yet dwelt on it at a time." Even Gilbert Tennent used the analogy of social and cosmic order, an argument which had been used for generations to justify the calling, to impress his audience with its significance.

To what, my Brethren, but Diligence, can we ascribe all the Works of Art, all the curious Structures and stately Ornaments which we behold the world beautify'd with? And isn't it this that has adorn'd the human Mind with the nobler Beauties of Science? I may add, that Diligence is commended to our Imitation by all Sorts of Examples. Universal Nature is a Glass in which we may behold the Necessity and Excellency of this Duty; the inanimate Parts of the Creation, are in a Course of their constant Labour to answer the Design of their Being.[40]

[39]Chauncey, *Seasonable Thoughts*, p. 305.
[40]Joseph Bellamy, "The Millenium" [1758], in *The Great Awakening*, ed. Heimert and Miller, p. 628; Tennent, *The Necessity of Studying to be Quiet*, p. 26.

The evangelicals, with their renewed concern about the way men acted, as well as about the spirit in which they acted, seemed to be drawing nearer to the nonevangelicals in their social ethics; but the evangelical clergy remained vague about the duty of men to work in this world.

After its secularization, the calling left an ethical legacy for men's attitudes toward work. One possible result of the loss of an awareness of Christian liberty, in which men were freed from "bondage to self and sin" in order to serve God properly, might have been the emergence of an ethic of economic individualism and a sanction for the satisfaction of natural desires. But, for several decades at least, these changes were less significant than certain parts of the social ethic of the calling which were perpetuated. The unrestrained self continued to be the chief object of moral concern, and work was habitually subjected as much to standards of justice as to standards of economic performance. Certain values associated with the calling—notably, industry and frugality—became autonomous ethical criteria for behavior, but the type of attitudes toward work which they were supposed to foster were not much different from those prescribed by the calling. The secularization of these values involved an effort to apply, not to accommodate, traditional standards of behavior in terms determined more by social realities than by religious ones.

III

THE RECOGNITION OF
COMMERCIAL LIFE

ESPITE THE LESSENED RELIGIOUS IMPORTANCE of the calling as a concept for understanding men's work, its social ethics of industry and frugality remained standards for the evaluation of economic behavior within the community. By the 1730s, society had come to be thought of as something more fluid and less prescriptive in its definition of duties than had been the case with the calling, and industry and frugality became matters more of virtue than of holy behavior. The secularization of these social ethics involved a process in which different strains of English thought—rigorist and benevolist ethics, republican ideology, and mercantilist economics—were combined to justify the values of industry and frugality. Idleness and extravagance, the terms which indicated a lack of industry and frugality, changed from offenses against God's will to offenses against oneself and society. One of the symptoms of this process of ethical secularization was the effort to incorporate the values of industry and frugality with a more empirical description of the organization and motivations of work. Industry and frugality were applied as terms for the understanding and regulation of life in a society in which commercial questions could be separated from religious questions but not from social and moral ones.

The tasks set for this moral regulation—the attainment of economic development and the alleviation of personal corruption—were at cross-purposes, though they seldom appeared so to the colonists, who assumed that the rationality of economic life was compatible with the rationality of moral responsibility. The tension in purposes corresponded to the colonists' economic situation.[1] America, especially from the second to the sixth decade of the eighteenth century, was the scene of an extraordinary economic expansion characterized by the involvement of the mass of the population in commercial life. Few Americans were self-sufficient, and nearly everyone was involved in the economic ties of the market and credit, a situation marked by the prevalent use and demand for currency from the 1720s onward. The interpretation which traditional values placed on such developments has already been sketched. But if American life was marked by the penetration of commerce it was also characterized by an economy which was primitive from the standpoint of growth. The gains had been those of extension, not structural change. The chief factor in the increase of production was population increase, and the sale of staple exports was the basic source of income. The lack of commercial banks, the confusion of earnings and capital gain, the shortage of liquid capital, unsophisticated business methods of cost accounting and organization, and a propensity for consumption rather than reinvestment of earnings obstructed capital formation that could have been used for development. In this situation of structural underdevelopment, however, Americans demonstrated the trait which is essential to the success of a market economy, a personal motivation to raise one's standard of living, a trait that simultaneously offended traditional values and encouraged analysis of economic behavior.

The Secularization of Industry and Frugality

The combination of acquisitiveness with an irrational use of wealth violated the ascetic prudence recommended in religious teachings and made it difficult for Americans to accept their prosperity. In his sermon on the ill effects of prosperity, John Danforth said that God had given New

[1] Two surveys of the colonial economy are Stuart Bruchey, *The Roots of American Economic Growth 1607-1861* (New York, 1965), and William S. Sachs and Ari Hoogenboom, *The Enterprising Colonials: Society on the Eve of the Revolution* (Chicago, 1965). On particular features of the economy, see Douglass C. North, *Growth and Welfare in the American Past* (Englewood Cliffs, N.J., 1966); George R. Taylor, "American Economic Growth before 1840: An Exploratory Essay," *Journal of Economic History*, 24 (1964): 427-44; D. A. Farnie, "The Commercial Empire of the Atlantic, 1607-1783," *Economic History Review*, 2nd ser., 15 (1962): 205-18; Bray Hammond, *Banks and Politics in America from the Revolution to the Civil War* (Princeton, 1957), chap. 1; E. James Ferguson, "Currency Finance: An Interpretation of Colonial Monetary Practices," *William and Mary Quarterly*, 3rd ser., 10 (1953): 153-80; Richard A. Lester, "Currency Issues to Overcome Depressions in Pennsylvania, 1723 and 1729," *Journal of Economic History*, 46 (1938): 324-75; *idem*, "Currency Issues to Overcome Depressions in Delaware, New Jersey, New York, and Maryland, 1715-1737," *ibid.*, 47 (1939): 182-217; Curtis P. Nettels, "The Origins of Paper Money in the English Colonies," *Economic History Review*, 3 (1934): 35-56; Theodore G. Thayer, "The Land-Bank System in the American Colonies," *Journal of Economic History*, 13 (1953): 145-59; Robert A. East, "The Business Entrepreneur in a Colonial Economy," *ibid.*, 6, suppl. (1946): 16-27; and Arthur H. Cole, "The Tempo of Mercantile Life in Colonial America," *Business History Review*, 33 (1959): 277-99.

England material blessings, and that the people, "overladen with Lusts," allowed the gifts of providence "to Overwhelm and Sink their unsanctifyed Hearts." He drew a simple lesson from this situation: "the Paradise of Prosperity is no guard against the Entrance of Sin." Like most American commentators of the early eighteenth century, Danforth was more suspicious of prosperity than of trade itself and he forthrightly opposed the extravagance he thought accompanied it. Extravagance alarmed him because of its traditional function as a symptom of an unrestrained self, and he was fearful of the chaotic and destructive energies that the ungoverned individual released. There was a "wilful Deafness of a Degenerate People, under prosperity," which was the result of "the Infatuating Influences that a Proud Worldly and Sensual Selfishness hath upon the hearts of the Degenerate." What such people ignored was "Christ's first Lesson of Self-Denial." Instead, they satisfied their "Carnal Self" with "Bodily Enjoyments, (to take their Ease, and to Eat and Drink, and be Merry, etc.)." Danforth thought that the situation had gone too far for self-imposed moderation to be feasible. He hinted at his hopes that the prevailing prosperity would lessen. "Prosperity Equips and mounts a proud man; affords Idols to the Covetous, and furnishes the Drunkard and Sensual Epicure to fill up his measure: *Vessels* exclusively and most richly Laden, do often sink with over-much *Weight*." Like the spider, which drew "nourishment for the *Poison* from the *wholsome Flowers*," "*Self-Idolizers*" ruined the "*Temporal Prosperity*" on which they thrived. It seemed to Danforth that sin was directly proportional to individual prosperity. "The more Money with many, the more sinful vanity and silly Gayety of Apparel: the more Estate, the fewer works of Piety & Charity."[2]

In addition to their anxiety about the consequences of prosperity, the colonists feared that they were not working in a socially useful manner. Work was a constant obligation, and no degree of success could relieve one of it. It was a violation of God's will to ignore this duty. "God's glory and the good of men" required of all men, no matter how "High and Rich in the World," that "their powers and abilities ought to be some way or other employed." To do otherwise would be to violate the "plain command of God, that Persons should *do their own business*, should *work with their own hands*, to supply their *own wants*."[3] Idleness was different from inactivity; it was usually discussed in reference to restless, purposeless activities like drinking and gambling.

Many New England clergymen took the opportunity provided by the earthquake of 1727 to explain to their congregations that pride manifested

[2] John Danforth, *The Vile Profanations of Prosperity by the Degenerate among the People of God* . . . (Boston, 1704), pp. 7, 35–36, 40.

[3] "Antigallican #2," *American Magazine, or Monthly Chronicle for the British Colonies* (Philadelphia, 1757–58), December, p. 119; Cotton Mather, *Bonifacius: An Essay upon the Good*, ed. David Levin (Cambridge, Mass., 1966), p. 9; Benjamin Wadsworth, *The Sin of Pride, Described & Condemned* . . . (Boston, 1718), p. 13; idem, *Vicious Courses, Procuring Poverty* . . . (Boston, 1719), p. 7.

in luxury or idleness was a provoking sin to God. Thomas Prince, a prominent Boston clergyman, explained that pride involved a willingness to exert selfishness in a disorderly fashion. "This Vice," he said, "consists in an high Conceit of our selves, in undervaluing & contemning our Neighbours, in Envying their Honours, and exalting our selves against the Glorious God." The sin often took the form of luxury. "It expresses it self in Boasting of and Praising our Persons or Actions [and] in extravagant Apparel, Building, Furniture, expensive and pompous ways of living." When men acted in these ways they gave the world more importance than they gave God, and according to Christian beliefs they were governed by their "*Sensual Appetites*" and "had come to live like *Beasts*." If the people of Boston continued to act in this way, they, like the inhabitants of Sodom, would be judged by God and suffer calamities.[4]

The concern with motive, as well as effects, in these matters of worldliness and frugality was essential as long as the problem was one of sin rather than vice. Thus, states of mind, like "an immoderate Love of the World," were indications of the sin of covetousness. Some men attempted to disguise an uncharitable reluctance to part with their riches "under the Specious Names of *Frugality*, and good Husbandry." Another writer on the same subject explained that the sin consisted in an "Excessive Esteem" of wealth and "an Idoletrous trust and confidence" placed in riches. Such desires indicated "a Discontentment with God's allotment, and an irregular Endeavour after more than God is pleas'd to allow us."[5]

The attacks on idleness and luxury depended in part on Christian beliefs about the transitory and unsatisfactory nature of earthly life. The notion of a providentially ordered world also provided a device for criticizing these failures as sins. After 1730, however, even religious figures often saw these failures less as sins than as personal failings and social vices. Throughout the late colonial period ministers denounced luxury, covetousness, and other forms of sensuality in much the same terms, whether they were treating religious problems or secular ones. There was a remarkable resemblance between the sin of pride and the vice of selfishness, which argues as much for a concern with the self as for objections to behavior proscribed on the basis of traditional codes. Thus an essayist in the *Virginia Gazette* could condemn frivolous upper-class manners in terms formerly used by pietistic moralists. "It is not monstrous! that a Man, because he is born to an Estate, is to imagine that the World was made for him alone?" But the writer drew a republican rather than a Christian moral lesson. He warned that there were "Vices . . . sufficient to spend an

---

[4]Thomas Prince, *Earthquakes the Works of God & Tokens of His Just Displeasure . . .* , 2nd ed. (Boston, 1727), p. 29; Nathaniel Gookin, *The Day of Trouble Near, the Tokens of It, and a Due Preparation for It . . .* (Boston, 1728), p. 21.

[5]Jabez Fitch, *The Work of the Lord in the Earthquake To Be Duly Regarded by Us . . .* (Boston, 1728), p. 13; Joseph Sewall, *A Caveat against Covetousness . . .* (Boston, 1718), pp. 3, 5.

Empire; and as Luxury creeps in, his Wants are greater; his Desires increase: Ambition, Pride, and Envy, are his constant Attendants."[6]

The extent of secularization in ethics is evident, for example, in a sermon by Charles Chauncey in which he advocated a stable currency as a necessity for social justice. He urged the "civil Fathers" to find some way to prevent "people's laying out so much of the fruit of their labour, in that which is *needless* and *extravagant.*" The excesses of "all ranks of people," he argued, needed correction. Like the preachers in the first decades of the eighteenth century, he attributed the excesses to pride, but in his application it was a pride without reference to God; instead, the simple fact of self-indulgence constituted a crime. Similarly, Andrew Eliot, minister of Boston's New North Church, while preaching about "an evil and adulterous generation," pointed out that pride was a "Sin of the Times." According to him, pride was any form of self-indulgence or self-righteousness. "It appears in our Dress, in our Furniture, and in all our Behaviour. Superiours treat those, who are below them, with Haughtiness and Contempt; and Inferiors affect to make as good as Appearance, as they do, whom Providence has placed above them." This reference to the providential source of civil authority was the only point at which Eliot indicated that pride was a sin against the divine order. In the rest of his sermon, the fact that luxury was a social evil was sufficient cause for its denunciation. "We all agree," he charged, "that *Frugality* is necessary, to retrieve us from the Difficulties in which we are involved; but no one is willing to begin, and to set an Example of that, which every one recommends to his Neighbour."[7]

By the late colonial period, idleness, like luxury, was usually treated as a vice rather than as a sin; there was a lull in self-denunciation during the 1730s which served as a transition. A minister in South Carolina, concerned about the "Abundance of Idleness" there, saw it as essentially a "Bane of Society" and an "Enemy of *all Righteousness.*" The leisure activities of the town's inhabitants, "Our *Billiard-Tables*, our *Cards*, our *Dice*," were constant reminders of men's idleness. "What else led Us into our *Balls*, our *Dances*, and *Night-Assemblies*, with their costly Apparatus & *Consumptions of Time*? Practices, to the last Degree, *Criminal!*" Far from indulging in a languid leisure, the idle in Charleston were very active in their vices, of which the chief one appeared to be gambling. An article

[6]"Monitor #15," *Virginia Gazette* (Williamsburg), 26 November 1736.

[7]Charles Chauncey, *Civil Magistrates Must Be Just . . .* (Boston, 1747), pp. 21, 62. Andrew Eliot, *An Evil and Adulterous Generation . . .* (Boston, 1753), p. 19. Not everyone of course, was intimidated by such sermons. Dr. Alexander Hamilton noticed an instance of such indifference at a sermon he attended in Albany. "This discourse, [the minister] told me, was calculated for the natural vice of that people, which was avarice and particularly for Mr. Livingston, a rich but very covetous man in town who valued himself much for his riches. But unfortunately Livingston did not come to church to hear his reproof." *Gentleman's Progress: The Itinerarium of Dr. Alexander Hamilton, 1744*, ed. Carl Bridenbaugh (Chapel Hill, 1948), p. 68.

in the *South Carolina Gazette* claimed that men gambled "from a Pretence of avoiding being intirely *idle*," but the result was that "They became intirely *wicked*." Gaming, the article pointed out, deprived men of the "Two Things the most conducive to the *Life* and *Well-Being* of Men," which were *"Time* and *Treasure."*[8] Men who made no effort to support themselves virtually "rob Society, or murder themselves." Such denunciations of idleness reflected a strictly secular conception of the evils involved; idleness was harmful to the individual and the society. But such secular social criticism was underpinned both by a confidence that there was in fact a proper order for men's work and by a conviction that ordinary prosperity required a man's fullest exertions; hence ease and surplus wealth were only transitory circumstances which led to disaster.

The notion that idleness and extravagance were offenses against God's will continued to be heard occasionally, but it was most likely to be expressed in peculiar circumstances, especially in times of external political threats and after natural disasters. At such times the familiar vices seemed to be blasphemous. For example, a note in the *South Carolina Gazette* complained about an advertisement for a ball. "What can the Advertiser mean! To make *Stoicks* and *Epicures* of us? Does he imagine us lost to all Sense of *Misery* and Reverence of a Diety! Is the *Small-Pox*, is the *fatal Fever*, is the Sword, &c. so soon forgot!"[9] It took such vivid troubles to remind men of the ultimate magnitude of their wrongdoing. More usually, denunciations of luxury and idleness related vices to social disorder and its origins in violations of the rationality and morality of economic activity.

As public virtues, industry and frugality had certain peculiarities. Fulfillment of them benefited the individual as well as the society; such mutual benefit was true prosperity. Practice of the two virtues was supposed to stimulate economic development, which everyone wanted; it also regulated selfishness and corruption, which everyone feared. Sermons against drunkenness often dealt with this relationship between individual prosperity and public virtue. Excessive drinking led men to *"neglect* diligent proper means, honestly to *Increase* [their] Outward Estate (which might

[8]Josiah Smith, *The Burning of Sodom, with It's Moral Causes: . . . A Sermon, Preached at Charlestown, South Carolina, after a Most Terrible Fire . . .* (Boston, 1741), p. 14; *South Carolina Gazette* (Charleston), 23 July 1737.

[9][Joseph Seccombe], *Business and Diversion Inoffensive to God, and Necessary for the Comfort and Support of Human Society . . .* (Boston, 1743), p. 11; "Laicus," *South Carolina Gazette,* 19 January 1740; Thomas Bacon, *Sermons Addressed to Masters and Servants, and Published in the Year 1743 . . .* (Winchester, Va., 1813?), p. 127. Some of the events of the Great Awakening constitute an exception to the generalization that, except for the stimulus of natural disasters and human catastrophes, idleness and luxury were usually thought of as vices rather than as sins in the late colonial period. James Davenport, whose uncanny sensitivity to the sinful nature of others made him anathema for the nonevangelical clergy, led one of the most extreme expressions of American "contempt of the world." In 1743 at New London he convinced the people of the town to make a pyre of all their luxuries in order to demonstrate "the great Necessity of Mortification." *Boston Evening Post,* 11 April 1743.

render [them] more *Serviceable* and Useful)." Such usefulness had a mercantilist ring; it referred the work of individuals to the broadest possible context. Industry and frugality, or the vices which negated them, characterized a whole people, not just individuals. "Industry is of great Account to the temporal weal of any Country, and without it no land can flourish. Idleness is the parent of all Vice, Misery and Wretchedness to any people."[10] It was only with reluctance that men would admit that certain social problems were the result of prevailing social and economic institutions rather than the supposedly more malleable material of individual morality.

Colonial Americans dwelt on the need for industry at such length because they often seemed to be on the verge or in the midst of a loss of that virtue. A writer who advocated the establishment of a market in Boston because it would "promote *Industry*, and prevent abundance of *Idleness*," cautioned his readers that "it is thought by *Strangers* who have observed the Industry of other places, that there is abundance of *Idleness* with us, and a manifest defect of Industry thro' the Country." Awareness of this danger led preachers and writers to point out that the vices of luxury and idleness were at the roots of most social deviance. It was assumed to be "morally impossible for any person to neglect the proper duties of life" and still avoid "falling into such practices as are positively criminal"; the idle person, in effect, "tempt[ed] the devil to tempt *him*." A poem in an almanac affirmed this fear of the destructive potential of idleness.

> Hard Labour's tedious everyone must own;
> But surely better such by far than none,
> The perfect Drone, the quite Impertinent,
> Whose Life at nothing aims, but—to be spent;
> Such Heaven visits for some mighty Ill;
> 'Tis sure the hardest Labour to sit still,
> Hence that unhappy Tribe who Nought pursue;
> Who sin for want of something else to do.

Idleness and extravagance were common explanations for criminal behavior. Men who "had nothing else to do but to loiter in idleness about the streets or lounge in the dram shops" eventually took to drink and then to stealing. The violent, self-destructive nature of idleness was demonstrated in the case of a man who had been a thief for twelve years before his execution (his punishment for the crime of burning down a jail while he was in it); at his execution he warned his listeners to "shun the paths of wickedness. . . . the love of money,

---

[10]Benjamin Wadsworth, *An Essay To Do Good: By a Dissuasive from Tavern-Hunting and Excessive Drinking* . . . (Boston, 1710), p. 4; Cotton Mather, *Sober Considerations, on . . . the Woful Consequences Which the Prevailing Abuse of Rum* . . . (Boston, 1708), p. 14; Samuel Danforth, *The Woful Effects of Drunkenness* . . . (Boston, 1710), p. 4; [Benjamin Colman], *Some Reasons and Arguments Offered . . . for the Setting Up of Markets in Boston* . . . (Boston, 1719), pp. 4-5.

the ruling principle of my mind, has brought me to the grave in the flower of my mind." The prophylactic properties of industry were often praised in the almanacs, and, as was often the case, Benjamin Franklin gave the idea its most concise expression. "Idleness is the Dead Sea, that swallows all Virtues: Be active in Business, that *Temptation* may miss her Aim: The Bird that sits, is easily shot."[11]

The back country, the western fringe of settlement running from Pennsylvania to South Carolina, presented the clearest case of the association of economic backwardness with the social dangers of idleness. In North Carolina the social detritus of the colonies had accumulated. "Excepting a few of the better Sort, its white Inhabitants have degenerated into a State of Ignorance and Barbarism, not much superior to the native *Indians*." The North Carolina frontier was the antithesis of a civilized society. There "Descendents of Freeborn Britons" lived in a "State of Barbarism and Degeneracy," and the cause of its troubles was idleness on the part of "profligate, audacious Vagabonds! Lewd, impudent, abandon'd Prostitutes Gamblers Gamesters of all Sorts—Horse Theives Cattle Stealers, Hog Stealers—Branders and Markers Hunters going Naked as Indians," all of whom had in common the fault of being "in-a-manner useless to Society." The experience of North Carolina was ominous for the rest of the colonies, for conditions there clearly revealed that it was men's virtue, not the economic condition of natural abundance, that determined prosperity; the people there were poor only because of "their extreme Indolence for they possess the finest Country in America."[12]

Though the situation in North Carolina was almost unthinkably extreme, fears that idleness and extravagance would corrupt American society were common by the late colonial period. Thus advocates of industry and frugality were as much social as economic reformers. It is in this context—and the more specific situation of wartime inflation and dislocation— that the apotheosis of the ethic of industry and frugality, Franklin's *Poor Richard's Almanac* of 1758, is to be understood. Franklin was objecting to the combination of unsystematic marketing with feckless spending, which too commonly passed for commercial life in the colonies. Father Abraham, whose speech took up most of the almanac, harangued a group waiting for the opening of "a Vendue of Merchant Goods" to the effect that the "badness of the Times" was their own doing, the result of their idleness and

[11]Jonathan Mayhew, *Christian Sobriety: Being Eight Sermons on Titus II.6* . . . (Boston, 1763), p. 157; Nathaniel Ames, *An Astronomical Diary . . . 1757* (Boston, 1756), pp. 3-4; Bacon, *Sermons Addressed to Masters and Servants*, p. 153; Isaac Frasier, *A Brief Account of the Life, and Abominable Thefts, of the Notorious Isaac Frasier* . . . (New Haven, 1768), p. 16; Benjamin Franklin, "Poor Richard Improved" [1756], *The Papers of Benjamin Franklin*, ed. Leonard W. Labaree, 17 vols. to date (New Haven, 1959-), 7: 83.

[12]James MacSparran, *America Dissected: Being a Full and True Account of All the American Colonies* . . . (Dublin, 1753), p. 10; Charles Woodmason, *The Carolina Backcountry on the Eve of the Revolution: The Journal and Other Writings of Charles Woodmason, Anglican Itinerant*, ed. Richard J. Hooker (Chapel Hill, 1953), pp. 121, 52.

extravagance. "We are taxed twice as much by our *Idleness*, three times as much by our *Pride*, and four times as much by our *Folly*" as by the taxes imposed by the government. Father Abraham also imparted a good deal of prudential wisdom. It is for these passages, and for the values of hard work, cunning, and economic calculation which they advocated, that the *Almanac* is best known. But the chief aim of the lecturer was to make his listeners understand that their self-interests were rightly understood only in relation to the welfare of the whole. What Father Abraham advocated was not unlimited acquisition but rather prosperity, which was the mid-point between the ruin of extravagance and the want of poverty. The living he envisaged was a decent, middling wealth, which could be attained only through unremitting labor and self-control. There was no very clear social model for becoming rich (as opposed to achieving a decent prosperity) without also becoming corrupted. Father Abraham thought that men did well if they provided themselves with the *"Necessaries of Life."* If one did so, he would be better off than "the Genteel," who by "Extravagancies . . . are reduced to Poverty, and forced to borrow of those whom they formerly despised, but who through *'Industry* and *Frugality'* have maintained their Standing." The listeners, however, paid no attention to the lecture, "just as if it had been a common Sermon," but instead "began to buy extravagantly" and thereby insure their ruin.[13]

One of the most concerted efforts of the colonists to deal with the detrimental social effects of idleness and extravagance was the Society for Encouraging Industry and Employing the Poor, which was located in Boston. The Society sponsored a workhouse for the manufacture of linen, a project that received widespread attention. Benjamin Franklin contributed money to it and sent Peter Collinson one of the Society's pamphlets. The Society's goal was to maximize the resources of the province by putting to work "our own Women and Children, who are now in a great measure idle." The spokesmen of the Society claimed that the workhouse did not represent a harsh attitude toward the poor, for there were "few Countries, perhaps none in the World, where [charity] prevails in a greater Degree than among ourselves." The Society did, however, aim to help "the Poor to maintain themselves," rather than encourage them in their poverty by providing them with alms. It was believed that the factory would accomplish two reforms. It would relieve the disorder of the city, to which "the Swarms of Children, of both Sexes, that are continually strolling and playing about the Streets of our Metropolis, cloathed in Rags, and brought up in Idleness and Ignorance" contributed. The Society would also contribute to public prosperity. "It is by Improvement in Arts and Trade, that they ['a flourishing People'] must grow in Wealth, and Power, and become possessed of the various Emoluments tending to the Benefit and Pleasure of Life." Economic and moral reforms were complementary.

[13]Benjamin Franklin, "Poor Richard Improved" [1757], *Papers*, 7: 341, 346.

The initial purpose of the Society was to stimulate a "Spirit of Industry and Frugality" among the poor, but more comprehensive changes were soon envisaged. The Society's annual sermons (like those of the Georgia Company) often addressed broad questions of social ethics and encouraged all the listeners to participate in a general effort to "banish Luxury and sloth. . . . then, and not till then, shall the State of our Affairs change for the better." The burden to work could not be shifted solely onto the poor, for it was "a shameful Thing for any to *eat the Bread of Idleness.*" Wealthy persons could "reasonably exempt themselves from the lower and more servile Parts of Business," but it was inherent in everyone's nature to be active. "We were made for Business. Both our Souls and Bodies are so constituted, as that Exercise is a great and necessary Means to keep them in a healthful and vigorous State; and without it we shall soon contract a strange Hebetude of Mind, as well as Inability of Body to all the Functions of Life."

The obligation of the rich to continue working did not necessarily imply that they should devote their energies to the accumulation of wealth; they should instead work for the public good. The sermons of the Society, though they encouraged an efficient use of human resources, did not equate efficiency with the maximization of wealth. As was often the case in such discussions, there was evidence of a suspicion of excessive riches. There was "a certain Proportion of Wealth, which when diffused among a People, renders them respectable among their Neighbours, and makes the Course of every Profession smooth and easy, and life itself comfortable and quiet." It was this "proportion" which the Society sought to achieve. There was also an excessive degree of wealth, "which when attained has been found by Experience dangerous and hurtful," for it exposed "its Possessors to Luxury and Profusion, and introduce[d] such Vices as in their Nature enervated and waste, render them contemptible, or even a Nuisance in God's Creation. . . . So that if a People are visited . . . with great Wealth; yet that will wear best, and last longest, which was attained by Industry."[14]

The Society's recommendations of industry and frugality marked both the continuity and the change which the social ethics of the calling had undergone during the late colonial period. Pride was no longer a horrifying challenge to God, but the sins which had been symptoms of pride were still offenses against the given order. This order was more social and economic than religious in its references, and work within it was evaluated in terms such as public prosperity and domestic tranquillity.

---

[14]*Whereas It Is Found by Experience* . . . (Boston, 1754), p. 1; *Industry and Frugality Proposed as the Surest Means To Make Us a Rich and Flourishing People* . . . (Boston, 1753), pp. 9–10, 14; Charles Chauncey, *The Idle-Poor Secluded from the Bread of Charity by the Christian Law* . . . (Boston, 1752), pp. 7, 11–12; Thomas Barnard, *A Sermon Preached in Boston . . . before the Society for Encouraging Industry, and Employing the Poor* (Boston, 1758), pp. 11–12.

PROVINCIAL MERCANTILISM

In part, the Society for Encouraging Industry was indicative of a widely prevalent cluster of attitudes toward colonial commercial life which might be labeled "provincial mercantilism." This group of ideas was often evident in discussions about general economic conditions, particularly in the course of currency disputes. Because of a lack of alternative means and terms of economic analysis, the colonists adopted the economic theory which was dominant in the mother country and applied it to their own situation. They quoted extensively from British economic writings, and, because they identified themselves with the interests that governed British economic policy, they cast themselves in roles that were the reverse of British conceptions of the colonies. The inhabitants of the various provinces considered themselves to be members of independent economic entities. Owing to their political subordination to Britain, the colonists' mercantilism was a false one because they were unable to give it full legislative form. They also recognized that the American situation differed from Britain's because their chief exports were staples and their chief imports were manufactured goods, which was the reverse of desirable trade according to mercantilist theory. But the colonists' basic economic ideas about the need for full employment and the benefits of low interest and a favorable balance of trade were the same as those of the British mercantilists.[15]

The Americans' mercantilism, like that of the British, reinforced the ethic of industry and frugality, and as such provided an economic measure of the utility of virtue. The "Opulency and Grandeur" of a nation, so the theory went, depended on *the Industry and Prudence of its Inhabitants.* The degree of industry applied by the inhabitants of a particular nation had to be sufficient to insure "that they will constantly prepare, either of the produce of, or Manufactures performed in their own Country, for Exportation in such Plenty, as that the value of them may be more than sufficient, to purchase everything that they want from abroad, to consume among themselves." It was assumed that the "overplus" of the value of exports would "be constantly drawing that which is used by the Traders for a Medium of Exchange, and make it plenty among them." Throughout the colonial period there were many statements to the effect that "Trade and Commerce is that which conduces much to the Prosperity and Enriching of both City and Country." The trade which such writers had in mind was the export trade. "The only solid Foundation which any Country has to erect a Trade upon, are such Commodities as may be spared from their own Occasions, and exported to supply the Wants of other Places," and the preserva-

---

[15]C. Robert Haywood has discussed the mercantilism of the colonists in several articles: "The Mind of the North Carolina Advocates of Mercantilism," *North Carolina Historical Review*, 33 (1956): 139-65; "Mercantilism and Colonial Slave Labor, 1700-1763," *Journal of Southern History*, 23 (1957): 454-64; and "The Influence of Mercantilism on Social Attitudes in the South, 1700-1763," *Journal of the History of Ideas*, 20 (1959): 577-86; see *Virginia Gazette*, 24 March 1739.

tion of such trade depended upon "the Diligence and Frugality of a people." The mercantilist explanation for the need of such industry and frugality was that "Silver and Gold will never tarry among us, till by retrenching our Expences and improving our Trade, we bring the balance in our favour."[16] Such statements demonstrated the colonists' conviction that mercantilism was the policy necessary for the protection of their interests.

The colonists' mercantilism determined the way in which they evaluated the economic importance of different types of work. Skilled manual laborers, for example, had the surest, if not the highest, claims on respect for their contribution to the commercial well-being of a society. Artisans and farmers produced the wealth of a country. It was a truism that "Labour and Manufactures are the Foundation of all Trade without which it cannot be carried on." The "Labourers and tradesmen" were likened to "the Heads [sic] which feed the Belly of the Commonwealth." Franklin reminded the readers of his almanac that "he that hath a Trade, hath an Estate." Husbandry, Jared Eliot asserted, "[is] the very Basis and Foundation of all nominal or artificial Wealth and Riches." "The poor Countryman and the industrious Mechanick" were truly useful, for their work enabled the merchant to conduct trade. If he fulfilled his role properly, however, the merchant made the indispensable contribution to prosperity. The promotion of "Trade and Navigation" could be carried out only by "men of good Stocks, with Skill and Ability for the Purpose."

Assertions of the social importance of merchants were often defensive and assumed that people might distrust merchants. These defenses usually emphasized the difference of roles in external and internal commerce. The merchant was essential to the prosperity of a society because he managed its foreign commerce. One currency tract stated that the proper function of a merchant was to "manage the Trade, so as that a good Proportion of *Silver* and *Gold* might once more find the way into New England." When a merchant combined this function with domestic trade, he could come in for criticism. Merchants were the objects of suspicion because they, along with "userers or money-jobbers, land-jobbers, and super-numerary officers . . . may all *very possibly* grow rich, while the rest of the community are oppressed and kept poor." It was a commonplace to contrast the merchant with the farmer in this respect. Landholders were thought to be the natural guardians of the public interest because they could not benefit themselves

---

[16][Thomas Paine], "A Discourse Shewing That the Real First Cause of the Straits and Difficulties of This Province . . . Is It's Extravagancy, & Not Paper Money" [1721], and [Thomas Hutchinson], "A Letter to a Member of the Honourable House of Representatives" [1736], *Colonial Currency Reprints, 1682-1751*, ed. Andrew McFarland Davis, 4 vols. (Boston, 1911), 2: 288, 290; 3: 160; *The Interest of City and Country To Lay No Duties* . . . (New York, 1726), p. 5; *The Report of the Committee of the Commons House of Assembly of the Province of South Carolina on the State of the Paper Currency* (London, 1737), pp. 15-16; and "Reflections on the Present State of the Province of Massachusetts Bay" [1720], *Tracts Relating to the Currency of Massachusetts Bay, 1682-1720*, ed. Andrew McFarland Davis (Boston, 1902), p. 329.

without benefiting society as a whole.[17] This notion that farmers could act only in the general interest depended on a paradigm for the domestic economy in which production was a real source of wealth and marketing was an artificial and frequently deceptive source.

The "shopkeepers" (retailers) best exemplified the perversion of commerce; and perhaps of all recognized types of work theirs came in for the most frequent disapproval. According to mercantilist analysis the shopkeepers, as middlemen, contributed nothing to the prosperity of a society. Whatever profit a shopkeeper made, "the *last* buyer and *user* pays it all . . . yet the *Province*, or *Publick* is not enrich'd *one Farthing* by their Labour. If they had been employ'd in Husbandry, or Handycraft-Business; there would probably have been some produce of their labour for the Publick good . . . but their meer *handing of Goods one to another*, no more increases any Wealth in the Province, then Persons *at a Fire* increase the *Water in a Pail*, by passing it thro' Twenty or Forty hands." Shopkeepers were also a positive menace because they sold tradesmen goods which they did not need and repaid merchants with depreciated notes.[18]

As orthodox eighteenth-century mercantilists, the colonists assumed, as did "all that understand Trade," that "the chief End and Design in carrying it on, is the making a Balance in Favour of those that do carry it on." They were not strict bullionists such as had opposed the ideas of Thomas Mun, but they believed that the final terms of a nation's prosperity had to be settled by specie payments. Thus it was the balance between the monetary value of exports and imports that determined the economic health of a particular province. Colonial spokesmen on economic matters did not think of foreign trade simply as a means of supplying the provinces with goods. On the contrary, they had a characteristically mercantilist "fear of goods," which meant that they were reluctant to import unnecessary items and eager to export the fruits of their own production in order to maintain employment. The primary reason for foreign trade was to accumulate credits, so that necessities could be imported without hurting the economy of the province. The principle by which the regulation of trade should be guided was simple.

If there is any one single Article that can be raised within the Community, for which they can find a market in any other Part of the World; . . . until such Times

[17][Cadwalder Colden], *The Interest of the Country in Laying Duties . . .* (New York, 1726), pp. 8-11; "A Discourse concerning the Currencies of the British Plantations in America" [1740], *Colonial Currency Reprints*, 3: 328; Benjamin Franklin, "Poor Richard, 1742: An Almanack," *Papers*, 2: 333; Jared Eliot, *Essays upon Field Husbandry in New England and Other Papers, 1748-1762*, ed. Harry J. Carman and Rexford G. Tugwell (New York, 1934), p. 99; *Advice to the Free-Holders and Electors of Pennsylvania . . .* (Philadelphia, 1735), p. 2; *A Dialogue Shewing What's Therein To Be Found . . .* (Philadelphia, 1725), pp. 31-33; "Objections to the Bank of Credit Lately Projected at Boston" [1714], *Tracts*, p. 103; [John Webbe], *A Discourse concerning Paper Money . . .* (Philadelphia, 1743), p. 7.

[18]"The Present Melancholy Circumstances of the Province" [1719], *Tracts*, pp. 188-89; "A Brief Account of the Rise, Progress, and Present State of the Paper Currency" [1749], *Colonial Currency Reprints*, 4: 392-93.

as they have brought every Individual Article to the greatest Perfection, and in such Quantities as that no Vent can be found for them, they have not arrived to that Perfection such a Community is capable; and therefore the consuming any unnecessary Articles, is the preventing that Community from arising to so great a Pitch of Grandeur and Stock of Riches, as it is capable of.

The colonies were obviously not in such a situation, and the primary evidence of their shortcomings was their difficulty in maintaining credit abroad.[19]

Certain complications were involved in applying mercantilist theory to the economic conditions of the various colonies. There was, for instance, the political problem of the Americans' subordination within the mercantilist system controlled by Great Britain. There was also a major commercial problem: the colonies' main exports were raw materials and agricultural products, and the economic theory of mercantilism recommended that, whenever possible, exports be composed of manufactured articles because of the increase in their market value over that of the original materials. The colonists sought instead to develop manufactures for the purpose of domestic consumption, which would reduce their dependence on imports. Frequent efforts were made to increase colonial production of linen and other cloths in order to reduce the importation of these goods. There were also objections to and regulations against the exportation of wool, hides, leather, grain, and candles because colonial production could not meet domestic demands for these goods, and their importation hurt each province's balance of payments.[20] Except for a few items which required only a crude technology, like rum, naval stores, and plantation staples, the colonists assumed that they would not be able to produce a significant surplus of manufactured goods. Had it been successful, their provincial mercantilism, like any mercantilist policy brought to its logical conclusion, would have had the effect of fostering internal market relations.

Because of the Americans' need and propensity to apply foreign credits to the purchase of manufactured goods and their lack of sufficient economic development to provide manufactured goods for exportation, provincial mercantilism stressed frugality more than industry. The colonists employed a strict mercantilist definition of usefulness—probably stricter than that of their contemporaries in Britain, where there was growing support for the idea that the consumption of domestically produced luxuries, though inefficient, at least increased employment. For the colonists, "useless," imports were usually items of conspicuous consumption. According to the Americans' economic ideas, imports should have consisted only of

[19]*The Good of the Community Impartially Considered in a Letter to a Merchant in Boston* . . . (Boston, 1754), p. 10; Roger Sherman, *A Caveat against Injustice, or an Enquiry into the Evil Consequences of a Fluctuating Medium of Exchange* . . . (New York, 1752), p. 13; [Oxenbridge Thacher], *Considerations on Lowering the Value of Gold Coins* (Boston, 1762), pp. 8, 25.

[20]"The Present Melancholy Circumstances," pp. 190, 196; *The Interest of New-Jersey Considered* . . . (Philadelphia, 1743), p. 7.

goods which men needed for subsistence and a moderate enjoyment of life, or else of goods which could be re-exported at a profit. Certain luxuries, like fine clothing, were considered to be useful if they helped maintain the social hierarchy by marking "Persons of publick note, and Trust, and plentiful Estates," but there was always a danger that the popularity of fashions would spread such consumption too widely.[21]

Because Britain was the chief source of the colonists' imports, there was a tendency for expressions of provincial mercantilism to treat the mother country as a foreign nation in matters of economic policy. Trade with Britain drained the colonies of their specie. One writer warned that, "if the *English Trade* will not be ballanced with the Produce of our Country, which may be readily purchased with Paper-money, that Trade will most certainly ruin us." Benjamin Franklin, writing about the causes of prosperity in nations, summed up the issues of provincial mercantilism in terms that implicitly questioned the notion that the economic interests of the colonies and the mother country were harmonious. "Foreign luxuries and needless Manufactures imported and used in a Nation, do, by the same Reasoning, increase the People of the Nation that furnishes them, and diminish the People of the Nation that uses them."[22]

Expressions of provincial mercantilism usually occurred during periods of economic distress, especially during recessions caused by excessive importations and the subsequent shortening of credit or in response to the related problem of a shortage of specie. Most of the time the colonists accepted their position of subordination in the British mercantile system because they appreciated benefits such as naval protection of trade and the facility in marketing which Britain's commercial connections offered. Because of their notion that Britain and the colonies had mutual economic interests the Americans could use provincial mercantilism as a means of understanding their economic situation. It seldom occurred to them that two different sorts of economic policy applied to Great Britain and the colonies. Mercantilist standards were the only ones available for the determination of economic well-being, and so the Americans used them to evaluate the efficient use of their resources. Provincial mercantilism was not a critique of the American involvement in the British system. Complaints about that system dealt with specific issues like currency and duties.[23] With the devel-

---

[21]Some of these "useless goods" were "Silver and Gold Lace . . . Velvet, Rich Silk, Sattin, Silk Stockings, Fine Broad-Clothes, Camlets, Perriwigs, Fine costly Shoes and Pattoons, Ribbons, Rich Lace, Silk Handkerchiefs, Fine Hats, Gloves . . . China Ware, very Costly-Looking-Glasses, Cane-Chairs, Costly Beds & Furniture." "The Present Melancholy Circumstances," pp. 285–86; "Antigallican #2," p. 118; [Paine], "A Discourse" [1721], p. 284; *South Carolina Gazette*, 25 March 1738; *The Chief Justice's Charge to the Grand Jury* (Charleston, 1741), pp. 10–11.

[22]*A Dialogue between Mr. Robert Rich and Roger Plowman* (Philadelphia, 1725), p. 2; Eliot, *Essays upon Field Husbandry*, p. 135; Benjamin Franklin, "Observations concerning the Increase of Mankind [1751], *Papers*, 4: 231.

[23]*To the Merchants and Manufacturers of Great Britain: The Memorial of the Merchants and Traders of the City of Philadelphia* (n.p., 1765), pp. 1-3; [James Otis], *Considerations on Be-*

opment of a nonimportation movement in the 1760s, however, the latent conflict over the locus of mercantilist interest surfaced and became part of the grounds for American alienation from Britain.

THE ECONOMIC MOTIVATION OF WORK

Out of recognition of the extent of commercialization in their society, colonial spokesmen sought to establish a psychological, empirical analysis of why men worked, and here too they looked to mercantilist theory. In application this realism did not include a moral neutrality; it was an amalgamation of British benevolist and mercantilist thought and involved an effort to coordinate public and private interests. This empirical analysis of the motivation of work did, however, have the potential to give a tacit legitimacy to some expressions of self-interest.

The readiness of Americans in the late colonial period to accept the economic basis of men's motivation to work represented a change from earlier, more strictly social valuations of work. Like provincial mercantilism, this readiness marked both an awareness of the fact that to live in society was to participate in the market and an interest in securing the economic benefits which it provided. Recognition of the market did not necessarily legitimize individual activities in it; on the contrary, provincial mercantilism made the notion of self-interest tolerable because it postulated the possibility that conflicts in the domestic economy were avoidable and showed that economic benefits were greatest when there was a harmony of interests.

The colonists believed that self-interest, in the form of economic imperatives, was the chief motive for most men's work. By the late 1740s Americans had worked out a scheme of enlightened self-interest which could take men's acquisitive inclinations into account. Because of the traditional fear of selfishness, this scheme often had to be justified in a way that reassured people that the values and patterns of behavior that had supposedly existed previously would be preserved. Benevolism taught that self-interest was a component of virtuous behavior, but it also left open the door for moral criticism by its recognition of an irrational form of selfishness. In a sermon to the Society for Encouraging Industry, Samuel Cooper, minister of the Brattle Street Church warned that, if it were possible for "a rational Creature, to extinguish the Principle of Self-Love," the result would not be "Vertue or Perfection," but rather "a gross and monstrous Defect in his Constitution." Cooper argued that "Self-Love" was as important as public virtue and complemented it. Both were necessary for "the Support and Happiness of the World" and were designed "by the Author of Nature" as such. "Our Lord has taught us to make the Love of ourselves, the Measure and Standard of Love to others." The crucial

---

half of the Colonists in a Letter to a Noble Lord (London, 1765), pp. 22, 29, 50. On the shift in American mercantilist perspective, see Max Savelle, "The Appearance of an American Attitude toward External Affairs, 1750-1775," *American Historical Review*, 52 (1947): 655-66.

problem in this scheme for "the Perfection of Vertue" was to maintain "a due Ballance" of the two types of love and to allow "to each it's proper Energy and Scope." Benjamin Franklin had a similarly benign view of self-interest. As in the case of Cooper, it was Franklin's confidence in a beneficent order that allowed him to espouse self-interest; Franklin believed that "Self-Love" gave the initial force to a "virtuous Mind" and acted "As the small Pebble stirs the peaceful Lake. . . . Friend, Parent, Neighbour, first it will embrace, His Country next, and next all human Race." In almost every case in which self-interest was positively espoused, it was considered to be legitimate only for men who were already predisposed to virtue. "*Personal* interest" motivated all men, but it did not "govern all Men alike: All Men are Sinners, but all Men are not the *greatest Sinners.*"[24]

The economic corollary of this approbation of self-interest was a belief that men would fall into evil ways if their desires for wealth were frustrated, and it is significant that the most frequent exponents of this belief were advocates of currency issues. They asserted the need for currency on the ground that everyone's interests were served by a readily available medium of exchange because they could then pursue their self-interests in ways that were rational and hence socially beneficial. Not surprisingly, these arguments usually appeared in times of trade stagnation, when credit was unavailable. It was assumed that men wanted to engage in economic activity. The frustration of these desires because of a "want of Business" would lead men into "an habit of Idleness." The extreme example of the consequences of a frustration of individual interests in economic life was the corruption of the slaves. By definition, they did not work according to their own interests: "the drudgery is theirs, and the profit entirely ours." Their deprivation had resulted in their depravity: "their temptations to ease or idleness, to drinking or riot, to filching for the supply of their pleasures and extravagance, or to any present gratification, increase in force as the means of satisfying them are further removed from their reach." It was assumed that men were "Laborious and Industrious while [they] work for themselves," but men who worked for the advantage of others became "mere Negroes [and] grow lazy and careless."[25]

The chief stimulus for the work of most men was the prospect of material success in commercial life. A contributor to a currency dispute wrote that the state of trade was the chief variable influencing the intensity of men's work. "For it is a Maxim pretty generally received, *That what is encouraging to Trade, is so to Industry.*" It was generally recognized that the

[24]Samuel Cooper, *A Sermon Preached in Boston, New England, before the Society for Encouraging Industry and Employing the Poor* (Boston, 1753), p. 2; Benjamin Franklin, "Poor Richard, 1745: An Almanack," *Papers*, 3: 5; "Appendix to Massachusetts in Agony" [1751], *Colonial Currency Reprints*, 4: 468; Thomas Warrington, *The Love of God, Benevolence, and Self-Love, Considered Together* (Williamsburg, 1753), pp. 11, 14, 20.

[25]"The Distressed State of the Town of Boston Once More Considered" [1720], *Tracts*, p. 359; Bacon, *Sermons Addressed to Masters and Servants*, p. 27; [Colden], *The Interest of the Country*, p. 16.

only possible means and the only justification for an increase in industry was "the advantage & encouragement of a profitable *Commerce*." This view indicated a significant shift in men's orientation to their work. Most of the discussions of labor in the early eighteenth century had assumed that men had to work very diligently simply to achieve a decent subsistence; the calling in particular was oriented to the efficient exploitation of meager resources. According to the traditional view, the primary trait of trade was the mutuality of exchanges of goods and services, and profit was a secondary benefit. By the late colonial period, many writers still assumed that individual prosperity might be hard to achieve and that most men did well just to satisfy their basic wants, but nearly everyone associated a decent prosperity with the conditions of trade. The explanation for men's motivation in work was that "none will Labour, but with a fore-sight of Profit; for Profit is the final Cause of Labour; and as there cannot be much profit by Labour without *Commerce*, so *Commerce* is the Cause of Profit by Labour." Mankind in its economic endeavors was an object of admiration; man was an "Active Projecting Creature," and "Men of Projecting Brains do most good to their Neighbours." Nearly everyone was eager to be industrious when there was a prospect of "quick profit," and such conditions did more "to reduce a People to a habit of Prudence and Industry than is possible to be effected by Whip, or Hunger or by all the penal Laws, that can be Invented for the Suppressing of Idleness."[26]

Most writers who favored paper money assumed that its increase would encourage commercial activity by lowering interest rates, a typical mercantilist goal. With money cheap, capital would be lent for use in trade rather than in usury, and people who "understand Business very well, but have not a Stock sufficient of their own, will be encouraged to borrow Money; to trade with, when they can have it at a moderate Interest." Presumably, there were great stores of industry, which could be put into action when economic conditions were satisfactory. "If Money were plenty [the farmers] could improve much more of their Lands, & consequently raise abundantly more, and their Lands would grow more valuable, and so could afford to Sell chaper to the Merchants, and yet be gainers by the Bargain." The advocates of plentiful paper currency were some of the earliest contributors to the tradition of American boosterism. Paper money was a panacea for a society's economic ills, and these ills were not just stagnation or depression but an inability to expand. It was necessary to "enjoy the Outward Blessings that Heaven has indulged us with," and this prosperity was simple to achieve. "The Means of our Relief are in our own Hands; and we can save our selves, as Easily, as to say the Word." It was axiomatic for the advocates of paper money that self-interest could "*neither*

---

[26]"Trade and Commerce Inculcated" [1731] and "A Few Remarks on the Present Situation of Affairs" [1734], *Colonial Currency Reprints*, 2: 361–62, 366, and 3: 133; "The Distressed State of the Town of Boston" [1720], *Tracts*, p. 244.

cheat or Lye: For that this is the String in the Nose (thro' the World) which governs the creature."[27]

Writers who dealt with motivation recognized that not everyone had a prospect of personal aggrandizement. What, then, was the motivation to work for men who were poor and likely to remain so? For certain groups in society economic opportunity did not exist. Servants and wage laborers, so it was thought, worked only hard enough to achieve a minimal subsistence because they had no prospect of long-term improvement. Their economic life was a series of short-term cycles of earning and spending. The pressure of material necessity was the only way to get such people to work. Once dependent on wages for their subsistence, men could be forced to work. For men who could profit in trade, prosperity was a stimulus to work, but in the case of wage earners too much success could lead to a reduction in labor. The problem of the inverse relationship between wages and industry fascinated Franklin; he believed that there was a "proneness of human Nature to a life of ease, of freedom from care and labour."[28] Other colonists also expressed this idea that hard work, though admirable, was unnatural; and it was generally believed that industry became habitual only when reinforced by the demands of society and stimulated by the expectation of goods and status as rewards.

Though the development of commerce depended on men's desires for wealth and goods in excess of basic necessities, there were some situations in which too much wealth could lead to a reduction of industry. Luxury was one symptom of such situations. The history of commerce was inherently a cyclical one because the development of trade led eventually to luxury, which brought about the decay of commerce as men reduced their exertions. In the course of the Seven Years' War, one writer warned his readers that such had been the experience of France, and that it could befall the colonists if they abused the fruits of victory. "Imitation and emulation, beget a spirit of industry. And thence the birth of arts and sciences. Thence also houses are erected; ships invented, and commerce propogated, the mother of opulence, the mother of luxury." The natural richness of

[27][John Wise], "A Word of Comfort to a Melancholy Country: Or, the Bank of Credit Erected in the Massachusetts Bay, Fairly Defended" [1721], and "A Modest Enquiry into the Nature and Necessity of a Paper-Currency" [1729], *Colonial Currency Reprints*, 2: 163, 219, 337. "A Letter, from One in Boston, to His Friend in the Country" [1714], and "A Letter from a Gentleman, Containing Some Remarks upon the Several Answers Given unto Mr. Colman's, Entitled, the Distressed State of the Town of Boston [1720], *Tracts*, pp. 138 and 292-93. The social basis of the desire for paper money is difficult to determine. There was general support for currency issues; the strongest opposition to paper money existed in Massachusetts, and there the matter was confused by conflicts over private versus public banks. Hammond, *Banks and Politics*, chap. 1; Joseph Dorfman, *The Economic Mind in American Civilization, 1606–1865*, 5 vols. (New York, 1946), 1: chap. 9; George A. Billias, *The Massachusetts Land Bankers of 1740* (Orono, Me., 1959); John M. Bumsted, "The Report of the Pembroke (Massachusetts) Town Committee on the Currency, March 24, 1740/41," *New England Quarterly*, 40 (1967): 550-60.

[28]James Logan, *The Charge Delivered from the Bench to the Grand Jury . . .* (Philadelphia, 1723), p. 10; Benjamin Franklin to Peter Collinson, 9 May 1753, *Papers*, 4: 480-81.

America was both a challenge and a danger to its industry. It could dull as well as stimulate men's economic motivations. One of the problems of America was that "the *Felicity* of our Country so much transcends its *Virtue.*" Thus an accurate analysis of men's motivations was necessary in order to discover the proper conditions for the preservation of industry and frugality. Luxury lessened the motivation to work. And luxury was not restricted to the rich; it characterized anyone who sacrificed industry to present pleasure.[29]

The economic valuation of work explained why individuals worked and described how the economy functioned. It did not (and by its nature could not) provide a moral priority of individual interests over social interests. Such attention to economic matters could, however, lead men to see their most important relationships as economic ones. Such a development was resisted. Industry and frugality remained personal standards for the conduct of work, and justice still applied to the realm of trade. The reasons for the retention of these traditional values depended on the attraction and repulsion which commercial life exerted on the American colonists.

[29]"Antigallican #1," *American Magazine*, November, p. 79; East Apthorp, *The Felicity of the Times* . . . (Boston, 1763), p. 21; Woodmason, *Carolina Backcountry*, pp. 204-5, 219, 226, 312; Robert Beverly, *The History and Present State of Virginia* [1705], ed. Louis B. Wright (Chapel Hill, 1947), pp. 296, 318-19.

IV

THE PRESERVATION OF COMMUNITY
IN A MARKET ECONOMY

B ELIEF IN THE INTERDEPENDENCE of economic and moral reforms was matched by an ambivalence about the economic context itself. An understanding of economic behavior was necessary in order to determine and encourage legitimate work, but economic valuations alone were not sufficient to confer legitimacy. Since the beginnings of the colonies, Americans had engaged in commercial life, but they persistently had difficulty in accommodating themselves intellectually to its effects. They were aware of commerce and the imperatives it posed for men's work, and they recognized that self-interest was the motive force in a life of trade. But they continued to adhere to an ethics which could give explicit legitimization only to activity which benefited the public. Commercial life had gained the Americans prosperity on a society-wide scale that was recognized at the time as being almost without comparison. In the midst of such prosperity men might be expected to voice their happiness with the direction of events, but worry was a much more common response. The colonists recognized that the extent of market relations in American society was increasing, but they complained of the effects of this increase on society as they wanted and understood it to be. There was anxiety about the erosion of the community, a conviction that mobility and wealth threatened social stability, a fear of the social destructiveness of economic individualism, and an awareness of the loss of the traditional priority of social considerations over economic ones in evaluating the worth of work. Basic to the colonists' social ethics was the notion that "work [was] a social activity performed in the context of a well-ordered community."[1] The price of prosperity appeared to be a loss of community allegiances and a disruption of traditional patterns of behavior.

A comprehensive explanation for the guilt the colonists experienced— or even of the censorious language with which they told themselves they ought to experience guilt—is probably impossible to retrieve solely from the surviving evidence of public expression. But it is feasible to reconstruct the pattern of thought by which they understood legitimate behavior. In doing so it is possible to gain some understanding of the fears which prevented the articulation of a new standard of behavior, one which would have been more harmonious with prevailing behavior and which would presumably have caused less anxiety. Part of this pattern involves the peculiar way in which they perceived economic reality and their work. The values which made up the boundaries of legitimate economic behavior in early American society gave meaning to both deviant and standard behavior, and thus revealed to men the significance of their work. The language in which these values were expressed shaped the way men identified their work with society.

The two elements of this language were, first, the Christian-Platonic notion of the ethical need for the denial of self in order to preserve justice and order and, second, the mercantilist-utilitarian orientation in which society was thought of as a realm for the efficient use (variously determined) of human and material resources. The tension between these two elements reflected and sustained the colonists' ambivalence about their own nature. On the one hand, the colonists viewed themselves as creatures of instinct and emotion whose selfish passions were a danger to themselves and to society. On the other hand, they identified the quality of being human with rationality, and commerce was an expression of rationality because it involved an improvement of natural resources.

How could the colonists reconcile their distrust of economic man and their fear of his destructive impact on society with an admiration and a sense of need for commerce as an integral part of their society? To understand their contrary views on these subjects, it is necessary to make a distinction between internal and external realms of commercial influence. The scene of injustice was local. As will be seen below, whenever the colonists criticized injustice and selfishness in economic life, they were implicitly referring to their immediate society. When commercial relations affected roles within the society, they had the unwanted effects of competition, exploitation, and luxury. When commercial relations were with other societies, these effects were thought to be absent or irrelevant. Mercantilist

---

[1]David Bertelson, *The Lazy South* (New York, 1967), p. 70. For a discussion of the awareness of cultural and moral deficiency in the late colonial period, see Jack P. Greene, "Search for Identity: Selected Patterns of Social Response in Eighteenth Century America," *Journal of Social History*, 3 (1970): 189–219.

thought conferred legitimacy on work related to external commerce, and so it was possible in that context to think of the members of society acting in concord for the common good because trade carried their products to the best markets and provided in return necessary goods which could not be produced domestically.

Discussions about the advantages of commerce sometimes implied that the development of trade would lead to a priority of economic over other social considerations. Some writers assumed that commerce was the *summum bonum* of society. Commerce was indispensable to the state; therefore, wrote Richard Jackson, Pennsylvania's agent in London, to Benjamin Franklin, "that Constitution of Government and that set of Manners which most effectually promote universal Labour and Application are, Politically speaking, the best Government and the best Manners," and so it followed that what "is necessary for Carrying on Commerce is Politically necessary to the Well being of a State."[2]

When analyzing situations in terms of such economic standards, which derived from British mercantilism, it was difficult not to neglect moral questions when they conflicted with practical considerations. The discussions of commerce implied a general commercialization of social ties, a picture of social relations which sharply contrasted with the supposedly traditional community allegiances to a stable, simple, interdependent and Christian social order. Because of their admiration and desire for the benefits of commerce, it was difficult for Americans to avoid the anxieties that arose from participation in it. The colonists usually attributed the problems arising from commercial life to deviant behavior rather than to the imperatives of that life. Yet the colonists were aware that, given man's acquisitive nature and given the market system in which he was so extensively engaged, there was little reason to expect him to act any differently. There was a conflict of distrust and esteem in attitudes toward commerce which was similar to the tension that resulted from application of the work ethic. In both cases execution of one valued activity caused a violation of other values. Fulfillment of the work ethic brought wealth and the temptation of personal indulgence; engagement in commercial life resulted in a weakening of the traditional community by competition and exploitation. By restricting their affirmations of commerce to situations in which foreign rather than domestic commerce was at issue, the Americans hoped to retain their allegiance to traditional values while benefiting from commerce.

When they discussed the problematic aspects of economic life the colonists referred to internal commerce; conversely, they referred to external commerce when they evaluated the benefits of commerce. As something that took place outside the society, commerce could be viewed in strictly economic terms. As something internal to the society, trade was not a

---

[2]Richard Jackson to Benjamin Franklin, 17 March 1754, Benjamin Franklin, *The Papers of Benjamin Franklin*, ed. Leonard W. Labaree, 17 vols. to date (New Haven, 1959–), 5:244.

single economic activity but rather the net effect of a variety of social functions like the exchange of labor for goods and the distribution of material necessities.

God's infinite Wisdom has made our Way of Living so agreeable to Love (when rightly used) that what a Man gains honestly is some Way for the *publick Good*, or such as deal with him are the better for it, so well as himself. What the *Farmer* raises on his Land makes so much the more Provision in the Country. The *Tradesman* serves his Customers as well as himself, and supplies what is needed in the Land, the *Merchant* brings into the Country what it needs, and disposes of their superfluities for them. . . . Thus Men need a Communion for the Good of each Party, to shew by Similitude the heavenly Communion.[3]

This perception of two different realms of economic activity perpetuated the traditional notions that economic autonomy of the individual was something to be avoided, if the interests of the community were to be preserved, and that social claims had priority over economic ones. Such prescriptions testified to more than a prudent concern for social order; they also indicated concern about the quality of affiliation itself and the possibility of self-fulfillment in a social context.

Americans seldom said that participation in a market economy was in itself bad, but there is abundant evidence of their discomfort with the world they had made. When they considered their society they were struck by the exploitive and impersonal relations among men. Travelers to American cities commented on the inhabitants' preoccupation with business to the exclusion of social pleasures and responsibilities. In Philadelphia, Dr. Alexander Hamilton, a traveler from Maryland, noted that the "chief employ, indeed, is traffick and mercantile business which turns their thoughts from these levities . . . so conducive to the improvement of politeness, good manners and humanity." In Albany the frugality he saw seemed anything but a social virtue. "They live in their houses in Albany as if it were in prisons, all their doors and windows being perpetually shut. But the reason of this may be the little desire they have for conversation and society, their whole thoughts being turned upon profit and gain which necessarily makes them live retired and frugall." By the time he arrived in Chester, Pennsylvania, the sights were familiar: "they have that accomplishment peculiar to our American colonys, viz., subtilty [*sic*] and craft in their dealings." Andrew Burnaby, an Anglican minister traveling in America, had the same impressions. "The Pennsylvanians, as to character, are a frugal and industrious people: not remarkably courteous and hospitable to strangers, unless particularly recommended to them; but rather, like the denizens of most commercial cities, the reverse." In the backcountry there was the same lack of concern with the welfare of others. John Urmston, a minister for the Society for the Propagation of the Gospel, was disappointed by the lack of

[3]Joseph Morgan, *Love to Our Neighbour Recommended; and the Duties Thereof Importunately Urged* . . ., 3rd ed. (Boston, 1749), p. 12.

Christian brotherhood in North Carolina. "My neighbours seem to like well of my industry but are far from affording me their assistance in anything[;] they love to see new comers put to their shifts as they themselves have been and cannot endure to see anybody live as well as themselves without having undergone the slavish part and I learnt to live independent of others." Nor was there much stability in social organization; instead of a division of labor by calling, men acted like undifferentiated economic atoms.

Men are generally of all trades and women the like within there spheres[;] . . . men are generally carpenters Joiners Wheelwrights Coopers Butchers Tanners Chandlers Waterman & what not[;] Women Soap makers Starch makers Dyes &c[;] he or she that can't do all these things or hath not slaves than can over and above all the common occupations of both sexes will have a bad time on't for help is not to be had at any rate everyone having business enoo' of his own[;] this makes tradesmen turn planters and these become tradesmen[;] no Society none with another but all seem to live by their own hands of their own produce and what they can spare goes for foreign goods.[4]

The colonists' economic interests had given impersonal and exploitive qualities to their social relations.

The articulate members of colonial society viewed such situations, which demonstrated the self-reliance and versatility so admired by American historians later, with an uncomprehending anxiety. It was difficult to sustain a belief in a natural harmony of private and public interests when conditions were so fluid and social relations so strained. Commercial imperatives prevented the practice of the social ethics of benevolence and self-denial. The opportunities for profit broke the bonds that were necessary to maintain social order. Just because the Americans took the type of society in which they lived for granted they found their behavior in it all the more unbearable. Perry Miller, describing the "declension of a bible commonwealth," summed up the situation thus: "they berated the consequence of progress but never progress itself."[5] What the Americans could not accept was the boundless nature of their own appetites.

The colonists needed a guide to behavior that was suited to the conditions of their particular society, one that was more tolerant of self-indul-

[4]Alexander Hamilton, *Gentleman's Progress: The Itinerarium of Dr. Alexander Hamilton, 1744*, ed. Carl Bridenbaugh (Chapel Hill, 1948), pp. 23, 73, 193; Andrew Burnaby, *Travels through the Middle Settlements of North America* [1759-1760], ed. Rufus Rockwell Wilson (New York, 1904), p. 96; Per Kalm, *The America of 1750: Peter Kalm's Travels in North America* [1748-1751], ed. Adolph B. Benson, 2 vols. (New York, 1937), 1:344; John Urmston to S.P.G., 7 July 1711, *The Colonial Records of North Carolina*, ed. William L. Saunders, 10 vols. (Raleigh, 1886-1890), 1: 764.

[5]Robert Carter to Peter Hedgeman, 22 June 1721, Robert Carter, *Letters of Robert Carter, 1720-1727: The Commercial Interests of a Virginia Gentleman*, ed. Louis B. Wright (San Marino, Calif., 1940), pp. 104-5; Perry Miller, "The Declension of a Bible Commonwealth," *Proceedings of the American Antiquarian Society*, 51 (1941): 68; Stephen Foster, "The Puritan Social Ethic: Class and Calling in the First Hundred Years of Settlement in New England" (Ph.D. diss., Yale University, 1966), pp. 189, 218-19.

gence in material prosperity and more adaptable to an open-ended view of the social consequences of individual activity. An alternative adaptation, but one that could leave few overt traces, was simply a less scrupulous and less self-conscious attitude toward their activities. Before the development of new attitudes toward work—and there is little public evidence to show that such attitudes were common before the Revolution—the Americans used an inherited ideology to mitigate their guilt by a series of confrontations with their wrongdoings. The jeremiads of tribal New England, the condemnations of worldliness in the Great Awakening, and the lamentations of the absence of a public spirit during the Revolution each served the dual function of making a bewildering situation understandable while maintaining a tie between justice and work.

THE DISTRUST OF ECONOMIC MAN

Faced with what they perceived as social disorder stemming from commercial life, the colonists were careful to demonstrate that economic interests were not necessarily synonymous with the public interest. They perceived economic life—or at least that part of it which was confined within their society—to be a part of social life. The distinction between private and public interest was basic to their social analysis. Their concern about public obligations was a function of their awareness of the inherent strength of men's self-interests; their constant ethical concern was to ensure that this basically destructive force be brought into harmony with the community's interest. They thought of men in their economic capacities as essentially selfish beings. Restraints on private interest required the greatest attention if order was to be maintained, for, when "*Self-Interest* becomes the *ruling Passion*, it is insatiable, and nothing can stand before MONEY and POWER." When private interest was unregulated, it was likely that "little of Kindness and Love will be shown." The public good was something other than the sum of individual goods; only when self-interest was guided by broader social interests was the public welfare served. Even grand schemes "under the Pretences of publick Spiritedness and Promotion of Trade" required careful examination, because projectors, under the guise of public service, "secretly carry on their private interest, and too often sacrifice the Publick to great Damage, if not Ruin."[6] Commercial life was the most dangerous field of action for self-interest because in it men could acquire both power and a specious legitimacy.

Though from some twentieth-century perspectives market relations are pre-eminently contractural ones—whereas the organization of production

---

[6]*South Carolina Gazette* (Charleston), 10 July 1736; "Appendix to Massachusetts in Agony" [1751], *Colonial Currency Reprints, 1682–1751*, ed. Andrew McFarland Davis, 4 vols. (Boston, 1911), 4: 468; *A Word of Advice to Such as Are Settling New Plantations* (Boston, 1739), pp. 9-10; *A Dialogue Shewing What's Therein To Be Found . . .* (Philadelphia, 1725), p. 7.

is seen to be based on power, and the exercise of consumption is taken to be an indulgence of freedom—in eighteenth-century America the idea of mutual benefit in commercial exchange was less prominent than the assumption that the structure of trade, domestic as well as foreign, depended on differentials in power which allowed some men to get others in their power. All three of the evils attending participation in commercial life—competition, exploitation, and luxury—involved the loss of autonomy as a result of the exercise of others' wills. If these evils were to be avoided, there had to be a high standard of morality in commercial exchanges; only in this way could the "negotiating life . . . be carried on without any mean or ill artifice, without impatient or tormenting designs, or tiresome and vexatious disappointments."[7] Yet the structure of commercial relations made competition seem to be inevitable, especially so in a staple economy where there was a lack of the flexibility in the allocation of economic resources which a truly rational contracturalism required. Competition in which one man's gain was not necessarily another's loss was possible only in situations where economic diversification was feasible, and these arose mostly in foreign trade. For example, the fear of inevitable competition led a writer from South Carolina to take a jaundiced view of plans to build a rice mill in the colony. He was sure that the wealthiest planters would build it and then further improve their position in the market and thereby "ruin all our middling and lesser Planters, who, destitute of these Advantages, must be obliged to sell their rough Rice to the more Wealthy, or lose by their Labour." Destructive competition seemed to be inherent in basic commercial activities like the extension of credit and the sale of goods. In trading with one another "we part with our most valuable Commodities for such *Bills of Credit* as are no Profit . . . and become a *Medium* whereby we are continually cheating and wronging one another in our Dealings and Commerce."[8]

Competition was bad enough, but it at least involved men in a rough equality. Outright oppression was a far more serious threat to community solidarity because it combined selfishness with unfair commercial advantage; the freedom to buy or not was crucial in an economy where the means and alternatives for subsistence were scarce. Nathaniel Gookin, a minister in Hampton, New Hampshire (who gained his parishioners' awe by preaching about a "day of trouble" several hours before the earthquake of 1727 occurred), described the different circumstances in which some men oppressed others in commercial exchanges as: "when they improve upon the *Necessities* of others to get excessive Prices for what they Sell, or upon

[7]Richard Lucas, *Rules Relating to Success in Trade . . . Taken from His Enquiry after Happiness* (Boston, 1760), pp. 19-20.

[8]"A Letter, from One in Boston, to His Friend in the Country" [1714], *Tracts Relating to the Currency of Massachusetts Bay, 1682-1720*, ed. Andrew McFarland Davis (Boston, 1902), p. 139; "Agricola," *South Carolina Gazette*, 3 February 1733; [Roger Sherman], *A Caveat against Injustice, or an Enquiry into the Evil Consequences of a Fluctuating Medium of Exchange . . .* (New York, 1752), p. 13; [William Gooch], *A Dialogue between Thomas Sweet-Scented, William Oronoco, Planters, and Justice Lovecountry* (Williamsburg, 1732), p. 12.

the *Ignorance* of the *Seller* to get things at an Under Rate, or of the *Buyer* to get more than the thing is worth; and especially, when their Trading is managed by *Lying* and *Deceit*." A man so indifferent to the needs of others was "Brother to a Thief." Economic advantage and foresight were insufficient justifications for oppression. Just as in the medieval municipality, there was hatred for the "huckster," the men who took advantage of the market by "forestalling, engrossing and buying up the Provision that comes into Town, which they buy almost at any rate, and then raise the price again as they please; for they know that many in the Neighbourhood must come to them." The individual profits from oppression were not worth their public costs. When men profited by oppression "the true harmony of the family appears to be in danger."[9]

Oppression was especially intolerable because it was naturally most effective against the weak, and in a society in which concern for the welfare of others was so highly esteemed the weak had special claims. The weak were a combination of widows, orphans, "Salary Men, Ministers, School-Masters, Judges of the Circuit, [and the] President and Tutors at Colledge." The well-being of the weak was controlled by money supplies and considerations of trade. If economic activity went unchecked, "the weakest always go by the walls, and become a prey to the strong; the Rich, Great, and Potent, with rapacious violence bear down all before them, who have not wealth, or strength to encounter or avoid their fury." Able-bodied men who remained idle when there was work available received little sympathy, but many expressed the belief that poverty was a matter beyond individual men's control. John Woolman thought that the mere existence of poverty was sufficient evidence to prove that someone was getting and keeping more than he deserved. "Were all superfluities, and the desire of outward greatness laid aside, and the right use of things universally attended to, Such a number of people might be employed in things usefull, as that moderate labour, with the Blessing of Heaven, would answer all good purposes." Woolman expressed in its pristine form the desire of many of his contemporaries to have economic matters be subordinate considerations in the affairs of society. But instead of such justice the poor served the rich: "The mony which the wealthy receive from the poor . . . is frequently paid to other people for doing business which is foreign to the true use of things."[10] In their condemnation of oppression the official elite acted

---

[9]Nathaniel Gookin, *The Day of Trouble Near, the Tokens of It, and a Due Preparation for It* . . . (Boston, 1728), p. 6; [Cotton Mather], *Instructions to the Living, from the Condition of the Dead* . . . (Boston, 1717), pp. 44–46; [Benjamin Colman], *Some Reasons and Arguments Offered* . . . *for the Setting Up of Markets in Boston* . . . (Boston, 1719), p. 6; Edward Holyoke, *The Duty of Ministers of the Gospel to Guard against the Pharisaism and Sadducism, of the Present Day* . . . (Boston, 1741), pp. 24–25; John Woolman, "Serious Considerations on Trade," *The Journal and Essays of John Woolman* . . ., ed. Amelia Mott Gummere (New York, 1922), p. 399; Samuel Hopkins, *An Address to the People of New England* . . . (originally pub. 1753; Philadelphia, 1757), p. 12.

[10]"The Present Melancholy Circumstances" [1719], *Tracts*, p. 193; "A Letter to an Eminent Clergyman" [1720] and [Thomas Hutchinson], "A Letter to a Member of the Honourable House of Representatives" [1736], *Colonial Currency Reprints*, 2: 234 and 3: 152–53;

as spokesmen for anyone who was a potential victim, and in a market society no one's position was secure.

The forms which exploitation took were varied, but they always involved unfair advantage being taken with market relations. The practices of trading by barter and taking payment in shopnotes were hated by small producers, who thought they were robbed of the fruits of their labor by the merchant, who would accept their trade only at a large discount and who insisted on making payment in goods rather than money. When merchants collaborated to refuse to receive the notes of other colonies or of land banks as currency, it was clear to others that they intended to exploit the weaknesses of poor people in a market situation. Merchants, "whose professed Aim, as such, is Gain," should not be allowed "to enrich themselves at the ruin of others."[11]

The encouragement of luxury was a more subtle exercise of power than either competition or exploitation, but this concomitant of commerce damaged the social fabric just as effectively. The vice of avarice motivated the colonists in those courses of action which were corrupting their institutions and their morals, and when avarice combined with pride it led inevitably to luxury. Whenever men met for business, "at Fairs, Markets, Country-Vendues, and almost all Times of Concourse," the acquisition of useless goods seemed to be their goal. Knowing men's weakness for luxuries, merchants did not hesitate to import vast quantities of rum, fashionable cloth and furnishings, and other frivolities. There was no middle ground between frugality and luxury, because the need for goods was self-sustaining. As men grew rich "they grew Ambitious, and as Persons in a Dropsy, the more they drink, the greater their Thirst, so the more Money they got, the more they coveted." When Samuel Davies looked upon the luxury which abounded in society, he saw men losing their humanity. "You see Avarice hoarding up her useless treasures, dishonest Craft planning her schemes of unlawful gain, and Oppression unmercifully grinding the face of the poor: you see Prodigality squandering her stores, Luxury spreading her table, and unmanning her guests."[12] With his feminine charac-

---

Thomas Prentice, *The Vanity of Zeal for Fasts, without True Judgment, Mercy, and Compassion* . . . (Boston, 1748), pp. 18-21; Charles Chauncey, *The Idle-Poor Secluded from the Bread of Charity by the Christian Law* . . . (Boston, 1752), p. 7; John Woolman, "A Plea for the Poor," *Journal and Essays*, pp. 402-4.

[11]On the "populistic paranoia" of the advocates of the Land Bank, see John M. Bumsted, "The Report of the Pembroke (Massachusetts) Town Committee on the Currency, March 24, 1740/41," *New England Quarterly*, 40 (1967): 550-60. See also "A Letter from a Country Gentleman at Boston" [1740], "A Letter from a Gentleman in Rhode-Island to His Friend in Boston" [1734], and "A Word in Season to All True Lovers of Their Liberty" [1748], *Colonial Currency Reprints*, 3: 45 and 4: 30, 362.

[12]*A Dialogue* (1725), p. 36; William Byrd, "The History of the Dividing Line" [1728], *The Prose Works . . . Narratives of a Colonial Virginia*, ed. Louis B. Wright (Cambridge, Mass., 1966), p. 173; "Massachusetts in Agony" [1750], *Colonial Currency Reprints*, 4: 440; Samuel Davies, "Religion and Patriotism" [1755], *Sermons on Important Subjects*, 3 vols. (New York, 1841), 3: 56-57.

terization of vices and his dire warning to the unwary, Davies was telling his audience that the accession of wealth, with its supposed power over others, could paradoxically result in a loss of autonomy.

With its changes in traditional ways of work and consumption, life in a market society was a strain on personal morality and on social ties. Commercial life divided the "several sorts of men . . . into two Parties; the man *Free from Debt* to his Neighbours; and the man *Involved in Debt.*" This awareness that commercial life, within a given community, required the interests of men to conflict—so that the gain of one came at the expense of another—disturbed the colonists because they believed that a harmony of interests was desirable and possible. "The unhappiness of all Societies of men" stemmed from the differences and conflicts of their interests.[13] It seemed to the colonists that they would have to give priority to social considerations over economic ones if they were to minimize the prevailing wrongs.

Many expressed the belief that moral obligations should have played a stronger part in economic life. Instead of profit, "we should desire to benefit others, as well as be benefitted by them"; instead of taking advantage of the chronic shortage of labor, "we should not Sell our Labour or the produce of it, for more than 'tis worth, according to the Rules of *Justice* and *Equity*: nor should we desire to have our Neighbours Labour or the produce of it, for *less* than the *just Value* of it." The economic advantage which arose from the possession of scarce goods was not be exploited, for "to Sell as high or dear, and Buy as cheap or low, as possibly we can, is no good rule for Christians to go by." In an effort to lessen competition and thereby reduce the social strains that resulted from commercial life, the colonists urged cooperation as a virtue in economic matters. Their proposals were usually exhortatory and only rarely did they make concrete recommendations for reform, but the amount of attention they gave to the matter indicated that the problem was real and that it aroused their anxieties. In arguing for leniency toward one another in business, a writer in South Carolina pointed out that all merchants faced the prospect of ruin. "If then the contingent Nature of Trade renders every Man liable to disaster that is engaged in it, it seems strange that Merchants should be outrageous and unmerciful to one another when they fall, and yet so it is."[14]

The colonists yearned for harmony and interdependence, for an integration of the individual with the community. Late in the colonial period people still clung to the notion that commerce could be a cementing force instead of a divisive one. Thomas Barnard, in a sermon to the Society for Encouraging Industry, explained that "a Life of industrious Pursuit of civil

---

[13]"The Second Part of South-Sea Stock, Being an Inquiry into the Original of Province Bills or Bills of Credit" [1721], *Colonial Currency Reprints*, 2: 323.

[14]"An Addition to the Present Melancholy Circumstances of the Province Considered" [1719], *Tracts*, p. 205; *South Carolina Gazette*, 13 March 1736; Thomas Warrington, *The Love of God, Benevolence, and Self-Love, Considered Together* (Williamsburg, 1753), p. 19.

Professions, has great Advantage for the strengthening of social Affections; By the constant Endearments of Family Relations; by the Exchange of good Offices in Vicinities; by friendly Conversations and mutual Assistance in Emergencies or under Sufferings: And tends to give clear Ideas of, and a firm Regard for Justice and Property, and an inward Feeling of Humanity, Benevolence and Mercy." A description of ideal working conditions showed a similar desire for a change in economic and social relations, and, even if the desires it expressed were outrageous in view of the conditions that actually prevailed, it at least provided an indication of what bothered the colonists.

The chearful Labourer shall sing over his daily Task, because he will be sure of his Wages, and his Employer shall punctually pay these Wages, because he will be sure they were earned. A general Satisfaction shall run through all Ranks of Men; good Offices shall be reciprocal and common; the Rich shall be better served and the Poor better paid. And what Heart would not leap at such a Prospect![15]

The traditional basis for these hopes was the notion "that every Man's particular Interest is comprized in the General." Because of their strong commitment to the preservation of community, it was impossible for the colonists to be sanguine about the competition which they saw about them and in which they themselves were engaged. There was as yet no intellectual framework in which the unhindered pursuit of individual interest could claim legitimacy. On the contrary, it was assumed "that how different soever [men's] Pursuits in Life may be, their interest is still the same, and that they ought to unite in pursuing the common good, which is the Good of every Particular." The union and dependence of the members of society upon one another was especially marked in commercial life, so "that one Individual cannot suffer, but some others must suffer with him." If monetary gain were the only measure of success, society would be deprived of the ties of benevolence and dependence. If status depended on wealth, "the Applause paid to some for their Success" would encourage others "to attempt and venture upon such like Enterprizes," and, since such attempts were likely to fail, resentment would increase and social ties would decline. History had shown that a society so divided could not last long. When the ancients lost sight of the public good and came "to look upon themselves as so many Individuals, distinct from the Public, they soon set up and pursued particular Interests of their own, and the Public was always neglected and often sacrificed to those private Pursuits when it came in Competition with them." With the destruction of their unity, their strength was lost, and the "Bundle became untied and those Arrows which,

---

[15]Thomas Barnard, *A Sermon Preached in Boston . . . before the Society for Encouraging Industry, and Employing the Poor* (Boston, 1758), p. 10; *Industry and Frugality Proposed as the Surest Means To Make Us a Rich and Flourishing People . . .* (Boston, 1753), pp. 14-15.

when united, could hardly be bent, now separate and single, were easily broken."[16]

Just as cooperation was urged as an alternative to competition, so there were hopes that charity would replace exploitation. In practice the rule of charity in economic life meant that one person should not gain at another's expense; too often the result of bargaining brought "no good to the publick, and [was] contrary to the Law of *Loving our Neighbour as ourselves.*" The wealthy Christian had special charitable responsibilities. Thomas Bacon preached to slaveowners that it was unlikely that God "hath entrusted us with this extensive authority for no other end than our own temporal gains." Instead of oppressing the weak, the Christians who were economically successful had a responsibility "to look on every Addition to [their] Fortune as an additional Obligation on [them] to assist and forward the Designs of those who, perhaps, are more indigent, tho' equally industrious."[17]

One of the most common opportunities for the exercise of charity in economic matters was in debtor and creditor relations. There was a persistent refusal to consider men only in their economic roles. *"For the Good of the Community"* there had to be some control over "the Tempers and Passions of Creditors," who otherwise "may ruin a valuable Man, his Family, and deprive Society of a useful Member; and all out of meer Humour, Will, Resentment, Spite, or Mallice." If a man "made use of rational Means for advancing his Fortune and answering Demands against him" and avoided "wanton Projects" and "improbable Schemes," then "he [might] . . . reasonably expect the Forbearance of his Creditors; and no considerate Man can refuse it." His character, not his success, entitled him to respect, "the one being at his own Command, the other at the Disposal of God."[18]

One response to the moral problems of life in a market economy was the recommendation to retreat from commerce. This appeal involved an outright rejection of luxury and encouraged a general simplification of economic life. It involved a new organization of work instead of simply urging

[16]"A Letter from a Gentleman, Containing Some Remarks upon the Several Answers Given unto Mr. Colman's, Entitled, the Distressed State of the Town of Boston" [1720], *Tracts*, p. 293; *South Carolina Gazette*, 10 July 1736; *The Ill Policy and Inhumanity of Imprisoning Insolvent Debtors* . . . (Newport, R.I., 1754), p. 4; *Industry and Frugality*, p. 4. Michael Zuckerman has found that in the towns of Massachusetts "neither conflict, dissent, nor any other structural pluralism ever obtained legitimacy . . . before the Revolution." In an effort "to establish moral community" the colonists strove for unanimity in decisions about the life of the town. "The Social Context of Democracy in Massachusetts," *William and Mary Quarterly*, 3rd ser., 25 (1968): 523–44.

[17]Morgan, *Love to Our Neighbour*, p. 12; Thomas Bacon, *Sermons Addressed to Masters and Servants, and Published in the Year 1743* . . . (Winchester, Va., 1813?), p. 14; *Debtor and Creditor: Or, a Discourse on the Following Words: Have Patience with Me, and I Will Pay Thee All* (Boston, 1762), p. 4; John Barnard, *A Zeal for Good Works Excited and Directed* . . . (Boston, 1742), p. 18.

[18]*The Ill Policy*, p. 34; *Debtor and Creditor*, p. 10; Cotton Mather, *Advice from Taberah: A Sermon Preached after the Terrible Fire* . . . (Boston, 1711), p. 32.

slightly different behavior in situations that in fact required men to act exactly in the ways that were causing psychological and social troubles. But the theory underlying such proposals was usually little more than a thoroughgoing application of the principles of provincial mercantilism for moral purposes.

The first stage in the simplification of commerce was to be the dismantling of the structure of monetary ties between men: "do but leave off Trusting [lending], or shorten Credit as much as possible, and this will make us all industrious, Frugal, and Prudent, whether we will or not." The second stage would involve a greater reliance on local and household production. The plan was to "raise & make as much as we can for our selves, of *Food, Raiment, Utensils,* &c. and buy no more of *Imported* Goods than *necessity* requires." The basic idea of such reform was to reduce market relations within the society because they were inherently corrupting, but some hoped that the simplifications would also result in a more favorable situation in foreign trade. Only trade whose direction was predominantly outward could be engaged in with safety. The bad consequences of trade within a society were plain for all to see. There was frequently an antitown and antimerchant bias in the analysis of these consequences; virtue could be sustained more easily by "a close following [of] the *Wheel* within doors and the *Plough* without" than by the *"Plotting heads, Proud hearts,* and *Idle hands"* of the town. Merchants were robbing the country people through the sale of imported goods, and corrupting them by spreading the "Boston distemper" of extravagance. In answer to the objection that *"to raise necessaries for our selves,* and buy no more than *necessity* requires of *Imported Commodities* . . . will spoil *Merchandizing* and *Trading,"* the reply was obvious, that "the good of the whole should be preferred to that of a part." The author of such ideas was at a loss, however, for a specific reform plan. He yearned for a return to the natural division of labor according to callings which he thought had characterized earlier American communities "It is not profitable to the Publick, to have *too many* of any *particular Trade* or *Calling,* for they must either be *idle* (when they might be imploy'd in proper business) or labour *for little or nothing,* which is unprofitable to themselves, and to the Publick therein."[19] The belief that a simplification of commercial life could reinstate a previous condition of virtue was given its most serious hearing when the nonimportation movement during the Revolution presented the Americans with an opportunity to put their desires for reform into effect.

The extreme case of the repudiation of commercial life came in the form of a counterimage to economic success, usually in the form of bucolic withdrawal. These arcadian fantasies represented a stylized personal dissatisfaction rather than a commentary on the structure of American economic

[19]"A Letter from a Gentleman," [1720], p. 274; "The Present Melancholy Circumstances," pp. 191–94.

life.[20] There were frequent expressions, often poetic, of a sense that work was essentially futile and could not give satisfaction. Each achievement only enabled one to pursue another goal or a higher status. "Capricious mortals! yet they all pursue Content, ease is the game they have in view, But never catch'd; a fair delusive cheat. This life affords no happiness complete." References to the futility of work applied especially to the market. In order to increase "Wealth, or Power, or Grandeur," a man had to give up the "Honesty, Plainness, and Sincerity" of a virtuous life and replace them with "Craft and Cunning." Economic life was uncertain by nature, but if a man made riches the object of his boundless efforts he was sure to remain unsatisfied. Even in the midst of success he would be unhappy, for the increase of wealth served only to "increase Men's Desires . . . which Thirst surely cannot be deemed a Branch of Happiness, but rather the contrary." Even men of business who appeared to be untroubled were really leading pointless lives; in order to remain successful they had to subordinate the rest of their life to business. If one were to ask a merchant "what it is he drives at in life, he would be at a loss for an answer."[21]

Primitivism colored much of this desire for a simplification of economic life. Stoic objections to the idea that worldly success could be satisfying were often expressed in terms that implied disapproval of artifice and sophistication. Wealth and manners disguised a man's true virtue. "Banish wealth but a moment from the world, and see how much more helpless the once opulent man would be, than the industrious poor; he is his own person, contributes to his own wants, whilst the other is indebted both to him, and the accidental circumstance of his riches." This appeal for contentment in work and a moderation of appetites often resembled the traditional notion of the calling. A life of "absolute Ease and Inactivity" was to be avoided because God had "designed every Individual to move in a certain Sphere, and to accomplish the Duties of a certain Station."[22]

The calling best suited to this hypothetical life of happy moderation was a rural one. Life in the country was a counterimage to the superficiality and corruption of the town, which was associated with an intense concern with economic matters. The apotheosis of colonial celebrations of rural life and retreat from commerce came in the imitations of John Pomfret's bucolic poem *The Choice*. The introduction to William Livingston's *Philosophic Solitude* recommended the poem because it took its readers

---

[20]For a discussion of this theme when it did constitute a criticism of the structure of economic life, see Leo Marx, *The Machine in the Garden: Technology and the Pastoral Ideal in America* (New York, 1964).

[21]*New York Gazette*, 9 April 1767; *Virginia Gazette* (Williamsburg), 23 September 1737; *The Folly and Vanity of a Life Spent in the Pursuit of Worldly Profit* . . . (Philadelphia, 1770), p. 6.

[22]*South Carolina Gazette & Country Journal* (Charleston), 23 January 1770; William Livingston et al., *The Independent Reflector: Or, Weekly Essays on Sundry Important Subjects* . . ., ed. Milton M. Klein (Cambridge, Mass., 1963), p. 407.

> To distant regions, and to happier climes;
> When native innocence adorn'd mankind,
> E'er fraud and lux'ry had debauch'd the mind.

Livingston's "happier climes" had practically nothing to do with society or work. The poem's persona expended almost all his energies on contemplation, and he had no evident means of support. He could retain the gentlemanly ideal of moderation and humanist cultivation only by removing himself totally from the realm of economic life. There was no recognition of social obligation in this poem; he longed to be

> From noise remote, and ignorant of strife;
> Far from the painted Belle, and white-glov'd Beau.
>
> . . . .
>
> Let ardent heroes seek renown in arms,
> Pant after fame, and rush to war's alarms;
> To shining palaces, let fools resort,
> And dunces cringe to be esteem'd at court.[23]

All of the espousals of rural life were part of a literature of retreat. Country life was happy because it avoided some of the discontents of work.

These repudiations of economic life reveal the nature of some characteristic colonial discontents. But, in comparison with the vast amount of moral suasion which sought to convince the colonists to reform, not to quit, their work, this language of retreat is chiefly significant for its scarcity. Discontented as they were, the colonists thought it was themselves and not society which needed correction. Until they came to believe that their wrongdoings were inevitable in their type of society, the dominant rhetorical theme would be self-criticism. Only when they had accepted the fact that society was simply the sum of the individuals who composed it could they come to accept themselves.

The economic imperatives of the market provided an approximation to a specific ordering of callings, yet activity in these callings seemed to be causing many troubles. When the colonists expressed their fears of competitition, exploitation, and luxury, they referred these evils only to market relations within their society. Economic man was feared because of the effects he had in the domestic realm of economic life. The colonists took it for granted that within the community economic justifications for action were insufficient unless they were compatible with established standards of justice.

[23]William Livingston, *Philosophic Solitude: Or, the Choice of a Rural Life* . . . (New York, 1747), pp. iv, 13–14. See also Benjamin Church, *The Choice: A Poem after the Manner of Promfret* [*sic*] . . . (Boston, 1757); Edwin T. Bowden, "Benjamin Church's *Choice* and American Colonial Poetry," *New England Quarterly*, 32 (1959): 170–84; Richard Bridgman, "Jefferson's Farmer before Jefferson," *American Quarterly*, 14 (1962): 567–77, points out that the appeal of rural life had aristocratic connotations before the Revolution, but he exaggerates the degree of contempt in which the ordinary farmer was held.

CIVILIZATION'S DEPENDENCE ON COMMERCE

Articulation of an effective critique of life in a market society was blocked by a strong persuasion that commerce was inherently a legitimate and valuable pursuit for men. Life would be wretched without the material benefits made possible by commerce, but, more important, economic life was intrinsic to rational self-expression. A poem quoted in an almanac made it clear that trade enabled men to transcend the limitations of their immediate environment.

> Commerce! We do they num'rous Blessings own,
> Thou bring'st the Fruit of other Nations home:
> The Taste of hot *Arabia's* Spice we know,
> Nor feel the scorching Sun that makes it grow:
> Without the Worm in *Persian* Silks we shine,
> And without Planting, drink of every Vine.[24]

It should be noted in this and the following examples of an admiration for commercial life, however, that in nearly every case the context referred work to foreign trade. In such trade, unlike commerce which was strictly domestic, men were free to treat others simply as economic beings from whom they sought personal gain.

Though moral indifference was at least acceptable in reference to external commerce, such work was also given more positive, ego-enhancing functions. Commerce facilitated rational self-fulfillment by providing opportunities for participation in the ordering of the world. The benefits of economic life were traced at least as much to exchange as to production. Mercantilist thought had taught the colonists that foreign trade was necessary for the preservation of the state and for the welfare of its inhabitants. One strategy to avoid the traditional moral objections to riches was to make recommendations for commerce in terms of a distinction between private and public prosperity, as did James Logan: "Riches it is true, are not always necessary to Happiness, in every private Condition, but it is otherwise in a State." It was a generally accepted principle that, "if *Wealth* be the Strength of a Country, and *Trade* the Source of Riches, it is certainly incumbent on a wise and free People, to be vigilant in preserving and promoting of *Commerce*, in all its Branches, as it is the Foundation and Pillar of their *Liberty*." Commerce was promoted by a refinement of the work ethic; in addition to industry and frugality, men should strive "to encourage and put [their] *Trade* under proper Regulations." The nature of commercial relations was such that the alternative to the encouragement of commerce was failure for societies as well as for individuals. "The Increase of Wealth and Power ['of all trading kingdoms'] has generally been propor-

---

[24]Nathaniel Ames, *An Astronomical Diary: Or, an Almanack for the Year of Our Lord Christ, 1762* (Boston, 1761).

tionate to the Enlargement of their Trade, and History fully proves, that Ruin and Desolation have always attended the loss of it."[25]

In addition to the political necessity of commerce, there was a belief that the order of the world required trade. John Wise, a Massachusetts minister who advocated an increase in paper currency, thought that "Temporal Commerce and Trade, is as necessary for the Conveniency, Comfort and Outward Profit of Man, whilst he holds his Tenure on Earth, as Civil Alliance and Cohabitation." This necessity arose from the uneven distribution of material resources. "All Men as all Nations dont raise all things that are for their Benefit & Comfort; therefore Trade is very needful." God had designed the world in this way in order to reinforce men's social nature with a mutual dependence for the necessities of life. George Whitefield concisely explained this relationship of God's will to man's social nature and his need for commerce. Creation was incomplete without company for man, and so God made it impossible that "communities be kept up, or Commerce carried on, without *Society*. . . . Providence seems wisely to have assigned a particular Product to almost each particular Country, on Purpose, as it were to oblige us to be social; and hath . . . admirably mingled the Parts of the whole Body of Mankind together." The mutual dependence of commerce and society demonstrated that the "one great End of our Existence, consists in being useful to each other in social Life, in a careful Discharge of all relative Duties incumbent on us." Some men believed that the imperatives of trade actually reinforced Christian life. For example, Benjamin Colman believed that a life of trade provided opportunities for the practice of charity. "One natural Benefit of Trade and Commerce to any People" was that "it *enlarges* Peoples' hearts to do *generous* things. . . . *Christianity* has been greatly serv'd by Trade and *Merchandise*, by means whereof a great Part of the World has been *gospelized*." In the writings of some pamphleteers commerce became a panacea for even the gravest immorality; indeed, the Bible would have been without one of its great examples of corruption "had *Sodom* and *Gomorrah* been Politick in *Trade* and accustomed to Manners of Civility & Magnificence according as the fertility of their Soil would have endured it, [because] they might have been diverted from the Sins of Idleness."[26]

The rightness of commerce was evident from man's rational nature as well as from his social need. It was in the nature of "rational creatures" to

[25]James Logan, *The Charge Delivered from the Bench to the Grand Jury* . . . (Philadelphia, 1723), p. 6; excerpt from the "Craftsman," no. 640, *Virginia Gazette,* 2 March 1739; Otis Little, *The State of Trade in the Northern Colonies Considered* . . . (Boston, 1749), pp. 7–8.

[26][John Wise], "A Word of Comfort to a Melancholy Country: Or, the Bank of Credit Erected in the Massachusetts Bay, Fairly Defended" [1721], and "Trade and Commerce Inculcated" [1731], *Colonial Currency Reprints,* 2: 165, 366; George Whitefield, *The Necessity and Benefits of Religious Society* . . . (Boston, 1740), pp. 5–6; Jared Eliot, *Essays upon Field Husbandry in New England and Other Papers, 1748–1762,* ed. Harry J. Carman and Rexford G. Tugwell (New York, 1934), p. 165; Benjamin Colman, *The Merchandise of a People Holiness to the Lord* . . . (Boston, 1736), pp. ii, 10.

be "most adapted for Society, Commerce, and Dealing," and so God had suited various "Climates for different Productions of Nature for a mutual Intercourse and Dependence on each other by exchanging the Growth of one Country with another, which is the Foundation of Traffick and Dealing." Commerce provided man with the opportunity to exercise his faculty of reason; commerce was natural to man, even though he did not always engage in it. It was possible for men to "Dwell in the Clefts of the Valleys, in Caves of the Earth, and in the Rocks, and digg *Juniper Roots* for their Meat, or [to] live upon *Acorns*," but such a way of life was "not at all agreeable with a wise and Bustling People, that would spend their Life, to the Height of Religion and right Reason."[27]

The rationality of commerce was evident in its ability to overcome physical limitations of space and time through the use of money. Without money people must either "sell their Produce for Shop Goods, or keep 'em and eat 'em all themselves; and that we can't allow of either, for then we must starve." The decline of prosperity would weaken society. "Children will be viciated for want of Business, and in another Generation will lose all that Spirit and Life, which distinguishes Free Men from Slaves." The problem with barter as a basis of exchange was its unpredictability and its susceptibility to forces other than economic rationality. If trade were based on barter, "Men will live by preying upon one another; like the Fish in the Sea, the greater will devour the less; the whole Trade will get into a few Hands in a short time, and the middling sort of People who are the chief Support of any Place, will soon come (many of 'em) to Poverty."[28] Without money, labor discipline broke down, the division of labor became impractical, and the allocation of resources by the market was impeded.

If trade was a measure of man's fulfillment of his capacities, then the history of commerce was a crucial part of the story of the development of civilization. Before the Age of Discovery, economic life had been less rational and more disorganized, and the variety of work had been more limited. "The Rich had no Commerce, the Poor no Employment; War, and the Sword, was the great Field of Honour, the Stage of preferment; and you have scarce a Man eminent, in the World, for any Thing before that Time, but for a furious outragious falling upon his Fellow Creatures." With the expansion of commercial life, people were able to live more rationally because they organized their resources for long-term needs instead of responding to immediate requirements. Thus in England the famines common to the medieval period had been prevented eventually by commerce, which could compensate for local shortages by facilitating the exchange of credits for goods over time as well as over distance. After the development of commerce, people were encouraged to maximize their production,

---

[27][Francis Rawle], *Ways and Means for the Inhabitants of Delaware To Become Rich . . .* (Philadelphia, 1725), p. 44; [Wise], "A Word of Comfort," p. 165.

[28]"A Letter from a Gentleman," [1720], p. 289; "Money, the Sinews of Trade" [1731], *Colonial Currency Reprints*, 2: 432.

but in previous times "there was no Encouragement to Raise it, more than to supply their own Wants: If they did Raise more, it must lie upon their Hands."[29]

The colonists, aware that a well-developed trade was a sign of civilization in a society, often saw their society in an unfavorable light because their economic life seemed to be poorly structured. An advocate for the construction of a canal from Philadelphia to the interior parts of Pennsylvania demonstrated this opinion when he argued that the project would enable the inhabitants "to cooperate and unite in promoting the wealth, the honour, the dignity and power, of a society." He evaluated his society in mercantilist terms and assumed that "the trade and commerce of the province . . . ought to increase with every addition of inhabitants." The purpose of this increase was to "augment the balance of trade in our favor." Because this balance, when favorable, could be paid only "in foreign specie," it would add to "the wealth and power of our country." The most important benefit of the canal, however, was its ability to civilize those frontier inhabitants who had succumbed to the wilderness.

Many of the back inhabitants are become uncivilized, and little better than Barbarians.—They are lazy, licentious and lawless—and, instead of being useful members of society, are become seditious, and dangerous to the community. They add nothing to the wealth of the province, because the little they raise, by their labour, is scarcely sufficient to support their families; and should there, by chance, be a surplus, it will not bear the present expensive carriage to market. . . . [But with the canal] the uncivilized will, by a communication with the civilized, lose their ignorance and barbarism. They will learn industry from the industrious, virtue from the virtuous, loyalty from the loyal; and thereby become useful members of society, and good subjects.[30]

This feeling of commercial backwardness was especially strong in the South. The use of technology in the processing of goods was assumed to be a sign of civilization, but the South seemed to engage in the production of staples to the neglect of manufacturing. In the back country things were so disorganized that it was hard to know where development could begin; commerce required social order, and social order was difficult to achieve without the orderly habits fostered by commercial life. Charles Woodmason, an Anglican minister in North Carolina, described these problems. "In our present unsettled Situation—When the Bands of Society and Government hang Loose and Ungirt about Us—When no regular Police is establish'd, but ev'ry one left to Do as seemth Him Meet, there is not the least Encouragement for any Individual to be Industrious—Emulous in Well Doing—or Enterprizing in any attempt that is Laudable or public Spirited. Cunning; Rapine; Fraud and Violence, are now the Studies and persuits of the Vulgar." The inhabitants of the more settled regions of the plantation

---

[29]*South Carolina Gazette*, 19 March 1737; Eliot, *Essays upon Field Husbandry*, p. 54.
[30]*Pennsylvania Chronicle* (Philadelphia), 8 January 1770.

colonies had some of the social order that Woodmason so desperately wanted, but these Southerners still felt that their society lacked commercial development. In addition to greater wealth, they sought commercial improvements because they sensed that their society was primitive.

Such calls for economic restructuring were never based on a real analysis of the comparative costs and benefits associated with alternative forms of production. Instead, appeals were couched in terms which identified economic development with the use of human potential rather than with material needs. Southerners, in their familiar role of exaggerating American traits, called for the duplication in the colonies of the economic life identified with the sophistication and civilization of Europe, and in so doing indicated that they admired the behavior and trappings of life in such an economy at least as much as they desired its more technical benefits. Many of the inhabitants of the plantation colonies were prospering, but there were frequent expressions of regret about the primitive simplicity and backwardness of their society's economic life. Such criticism asserted that the manufacture of finished articles and goods was a more civilized and rational activity than the growth and sale of staple crops, but no one proved that it would be more profitable. The alternative to these improvements was evident in the surrounding wilderness. "Let us but turn our Eyes to the numerous Tribes of *Indians* surrounding us, and there view the Miseries and Wants of a People unciviliz'd by Arts, and barbarous for *want* of proper *Manufactures* to employ themselves in."[31]

The contrast between potential and actual development was a source of distress to Southerners. A description of the "Present State of Virginia" noted with disappointment that in the natural state Virginia was "certainly one of the best countries in the world," but that when one looked for signs of civilization, "for well built Towns, for convenient Ports and Markets, for Plenty of Ships and Seamen, for well improv'd Trades and Manufactures . . . for an industrious and thriving People . . . and in short, for all the other Advantages of human Improvements, it is certainly for all these Things, one of the poorest, miserablest, and worst Countries in all *America*, that is inhabited by Christians." In order for the plantation colonies to develop societies in which men could enjoy the fullest economic opportunities, there were two related needs which had to be satisfied, the growth of towns and the diversification of economic activities. The plantation colonies relied too much on the export of staple crops. In periods of trade depression complaints were usually made that the plantations had reached the point of diminishing returns in the production of their particular crops;

[31]Charles Woodmason, *The Carolina Backcountry on the Eve of the Revolution: The Journal and Other Writings of Charles Woodmason, Anglican Itinerant*, ed. Richard J. Hooker (Chapel Hill, 1953), p. 226; Henry Hartwell, James Blair, and Edward Chilton, *The Present State of Virginia, and the College* [1727], ed. Hunter Dickinson Farish (Williamsburg, 1940), pp. 4, 12-13; Robert Beverly, *The History and Present State of Virginia* [1705], ed. Louis B. Wright (Chapel Hill, 1947), pp. 70-71; Bertelson, *Lazy South, passim.*

further increases in production resulted only in proportionately lower prices. There were frequent proposals for cooperative or coercive efforts for the restriction of production in order to restore high prices, but they inevitably brought further disadvantages to those who took part in them because other men refused to cut back production. One of the arguments for the encouragement of towns was that they would make such controls of the market easier.

Towns were also necessary for economic efficiency and diversification. By consolidating trading facilities in towns the costs of storage and shipping would be reduced. Proposals were made in Virginia that planters with poor land, who had been glutting the market with their cheap tobacco, should move into the towns and take up more specialized jobs in transportation, trade, and manufactures. Only with the growth of towns could there be more prosperity and security; without "Towns, Markets, and Money, there is but little Encouragement for Tradesmen and Artificers, and therefore little Choice of them, and their labour very dear in the Country." Southerners hoped that, once there was a sufficient income from agricultural production to support the specialized labor of a town, the actual manufacture of goods for export could begin.[32] Such a development would improve their claims to be civilized men.

THE BENIGN ATTITUDE TOWARD A MARKET SOCIETY

Despite modifications, the traditional work ethic, with its subordination of personal interests to public ones and its priority of social considerations over economic ones, continued to evoke affirmations throughout the colonial period. But occasionally there were hints of a more benign understanding of work, an understanding that accepted the prevailing economic individualism and recognized the incapability of the old social ideals to contain it.[33] There was no clear chronological pattern to these hints; they were likely to be expressed in certain situations but not necessarily to in-

[32]Francis Makemie, "A Plain and Friendly Persuasive to the Inhabitants of Virginia and Maryland for Promoting Towns and Cohabitation" [1705], *Virginia Magazine of History and Biography*, 4 (1897): 263; Hartwell *et al.*, *The Present State of Virginia*, p. 9; Hugh Jones listed the goods which he hoped Virginia could export as follows: "leathern and woolen manufactures, hempen and flaxen goods, pitch, tar, timber for ship and house-carpenters, and cabinet-makers . . . masts, yards, ships and all sorts of naval stores . . . also hops, wines, hoops, cask, silk, drugs, colours, paper." *The Present State of Virginia* [1724], ed. Richard L. Morton (Chapel Hill, 1956), p. 148; *South Carolina Gazette*, 8 October 1744. Benjamin Franklin observed that the Indians "have few but natural wants and those easily supplied. But with us are infinite Artificial wants, no less craving than those of Nature, and much more difficult to satisfy." Franklin to Peter Collinson, 9 May 1753, *Papers*, 4: 482.

[33]The sporadic appearance of these more "realistic" views is similar to the situation which Bernard Bailyn discovered in studying *The Origins of American Politics* (New York, 1968), pp. 124-31. He found that factions and interests were basic to the operation of colonial politics, yet the values to which men paid allegiance held that political behavior based on factions and interests was illegitimate. Only occasionally did men argue that the public interest was objectively indeterminant and in practice could be decided only by the competition of interests.

crease in frequency over time. These expressions of a more benign view of commercial society in America combined nonprescriptive and utilitarian measures of social behavior with a defense of individual economic interests. They were nonprescriptive in the sense that work was considered to be an instrumental activity to which standards of justice were difficult to apply; the traditional view that social utility was a measure of the legitimacy of an individual's work was subordinated to a utilitarianism that was more personally oriented. Such expressions implied that domestic economic life had a moral autonomy that was usually extended only to commercial relations outside the community.

Only rarely did someone espouse the point for which Mandeville became infamous—namely, that private vices could result in public benefits. Joseph Morgan, a New Jersey minister and friend of Cotton Mather who contributed some of the most unorthodox economic writings to colonial thought, articulated a perverse defense of individualism, which recognized that "*Covetousness* (which is Idolatry) must be the support of the World, and the Misery of it both." If men truly sought "the Good of others," there would be a natural harmony of needs and production, and "no *Price* would be talked of." But for sinful men, who "love none but themselves, such a thing would be vain to talk of" because everyone would be lazy and depend on others for his subsistence. The institution of private property gave men the security they needed to unleash their avarice. Covetousness remained for him a wicked trait, but men nonetheless "cannot gain Riches and use 'em, except they help others by it." Morgan was able to reconcile the old moral standards for economic behavior with the recognized material need of society for commerce. But the idea that "a rich Man is a *Slave* to others while he thinks others are Slaves to him" was not very suitable as a legitimization of the pursuit of economic interest. Morgan found prosperity to be proportional to unhappiness, and he condemned as immoral those who aided society the most.[34] Yet the conflict of values and behavior which he recognized and for which he found a unique reconciliation was a common one.

Some writers eliminated the conflict of social and economic interests simply by assuming that a special morality applied in the economic realm. A belief in the moral autonomy of economic life was evident in arguments which defended free trade as the most efficient means to serve the public interest, which in such cases was usually assumed to be little more than economic growth.[35] Economic liberalism was more often evident when in-

[34]Joseph Morgan, *The Nature of Riches* . . . (Philadelphia, 1732), pp. 4-6.
[35]*Pennsylvania Gazette*, 22 April 1736; [Cadwalder Colden,] *The Interest of the Country in Laying Duties* . . . (New York, 1726), pp. 6-7; Richard L. Bushman found that some of the "rationalists" after the Great Awakening defined the public good as the sum of individual goods. "The rationalists who made the satisfaction of human desires the main end of government seemed to think that self-interest, if enlightened, could be given a free rein and made the very foundation of civil society." *From Puritan to Yankee: Character and the Social Order in Connecticut, 1690-1765* (Cambridge, Mass., 1967), pp. 278-79.

dividual interests were threatened. In Massachusetts in 1754 the proposal of an excise on imported liquors, which would bear most heavily on the rich, stimulated the writing of several pamphlets in opposition to the measure. It was, wrote one opponent, "the most pernicious Attack upon *English Liberty* that ever was attempted," because the "particular Advantages of distinct Communities were forgot upon this Occasion; and Liberty, Heaven-born Liberty, the Source of Virtue, the Nurse of Industry, Wealth and Contentment, the Concern not of a few, but of every Individual, was the sole motive to the Opposition." Another writer was more candid and more specific in his objections; it was, he thought, a "very poor Encouragement for Industry, that those who have taken honest Pains to acquire a Fortune, with hopes of enjoying it themselves, and serving the Publick in the Way they may chuse, (which is I think at least consistent with English Liberty) should be oblig'd to pay such a Part of it, whether agreeable or not to their Inclinations, towards the Support of such as perhaps do not care to use the same Industry to promote themselves." The duties of stewardship had little importance for this man; he intended to part reluctantly with his wealth. The supporters of the excise were aware that their opponents held a powerful position when they based their arguments on the grounds of the sanctity of property and self-interest.

But say others, [to the argument that a community must be prevented "from arising to so great a Pitch of Grandeur and Stock of Riches"] to what Purpose is it, that Mankind *Work* and *Toil*, and *Slave* themselves, unless they may be allow'd to enjoy all the Comforts of Life . . . To which I readily agree, that it would be to no Purpose; for the Enjoyment of Property is the Aim of all Mankind; and the Foundation of their entring Societies; but it must be remember'd at the same Time, that the keeping such Societies together is attended with considerable Expence, which must be borne by the Members of Society.

It was difficult to contradict a forthright assertion of self-interest in a political context because everyone believed that liberty depended on security of property. What is surprising is that such assertions were not made more frequently and that the ill consequences of the pursuit of self-interest, which was so irresistible a motive, were bemoaned so often.[36] The access to property in America and the extent of freedom in its use were extraordinary by comparison with Europe and made doctrines of laissez-faire less relevant to the needs of economic life in the New World than to those in the

---

[36]James Lovell *et al.*, *Freedom, the First of Blessings* (Boston, 1754), p. 1; *A Letter from a Gentleman to His Friend upon the Excise-Bill* . . . (Boston, 1754), p. 2; *The Good of the Community Impartially Considered in a Letter to a Merchant in Boston* . . . (Boston, 1754), p. 12. It may be important to note that the opponents of the excise based their arguments primarily on a defense of political liberty, not economic liberty. It may also be significant that they were unsuccessful. Paul S. Boyer, "Borrowed Rhetoric: The Massachusetts Excise Controversy of 1754," *William and Mary Quarterly*, 3rd ser., 21 (1964): 328-51. For a discussion of the populist element in the excise controversy, see Robert Michael Zemsky, "The Massachusetts Assembly, 1730-55" (Ph.D. diss., Yale University, 1967), pp. 280ff.

Old; such doctrines had an appeal in late eighteenth-century Britain which they lacked in America.[37]

Because the strongest defenses of economic self-interest occurred when the property interests of individuals were contravened, it was no coincidence that the early colonists of Georgia, whose whole economic life was circumscribed, made some of the clearest statements about the priority of individual pursuits over questions of public interest. The opponents of the Georgia plan simply equated their self-interest with the opportunity to get rich in commercial life in whatever way they could. The Georgia settlers, at least in the representations of their complaints, considered morality and economic life to be separate concerns. For example, in his opposition to the administration of Georgia, Thomas Stephens, son of one of the trustees, articulated his self-interest and disregarded the public interest with an explicitness which was rare during the colonial period. Commercial, not moral, questions were his first concern, and for him slavery was an instrumental matter, not a threat to the ethical conditions of work. "In spite of all endeavours to disguise this point," Stephens wrote, "it is as clear as light itself, that negroes are as essentially necessary to the cultivation of Georgia, as axes, hoes, or any other utensil of agriculture." Lord Egmont and Stephens met and argued over the introduction of slavery, an argument during which they showed very different attitudes toward membership and work in society.

I [Egmont] said if Negroes were allow'd, there would be a necessity of granting a liberty of alienation of lands, for otherwise the Negro merchant would have no security for the slave he furnished; but if the Inhabitants are really so poor as he pretended, they would most of them sell their lots if allow'd to alienate and abandon the Country, and the lands would fall into the hands of a few rich men. . . . He [Stephens] reply'd, what if they did, what was it to England whether the lands were in a few or many hands.

Egmont was concerned with the preservation of a community and the protection of its members from economic disorder and exploitation. Stephens and the others who were discontented with conditions in Georgia wanted themselves to have the fullest opportunity possible to become rich, and they did not pale at the prospect that in such conditions some men would necessarily "be undone, whilst many others would thrive." The satirical dedication to Lord Egmont of the *True and Historical Narrative of the Colony of Georgia* showed that his opponents understood his principles well and found their foolishness contemptible.

You considered Riches like a Divine and Philosopher, as the *Irritamenta Malorum*, and knew that they were disposed to inflate weak Minds with Pride; to pamper

[37]Oscar Handlin and Mary Flug Handlin, *Commonwealth: A Study of the Role of Government in the American Economy: Massachusetts, 1774–1861*, rev. ed. (Cambridge, Mass., 1969).

the Body with Luxury, and introduce a long Variety of Evils. Thus have you *Protected us from ourselves*, as Mr. *Waller* says, by keeping all Earthly Comforts from us: You have afforded us the Opportunity of arriving at the Integrity of the *Primitive Times*, by intailing a more than *Primitive Poverty* on us: The Toil, that is necessary to our bare Subsistence, must effectually defend us from the Anxieties of any further Ambition: As we have no Properties, to feed Vain-Glory and beget Contention; so we are not puzzled with any System of Laws, to ascertain and establish them: The valuable Virtue of Humility is secured to us, by your Care to prevent our procuring, or so much as seeing any *Negroes* (the only human Creatures proper to improve our Soil) lest our Simplicity might mistake the poor *Africans* for greater Slaves than ourselves: And that we might fully receive the Spiritual Benefit of those wholesome Austerities; you have wisely denied us the Use of such Spiritous Liquors, as might in the least divert our Minds from the Contemplation of our Happy Circumstances.[38]

That the dedication, with the exception of the sarcasm of the concluding lines on slavery and drink, might credibly have been written by Egmont as an accurate indication of the merits of Georgia showed how far apart the planners and some of the settlers of Georgia were in their views on work and society.

Advocates of less prescriptive and more utilitarian measures of social behavior than the prevailing ones argued that merchants were peculiarly suited to act for the public interest, which was an easy point to make because such advocates usually assumed that interest to be equated with increases in the material welfare of individuals, increases which were thought to be possible only through the medium of commerce. For example, a letter in the *South Carolina Gazette*, in a discussion about an election to fill a vacant seat in the province's House of Commons, urged that a merchant be elected because of his economic wisdom. "Those who are immediately and actually engag'd, and continue to engage in Trade . . . ought to be better Judges of the Concerns of it, and of the Consequences which flow from particular Laws made relating thereto, than those who are unskilled in the Practice, and have their Learning therein only from Books and casual Conversation." A speaker in the Massachusetts General Court who dealt with this same question about what sort of man could best determine the public interest took a more radical position. He denied the notion that society had a proper order and implied his willingness to have the social utility of various interests decided through competition. He assumed, and was not very concerned with the fact, that merchants would only follow their own interests. "The Merchants in general are a Set of wise and

[38][Thomas Stephens], "A Brief Account of the Causes That Have Retarded the Progress of the Colony of Georgia in America" [1743], *Collections of the Georgia Historical Society*, 2 (1892): 93; "Journal of the Earl of Egmont," *The Colonial Records of the State of Georgia*, ed. Allen D. Chandler, 26 vols. (Atlanta, 1904–16), 5: 304; Patrick Tailfer *et al.*, *A True and Historical Narrative of the Colony of Georgia . . . with Comments by the Earl of Egmont* [1741], ed. Clarence L. Ver Steeg (Athens, Ga., 1960), p. 4.

useful Men, yet they are not always the best Judges of Trade, *as it relates to the Good of their Country*—the Business of a Merchant, *as a Merchant,* is to find out that Branch of Trade which will yield him the greatest Profit; and it never enteres into his Mind *when two legal Branches of Trade* lie open befor him, which of them is for the greatest good of the Country." The writer had only a lame suggestion for discovering and preserving the public interest. "A Gentleman no Ways interested in Trade, was better capable of judging of it, *as a Science,* than the Merchant himself, because he sees Things in a different Light, and having no Bias in his Mind, views them with a Degree of Evidence, which the Merchant never thinks of."[39] But if everyone had compelling interests, how could he set them aside?

In a similar discussion about the legitimacy of self-interest, Robert Livingston, head of his family's manor in New York, showed that, if one adopted nonprescriptive and utilitarian standards of behavior, he must resign himself to accept the outcome of competition as the natural social order. This conclusion was unavoidable if one assumed, as Livingston did, that "any country . . . [was] divided into several Parties, contending for the Superiority with the greatest Eagerness, not only by advancing their own Interest, but by oppressing their Antagonists, and as often as an Opportunity offers to do both at a Blow, they are sure to embrace it, without regard to any thing which Reason or Justice might object." The assumption seemed well warranted by the American experience. "In New York [so Livingston thought] we are naturally divided into a Landed & monied Interest"; these interests were the occasion of competition because "it is the Nature of Man never to be satisfied. Tho' this Station be ever so agreable & he is sure to enjoy it during Life, Yet there will be Something wanting if he has it not in his Power to leave it to his Heirs, Nothing less than a Fee [*sic*] will satisfy his Ambition."[40] Livingston shared the views of his fellow colonists about the vice inherent in human nature; what was remarkable about his outlook on social and economic questions was his indifference to the traditional problem of directing that wanton nature into prescriptive patterns of behavior.

One repository of such indifference was folk wisdom, such as could be found in the prudential advice of the almanacs. The almanacs were a hodgepodge of borrowed verse and conventional wisdom, but they frequently displayed a hard-headed attitude toward money and acquisitiveness, combined paradoxically with urgings to accept one's lot and comments on the transitory nature of earthly existence. Self, not public, interest was the main concern in such sayings as "Industry will make thee wealthy" or

[39]*South Carolina Gazette* [postscript], 7 November 1741; *Boston News Letter,* 30 June 1754.

[40]Beverly McAnear, "Mr. Robert R. Livingston's Reasons against a Land Tax," *Journal of Political Economy,* 48 (1940): 82–83. McAnear also cites other expressions of the idea that self-interest was ineradicable.

> Up, and be doing, honest Ned.
> There's little got by lying in bed.

There was also an easygoing attitude toward gain.

> Those are fill'd with sorrow
> Who neither Money have, nor none can borrow.

Likewise, "Today is thine, Tomorrow is in the Womb of Futurity, and thou knowest not what it may bring forth; therefore use the present Time, and lament not a lost Opportunity."[41]

The classic spokesman both for the tradition of folk wisdom and for stoical indifference toward the ethics of prescriptive social order was Benjamin Franklin. His attitude toward the rhetoric of community was irreverent. Other publishers of almanacs prefaced their works with pious statements of their desire to perform a public service. Franklin introduced his first almanac by saying: "The plain Truth of the Matter is, I am excessive poor, and my Wife . . . has threatned more than once to burn all my Books and Rattling-Traps (as she calls my Instruments) if I do not make some profitable Use of them for the good of my Family. The Printer has offer'd me some considerable share of the Profits, and I have thus begun to comply with my Dame's desire." He had a fondness for startling opinions, as he revealed when he pretended that frugality and industry were irrational standards of behavior. "Who is there that can be handsomely Supported in Affluence, Ease and Pleasure by another, that will chuse rather to earn his Bread by the Sweat of his own Brows?" The candor with which he discussed the pursuit of self-interest distinguished him from other men, and his attitudes, like Livingston's, derived from an acceptance of the social consequences of commercial society.[42]

One of the most remarkable colonial statements about the moral isolation of economic life from questions of social justice occurred in a letter from Richard Jackson to Franklin. Jackson took a Lockean view of motivation and natural right; he assumed that "the end of every individual is its own private good" and asserted that "the happiness of individuals is evidently the ultimate end of political society." He recognized that reliance

---

[41][Theophilus Grew], *The Virginia Almanack . . . 1753 . . .* (Williamsburg, 1752), pp. 7, 13; John Jerman, *The American Almanack . . . 1747 . . .* (Philadelphia, 1746), p. 6; Titan Leeds, *Leeds, 1717: The American Almanack . . .* (Philadelphia, 1716), p. 10.

[42]Benjamin Franklin, "Silence Dogood, No. 5" [1722], and "Poor Richard, 1733: An Almanack," *Papers,* 1: 19, 311. A study of Franklin's extensive borrowings from Lord Halifax revealed that the stoical sayings of Halifax, which Franklin obviously admired, simply could not be used in Father Abraham's speech. Robert Newcomb, "Poor Richard's Debt to Lord Halifax," *Publications of the Modern Language Association,* 70 (1955): 535–39. For a discussion of the connection between stoicism and economic liberalism, see William D. Grampp, "The Moral Hero and the Economic Man," *Ethics,* 61 (1951): 136–50. Franklin's prudential wisdom needs to be placed in this broader intellectual context. "In his vision of the Virtuous Orders, Franklin saw a benevolent society, where self-interest would be eclipsed by solicitous mutual concern. . . . he rested his case for productivity upon two of its effects—prevention of social delinquency and the increase of consumer goods." Paul W. Conner, *Poor Richard's Politicks: Benjamin Franklin and His New American Order* (New York, 1965), pp. x, 42.

on devotion to the public good for the organization of economic activity was no longer adequate, "for commerce is at this day almost the only *stimulous* that forces every one to contribute a share of labour for the publick benefit." He also thought that the material advantages of life in commercial society required certain social costs. "We see industry and frugality under the influence of commerce, which I call a commercial spirit, tend to destroy, as well as support, the government it flourishes under. . . . Commerce perfects the arts, but more the mechanical than the liberal, and this for an obvious reason; it softens and enervates the manners. Steady virtue, and unbending integrity, are seldom to be found where a spirit of commerce pervades every thing." The impact of trade on society was uncontrollable; the "perfection of commerce" was not complete until "every thing should have its price." The progress of commerce involved both benefit and detriment. "Things that *boni mores* are forbid to be set to sale, are become its objects, and there are few things indeed *extra commercium.* The legislative power itself has been *in commercio.* . . . Luxury and Corruption . . . seem the inseparable companions of Commerce and the Arts."

Jackson recognized that a new economic and social order, a market society, had appeared. In the clarity of this perception he was unusual; he was also special because he had come to terms with the change and accepted it, perhaps reluctantly, in order to recommend the behavior that could most realistically preserve a decent social order. But the social ideal that illuminated his thought was not very different from that of the more confused colonists. Only education, he thought, could "stem the torrent" of economic change "and by rendering ancient manners familiar, produce a reconciliation between disinterestedness and commerce." It is possible only to conjecture why the "benign view" of life in commercial society was not more common. The case of Jackson suggests that, however reasonable the acceptance of change might have been, men were reluctant to give up their traditional social identities as members of a mutually interdependent community.[43]

The benign attitude toward commercial life was significant in several respects. First, in its scarcity it showed the continuing hold of traditional standards of social legitimacy on men's minds. Second, by its presence it demonstrated that an alternative vocabulary for dealing with moral questions about men's work was available for use had it been desired. Third, by its nature it revealed the way in which these values could, and probably did, change. The most noticeable feature of the benign view was its moral indifference rather than its assertion of a new morality. This indifference derived from the pessimistic streak that had run through the highly moralistic evaluation of man as a social creature. The work ethic, as it has been discussed so far, was primarily concerned with men's innate and dangerous

[43]Richard Jackson to Benjamin Franklin, 17 June 1755, *Papers*, 6: 76, 81-82. See Fred Weinstein and Gerald M. Platt, *The Wish To Be Free: Society, Psyche, and Value Change* (Berkeley, 1969).

selfishness. The benign attitude depended on an acceptance of the fact that moral reform could not eliminate or effectively control this selfishness. Combined with this pessimism about human nature, however, was an optimism about the ability of society to survive the activities of selfish men. In the context of eighteenth-century thought, the significant innovation was a morally neutral view of work, not a glorification of economic individualism. A coherent articulation of such neutrality, however, emerged only after post-Revolutionary disillusion, for the Revolution itself involved high hopes of moral reform.

V

THE NONIMPORTATION MOVEMENT
AND AMERICAN SELF-AWARENESS

IN RESPONSE TO THE CRISIS in imperial relations during the 1760s and
1770s, American colonists resorted at various times to extralegal
agreements to reduce their importation and consumption of foreign
goods and to increase domestic production of manufactured goods.[1] The
initial reasons for these actions were political. In several places, notably
New York and Philadelphia, part of the opposition to the Stamp Act took
the form of boycotts of British goods in an effort to pressure British merchants to appeal to Parliament for the repeal of the act. The agreements
which followed the Townsend Acts had this same purpose, but this time the
regulations were more comprehensive and were directed as much toward
internal reform as toward external reform. The first Continental Congress
also employed a nonimportation agreement, in the form of a Continental
Association, to bring political and economic pressure against the British.
An examination of the nonimportation movement of 1767–1770 is particularly revealing of reform efforts in the Revolution because it was more

---

[1]For the political context of the nonimportation movement, see Arthur M. Schlesinger,
The Colonial Merchants and the American Revolution, 1763–1776 (New York, 1918);
Charles M. Andrews, "The Boston Merchants and the Non-Importation Movement,"
Publications of the Colonial Society of Massachusetts, 19 (1917): 181–249. For an analysis
of the way in which social values applicable to economic life reinforced political demands
for liberty and prepared the colonists for independence, see Edmund S. Morgan, "The Puritan Ethic and the American Revolution," *William and Mary Quarterly,* 3rd ser., 24 (1967):
3–43.

extensive and lasted longer than the one after the Stamp Act and because its purposes did not have to be accommodated to the needs of war as was shortly the case with the Continental Association.

The organization and rhetoric of these programs revealed that they involved more than a need to influence Parliament. The programs were part of an exercise in moral criticism and an effort to reform the prevailing ways of life in American society. Hundreds of letters and essays in the various colonial newspapers contributed to this criticism.[2] The popularity of the programs, which relied for the most part on informal arrangements and community good will for their success, depended on a widespread recognition of long-established vices and a conviction of the possibility of their correction. Selfishness, luxury, avarice, and idleness all needed to be reduced. The imperatives of the political situation, which called for immediate and coordinated action, required that reform of these vices consist of something more than the usual public voicing of discontent.

It was the concreteness of the patriot program—with its subscription lists for adherents to the nonimportation resolutions, its conspicuous nonconsumption in the form of the fashionable homespun, and its public proscription of wrongdoers—which gained it public favor. For decades Americans had told themselves that work should be a contribution to the needs of the community, but the ways in which most men could actually work in commercial life seemed to be individualistic and selfish. The nonimportation movement allowed people to identify their work and their self-denial with the public good and thus to legitimize themselves in their ordinary social capacities. The movement encouraged personal identification with the community and thereby presented opportunities for self-fulfillment through self-denial, for autonomy through participation—just that harmonious relationship between the rational self and society which was sought so often in the colonial period. This awareness that the nonimportation and domestic manufactures movement presented a unique opportunity for moral reform on a large scale gave the movement its significance in the history of early American attitudes toward work. The movement fostered self-awareness both socially and personally; it obliged Americans to consider the course of their social development, and it required them to assess their individual contributions to that development.

For all the emotional intensity of demands for changes in the economic relationship of the self to society, however, the nonimportation movement chiefly involved the application of a gloss of political virtue to existing social and economic arrangements. As was the case throughout the colonial period, reform was conceived primarily as moral alteration within the existing social and economic framework. This posture corresponded to the

[2]On the diffusion of political rhetoric, see Arthur M. Schlesinger, *Prelude to Independence: The Newspaper War on Britian, 1764-1776* (New York, 1958); Carl F. Kaestle, "The Public Reaction to John Dickinson's *Farmer's Letters*," *Proceedings of the American Antiquarian Society*, 78 (1969): 323-59.

preoccupying fears and doubts about the self and to the conviction that its fulfillment required harmony with the society at large. Yet the motivation for reform did not depend just on the colonists' assessment of their individual natures; they were also concerned about the peculiar structure of activity which had evolved. Rather than seek structural changes in society, revolutionary expectations focused on changes in scale in the direction of greater economic simplicity. The hopes for structural changes took a political direction.

THE NEED FOR REFORM

The Townsend Duties made the colonists more aware than usual of their own shortcomings and of those of their society. They recognized that their political and commercial problems were not just externally imposed; rather, they had in part brought them on themselves. Writers often pointed out that the unconstitutional acts could in the long run benefit the colonies if the inhabitants drew the required lessons from the situation. Perhaps the "unconstitutional and oppressive Revenue Acts" could "excite a Spirit of Frugality and good Oeconomy, and thereby decline the Use of luxurious Importations." One newspaper contributor, supposedly from England, expressed the hope that the dispute would eventually "turn out to the Advantage of the Colonies," but summed up the troubles which the crisis had brought to light. "Your Traders before were too forward to run deep in Debt with our Merchants, and thereby involved themselves in great Difficulties. They were too fond of the Fashions and Follies of England, and too negligent of the natural Advantages of their own Country: Trading so much upon Credit, and aping the Extravagancies and Luxuries of the rich and opulent, have already done the Colonies irreparable Damage, sunk their Character, and sapped their Virtue." This pattern of consumption mocked the supposition that autonomy followed from wealth. The imperial constitutional crisis taught the colonists that group and individual fates in America were being determined elsewhere, often with the willing cooperation of the victims. It was generally recognized that the various colonies were in a common state of "Misery and Ruin, as a Consequence of the unnecessary Imports of European Goods." For example, the committee of merchants in New York declared "that the Colony in general is in a State of Poverty and Distress, chiefly arising from the Decline of Commerce, and a vast Consumption of British Manufactures and foreign Commodities, although incompatible with our present calamitous Circumstances."[3]

In its most immediate form the problem was economic. The colonies were in a chronic condition of debt in their trade relations with Britain. Moreover, local depressions occurred in several of the colonies in the after-

[3]*Pennsylvania Gazette* (Philadelphia), 17 May 1770, 23 February 1769, and 10 December 1767; *The Committee Appointed by the Inhabitants . . . on Wednesday the 29th of December Last . . .* (New York, 1768).

math of the Seven Years' War. (Or so it was perceived; actual trade conditions varied considerably from colony to colony and between town and country.) The preacher of an election sermon in Connecticut in 1768 listed the elements (which could have been reiterated in other colonies) of that province's distressed state as "our amazing debts; the want of a sufficient medium of trade; the uncommon multiplication of lawsuits, and singular protraction of their issues, in the courts of justice; and the astonishing consumption of spiritous liquors." The basic cause of "these embarrassed circumstances" was the extensive "Luxury and extravagance in the use of British and foreign manufactures and superfluities." The essential measures to correct these economic distresses were "oeconomy, industry, and application to American Manufactures."[4]

The recommendation of industry and frugality revealed that the economic issues of the constitutional crisis were inseparable from moral considerations of work and its rewards. The vice of "luxury" was rich in connotations which wove together matters of personal morality, public virtue, political history, and mercantilist economics. Luxury was associated with illness and ruin. Dr. Tissot, a French physician whose handbook on health was popular in England and America, wrote that luxury was one of the chief causes of the depopulation of states; "the irregular manner of life which it introduces, depresses health; it ruins the constitution." Americans constantly warned one another that they were coming under the influence of this vice. The republican element in English oppositional political thought had taught them that luxury was an insidious vice. "It puts on the appearance of conveniency, and entangles the unwary by the show of something useful, until the retreat from its snares is cut off, by fears of supposed inability." In many of the public agreements for nonimportation there were confessions to indulgence in the vice of luxury. Indeed, a theme of self-mortification runs through the rhetoric of the nonimportation movement. The Annapolis agreement stated that the subscribers had "too much indulged" themselves in the consumption of "foreign Luxuries and Superfluities . . . to the great detriment of [their] private Fortunes." This statement was typical of agreements in other colonies in its assertion that the need to eliminate luxury had existed prior to the imposition of the Townsend Duties and that the economic and constitutional troubles these duties produced made "a Habit of Temperance, Frugality, Oeconomy, and Industry . . . more particularly necessary at this time."[5]

There was a direct connection between the need for public virtue and the need for industry and frugality; together they were the remedies to

---

[4]Richard Salter, *A Sermon Preached before the General Assembly* . . . (New London, 1768), pp. 34–35; *Newport Mercury*, 7 December 1767; Andrews, "Boston Merchants," pp. 181–82.

[5]Simon André Tissot, *Advice to the People in General with Regard to their Health . . .* , trans. J. Kirkpatrick (London, 1765), pp. 4–5; "Atticus," *Pennsylvania Chronicle*, 14 December 1767; *Maryland Gazette* (Annapolis), 29 June 1769.

luxury. A writer in Boston reminded his readers of their ancestors' virtue, which he associated with their willingness "to eat [their] bread, with sweat of brow and sorrow of heart." This writer praised the "disinterested conduct" of the merchants in their reduction of imports, but stressed that the success of nonimportation depended on "the virtue of the people." Nonimportation gave the notion of the common good a welcomed concreteness. Behavior which, if not innocent, had at least been difficult to condemn outright was now more susceptible to criticism. It became apparent that the colonists, through a laudable fondness for their mother country, had "foolishly and unguardedly adopted her customs, mode, and manner of living, even to an extreme, so as to exceed [their] abilities." In order to re-establish public virtue and thereby protect their constitutional rights and foster prosperity, the colonists needed to moderate their desires and cease "aspiring after things unnecessary or inconvenient for them." If they could do so, Great Britain's "unkindness" would lead them "to discover, in [their] *industry* and *frugality*, surprising remedies."[6]

Ministerial tyranny served the beneficial function of bringing the colonists to their senses before they were completely dulled by luxury. Ironically, the self-indulgence of the colonists in the first place had led the ministers to believe that America had sufficient wealth to make it a good source of extra revenue. The Americans had been especially ostentatious with their new wealth after the last war, and in England "*Tax America* became the popular Cry." During the nonimportation movement the colonists agreed that such prodigality was unwise, not only because it aroused the envy of the British, but also because luxury would prevent the growth of "a young people." The various nonimportation agreements reflected this awareness of the dangers of the existing luxury by specifying those "super fluities" which people were to refrain from importing in lists that contained such items as carriages, ready-made clothes, household furniture, gloves, gold and silver thread, exotic cloth, jewelry, and silver.[7] Other items in such lists were necessities which the colonists wanted to produce domestically in order to relieve their commercial dependence on England.

In addition to the condemnation of excessive consumption, there was also criticism of the luxury involved in institutions like slavery and the theater, two of the most highly visible forms of self-indulgence. Some writers cited slavery as an evil because of its injustice, and pointed out the colonists' hypocrisy in opposing their enslavement by the British while they enslaved others. "If you say interest and power do not make an action

[6]"Pro Aris et Focis," *Boston Gazette*, 11 September 1769; "A Lover of His Country," *Pennsylvania Gazette*, 14 January 1768; *South Carolina Gazette and Country Journal* (Charleston), 3 April 1770; John Dickinson, *Letters from a Farmer in Pennsylvania to the Inhabitants of the British Colonies* (Philadelphia, 1768), p. 67.

[7]*The Power and Grandeur of Great Britain, Founded on the Liberty of the Colonies . . .* (Philadelphia, 1768), p. 7; "Pro Rege & Grege," *Boston Gazette*, 26 October 1767; *At a meeting of the Freeholders and Other Inhabitants . . . the 28th of October . . .* (Boston, 1767).

lawful and right (as they really do not) you condemn yourselves." But the most common objection to slavery dealt with its function as a stimulus of idleness and luxury. The slaveowner became too proud to labor himself, and "this indulgence . . . lays the most certain foundation for indolence while it opens a door to luxury and extravagance."[8] The theater had a similar effect because it challenged people to demonstrate "their great opulence and leisure" and to show their "taste and judgment." The political imperatives of the nonimportation movement provided a clear standard for the condemnation—in the name of *"Industry, Virtue,* and *Moderation"*— of such seemingly disparate practices as the theater and slavery, which had been the source of uneasiness during the colonial period.[9]

The constitutional dispute caused by the Townsend Duties reminded the colonists that widespread selfishness, of which luxury was the chief symptom, usually resulted in a loss of liberty. The Americans' reading of British political writings had taught them that luxury inevitably led to slavery unless it was checked, because it substituted selfishness for public virtue as a guide for public behavior. True prosperity was public, and it depended on *"virtue* and *commerce* . . . under the softening influence of *liberty."* Slavery, which was the negation of Liberty, led to the ruin of trade and the corruption of morals, and it was believed to be "proved, beyond controversy, that a state of slavery is necessarily accompanied with idleness, profligacy, and irreligion." According to this view, the immorality of luxury was not solely an individual concern but rather a matter whose public nature directly affected economic and political life. During the period of the nonimportation movement, the colonists often reminded each other of the serious consequences of their lack of public virtue. To this purpose they quoted works like *Cato's Letters,* which warned that "Men, who, from the Bait of present Wealth and Place, helped to overthrow the Constitution . . . were not only the Parricides of their Country, but the Murderers of their own Children and Families." The point of such warnings was that "the general Security is the only certain Security of Particulars." In the *Farmer's Letters* John Dickinson warned that it was common for states to lose their liberty through "the decay of virtue," and that a people was well on the way to such decay "when *individuals* consider *their* interests as distinct from *those of the public."* Virtue's most sinister and aggressive enemies were few in number in comparison with the people at large, whose vice was usually a simple matter of indifference to public responsi-

---

[8]*Newport Mercury,* 11 January 1768. In contrast, a South Carolinian made the same direct comparison between Great Britain's power over the colonies and the colonists' command of their slaves, but saw a wrong only in the political example; *South Carolina Gazette,* (Charleston), 22 June 1769. Cf. *Extract from an Address in the Virginia Gazette of March 1767 by a Respectable Member of the Community* [Philadelphia, 1770?]; *New York Gazette,* 14 March 1768.

[9]"Pennsylvaniensis," *Pennsylvania Chronicle* (Philadelphia), 9 November 1767; "Philaretes," *New York Mercury,* 7 December 1767.

bilities, as when they sought "to increase their own *wealth, power,* and *credit,* without the least regard for the society, under the protection of which they live."[10] During the constitutional crisis, however, such banal selfishness had taken on a new and dangerous political dimension.

In their response to the Townsend Duties, the colonists generally considered frugality to be a moderation of established patters of behavior. But during the period from 1767 to 1770 there were also many appeals which called for basic reforms in the commercial life of the colonies. These appeals recognized the need for frugality, but they also stressed the need for industry if frugality were to be practical. The efforts to establish domestic manufactures involved a recognition of the fact that "this country never call'd louder for industry than at present." Not only were manufactures necessary in order to reduce the Americans' dependence on England, but they were also required by the state of social development which the colonies had reached. "Colonies settled in new countries may for a time do very well, without manufactures, But old colonies, in time, must, and will, as necessarily, and as naturally swarm, as the original hive."[11]

Some appeals to industry argued that self-sufficiency was needed because it would eliminate some of the undesirable social and moral effects of trade. Unlike Britain, which was dependent on trade because it was an island, America was rich in land and natural wealth. In American towns there were too many "shopkeepers and retailers," who contributed nothing to the society's wealth and whose economic life was precarious. If they were to take up agriculture, they would live a simpler but more useful life. Although America already had "too much trade," it still had a chance to learn from the experience of England, which had "overtraded herself" and thereby permitted "too many inlets for luxury and debauchery." If America did not act to reform its commercial life, it might soon resemble England in its corruption. A consideration of "the commercial conduct" of New York led one writer to reconsider whether or not trade was an unqualified good for a society. He agreed with Montesquieu that it "is a bad kind of Riches which depends on Accident, (meaning Trade), and not on the Industry of a Nation." He argued that the simultaneous experience of trade depression and ministerial tyranny ought to lead people to reconsider what was "generally laid down as a self-evident Proposition, that Trade is the Road to and Fountain of Riches." Everyone who could, "turns Merchant," but whether "they serve themselves and their Country" in their "Commercial Pursuits," or "whether it has not a direct contrary Effect on both," was an important question about American economic life. This writer emphasized the difference between internal and external com-

[10]"A.L.," *Pennsylvania Chronicle,* 30 May 1768; *Boston Gazette,* 23 October 1769; Dickinson, *Letters,* p. 65.

[11]"Philander," *New York Gazette,* 10 April 1769; "North American, No. II," *Boston Gazette,* 9 January 1769.

mercial development and reminded his readers that large importations were not "a Mark of their great Riches; when it is Exports alone that makes a Country rich."[12]

The rhetoric of the nonimportation movement presented the situation as an alternative between the ruin and the salvation of American society. The first step toward salvation was an agreement not to import goods from Britain; such an agreement was "the only probable means of averting so horrid a train of evils as are staring us in the face." This agreement would have the important economic benefits of "inclining us to be more frugal, affording our Merchants Time to collect their Debts, and enabling them to discharge those they owe to the Mother Country." Similarly, the program of domestic manufactures promised to contribute to the revival of American economic life.

The greater part of the mechanicks, day-labourers and mariners, will be employed as usual; add to this, manufactures will naturally and necessarily increase among our selves, both sexes and all sizes of the poor will find a ready and sufficient employment, our supplies for home consumption will increase beyond the demand for them, new articles for export will thence arise, a more extensive trade will result, and soon very soon, we may rival our present masters in many beneficial articles of commerce; which they are so thoroughly apprehensive of, that to prevent the growing malady, they make use of every artifice.

This disappointing contrast between America's economic promise and its accomplishments encouraged the colonists to denounce their backwardness in social attainments. It was degrading that "Britons . . . who carried with them *Arts* and *Sciences*" and who lived in a land which was "capable of every Production that any Part of the World is known to afford" "should have Recourse to Europe."[13]

The note of self-condemnation that ran through most of the appeals for industry and frugality was balanced by a conviction that reform was possible. The constitutional crisis provided an opportunity for a simultaneous indulgence in self-criticism and assertion of self-righteousness. The newspapers were filled with essays stating that America had reached a point of crisis in its economic, political, and moral life. The people were pursuing a path of corruption, but if they reformed their behavior they could be redeemed. The test of an individual's patriotism became a matter of whether or not he had "vanquished luxury and subdued the worldly pride of his heart."[14] Drawing on these traditional terms of social legitimization—self-denial and public virtue—the moral force of the movement derived from a

[12]"A Citizen," *Pennsylvania Chronicle*, 16 November 1767; *Newport Mercury*, 21 December 1767; "A Friend to This Colony," *Providence Gazette*, 14 November 1767; *The Commercial Conduct of the Province of New York* . . . (New York, 1767), pp. 6, 16.

[13]*South Carolina Gazette*, 22 June 1769; *Pennsylvania Gazette*, 31 March 1768; *Boston Gazette*, 26 October 1767; *Commercial Conduct*, p. 9; Rind's *Virginia Gazette* (Williamsburg), 14 June 1770.

[14]"Pro Rege & Grege," *Boston Gazette*, 3 October 1768.

widespread desire to reaffirm the importance of men's work to the community.

THE COUNTERIMAGE OF ENGLAND'S VICE

The colonists were especially sensitive to the possibility of corruption in their society because England presented them with an example of the disastrous consequences of extremes of luxury and vice. The need to defend their liberties against ministerial tyranny imposed certain limits on the Americans' self-denunciation. No matter how corrupt America was, conditions in England were even worse, and therefore the Americans had an opportunity to reform their ways and restore their virtue before they reached rock-bottom.

The colonists' ambivalence about the existence of vice in their society was especially evident when they were subjected to English criticism of their lack of virtue. Thus the Americans felt a strong need to defend themselves in 1767 when a preacher at the annual meeting of the Society for the Propagation of the Gospel accused the colonists of living "without any divine worship, in dissolute wickedness, and the most brutal profligacy of manners." The preacher argued that it was impossible for the colonists to fulfill both of their professed goals, the expansion of commerce and the propagation of Christian faith; men "who with desperate hardiness invade unknown difficulties and dangers in quest of gain, could not be supposed to be much concerned about spiritual interests. Religion is but an impediment in the way of avarice." The only moral benefit of the colonization of America, the preacher sarcastically suggested, was the opportunity it presented for the "double occasion of propagating christianity among the native heathen of those regions, and among themselves also, who soon become heathens."[15]

Because Americans had already made many of these criticisms of themselves, it was difficult for them to make an outright refutation. Instead, they chose to interpret the sermon as an attack on the motives and virtue of the founders of the colonies; to the colonists this was plainly an outrageous falsehood, because their forefathers, archetypes of virtuous living, had provided a standard against which to measure the shortcomings of later generations. The responses to the S.P.G. sermon conceded that the Americans had "too far departed from the simplicity, piety, and strict virtue of their fathers." But, whatever moral corruption there was in America, "true Christianity" was *more generally* better practiced" there than in England, where the people were inferior "in purity of morals" to the Americans.[16]

---

[15]John Ewer, *A Sermon Preached before the Incorporated Society* . . . (New York, 1768), pp. 5–6.

[16]Charles Chauncey, *A Letter to a Friend* . . . [about a Sermon by] *John, Lord Bishop of Landaff* . . . (Boston, 1767), pp. 16, 37; William Livingston, *A Letter to the Right Reverend* . . . *John, Lord Bishop of Landaff* . . . (New York, 1768), pp. 4, 9, 11.

The way in which the Americans perceived the vices of England both demonstrated the dangerous outcome of their present course of behavior and provided them with a sense of moral superiority over the English. American newspapers readily reprinted English self-accusations of corruption. An article from the *British Chronicle* described the English as "a people stupified by luxury and the opium *vice*" who had thereby lost their public virtue. Because of this loss of virtue, the English were beginning to view the Americans in the same way that the French had viewed the Corsicans: "Every Englishman considers himself as King of America, and peculiarly interested in our Subjection; it gratifies his Pride, and he is at the same Time free from Apprehensions of suffering himself." Such reports led George Mason to the view, widely reprinted in his "Atticus" articles, that "Luxury, Venality, and Corruption, are arrived at that enormous Height, that *Great-Britain*, like ancient *Rome*, seems ready to sink under her own Weight."[17]

It appeared to the Americans that they were supporting the extravagance and corruption of England. Because the leaders of England were so idle and self-indulgent, they were obliged to live off the industry of the colonists. The Americans associated the Townsend Duties with the "iniquitous Extravagance" of ministers who sought superfluous offices. "The present involved State of the British Nation, the Rapacity and Profuseness of many of her great Men, the prodigious Numbers of their Dependents, who want to be gratified with some Office which may enable them to live lazily upon the Labour of others, must convince us, that we shall be taxed as long as we have a Penny to pay." In the *Farmer's Letters* Dickinson warned that, if a precedent for the taxation of the colonists were established, America would find itself in the same condition as Ireland, the victim of " 'pensionary vultures.' " During the late 1760s any increase in English colonial officialdom was greeted by the Americans with suspicion and contempt. An opponent of the projected American episcopate questioned whether it was an appropriate time "to think of episcopal palaces, of pontifical revenues, of spiritual courts, and all the pomp, grandeur, luxury and regalia of an American Lambeth." Such criticism of the excesses of English grandeur occasionally implied that they were symptoms of imperial decline and that England's economic control over the American colonies was the only means whereby she could maintain commercial dominance over the other countries in Europe.[18]

The American's favorable self-image of autonomy derived in part from this notion that England depended on her colonies for her prosperity. John Dickinson quoted the mercantilist writings of Davenant, Child,

[17]*New York Journal*, 15 September 1768; *Pennsylvania Gazette*, 6 September 1770; "Atticus," *Maryland Gazette*, 4 May 1769.

[18]Thomas Bradbury, *The Ass: Or, the Serpent* . . . (Boston, 1768), p. 12n; Dickinson *Letters*, pp. 51–52; "American Whig #1," *New York Gazette*, 14 March 1768; "Atticus," *Maryland Gazette*, 11 May 1769.

Postlethwayte, and Tucker to show that the "wealth, power and glory" of England were based on the colonies. In a letter to the provincial agent in England, the Massachusetts House of Representatives made the same point; the colonies were "the sources of opulence and strength to Britain." Advocates of the nonimportation movement often proposed that the economic ties between England and the colonies, which had long been taken for granted, were due for re-evaluation. Great Britain had acquired her riches "by her *exclusive* trade with her Colonies, which [was] an *amazing incidental* tax that [the colonists] have always hitherto chearfully borne, as being *merely and naturally* such." The Americans had previously been willing to depend on England for manufactured products, but the Townsend Duties demonstrated that their political liberties were compromised by their economic dependence on England. "From the Manner in which she tied up our manufacturing Hands, [England] not only received the entire Produce of the Lands and Labour of these Countries, but has besides involved the People here in a heavy Debt, which Agriculture, without Arts, and a Trade so confined, will probably never pay." The colonists began to perceive a pattern of economic exploitation in their imperial relations with England; their trade, manufactures, and currency could be manipulated to their disadvantage. A contributor to the *South Carolina Gazette* warned that the influence of England in the economic life of the colonies was so great that it could and probably would act to prevent the Americans from becoming too prosperous or self-sufficient. An article reprinted from the *London Chronicle* pointed out that the English were playing "a losing game." "The Americans are forced into measures which must in the end turn to their advantage. These taxes will put an end to their dissipation and luxury. Trade being greatly lessened among them, many must retire into the country, and lay out in improvements and population, the money formerly employed in trade, and thus make a more lasting, perhaps a greater, acquisition of fortune." In order to retain their liberties the Americans needed to eliminate the "Necessity of using the Manufactures of Britain."[19]

As they articulated their complaints about the economic consequences of their commercial dependence on England, Americans became aware that such a relationship inherently involved them in the follies and luxury of England. The colonists considered their imports from England to be superfluities, and they assumed that England would of necessity remain dependent on the colonies for raw materials. England had been "strength-

[19]Dickinson, *Letters*, pp. 25-26; *Extract of a Letter from the House of Representatives of Massachusetts to Their Agent Dennys de Berdt . . .* (London, 1770), p. 16; *South Carolina Gazette*, 1 June 1769; "To the Public," *Maryland Gazette*, 20 April 1769; *From the Merchants and Traders of Philadelphia . . . to the Merchants and Manufacturers of Great Britain* (Philadelphia, 1770); "A Citizen," *South Carolina Gazette*, 18 April 1768; "A Briton," *Pennsylvania Gazette*, 9 February 1769; "Monitor #1," *The American Gazette: Being a Collection of All the Authentic Addresses, Memorials, Petitions, and Other Papers . . .*, 6 vols. in 1 (London, 1768-1770), 4: 191.

ened by the luxury of the colonies," but as the colonists became more "prudent, frugal and industrious" they would be able "to subsist without the manufactures of Great-Britain." During the imperial crisis the colonists could conveniently claim that "play-houses, cock-fighting, fox-hunting, horse-racing, and every other expensive diversion" were "all of British extract." By associating their rights with the conditions under which the colonies had been settled, and by seeing themselves as the inheritors of these rights, the colonists were able to compare themselves favorably with the rigorous virtue they had habitually ascribed to their forefathers. "The present Inhabitants, tho' more happily circumstanced than their Ancestors, and though some among them, especially in the trading Towns, may live in Affluence, yet, from the Operation of the same causes . . . are now able with all their Labour, to obtain but a comfortable, and many of them but a slender, Support for themselves and Families." Thomas Pownall, in a speech at the House of Commons which was reprinted several times in the colonies, described the origin and nature of the Americans' affectation of English life and pointed out that these habits could change radically in the current crisis. "The only sacrifice they have to make is that of a few follies and a few luxuries.—It is not necessity that is the ground of their commerce with you; it is merely the affectation of our modes and customs— the love for home, as they call England, that makes them like everything that comes from thence; but passion may be conquered by passion, and they will abominate as sincerely as they now love you; and if they do, they have within themselves every thing which is necessary to the food, raiment, or the dwelling of mankind, and have no need of your commerce."[20] The process of defending their liberties forced just such a revaluation of economic and moral status upon the colonists.

THE POSSIBILITY OF AMERICA'S SALVATION

The appeals for industry and frugality during the imperial crisis held out the alternative of social redemption or social ruin. The preacher of a fast-day sermon in 1769 pointed out that the freedom and happiness of individuals depended on public virtue. "A people can never be free and happy but in proportion as they are virtuous—vice is slavery, misery and certain ruin." The colonists had arrived at a juncture where they would have to choose between liberty and slavery because, if they persisted in their established ways for much longer, they would succumb to vice and no longer have such a choice. An essay in the *Virginia Gazette* explained what was involved in such a change. Liberty was a quality that influenced every aspect of a man's life, especially his work. "In times of liberty, a

[20]*Observations on Several Acts of Parliament* . . . (Boston, 1769), p. 24; *New York Gazette*, 20 August 1767; "The Petition of the House of Commons . . . of the Major Part of His Majesty's Council of the Province of Massachusetts-Bay," *Letters to the Right Honourable the Earl of Hillsborough* . . . (London, 1769), pp. 139–40; Thomas Pownall, *The Speech of Th–m–s P–wn–ll . . . in the H—se of C–m—ns, in Favor of America* (Boston, 1769), p. 10.

man depends upon himself, his eloquence, integrity, spirit, ingenuity, and every virtue have incentives to kindle and enflame them, a proper field to display themselves, and to operate to his own emolument and his country's glory."[21]

America was fortunate that, though "reduced to the brink of ruin by prodigality and dissipation, [and] by selfishness and ambition," it still retained a glimpse of the benefits of liberty and therefore could be "rescued from the destruction that visibly impended over it." What would appear to the modern reader as a political problem was often discussed at the time in the terminology of Christian salvation and the morality of self-denial. A broadside addressed to "the Tradesmen, Farmers, and other Inhabitants" of Philadelphia alerted its readers that "the Ghosts of our Ancestors" were watching them on "this the only Day of your Salvation." A simple part of the boycott, the wearing of domestically manufactured cloth, became "a Sacrifice of . . . Pride and Vanity." A public apology for the transgression of a nonimportation agreement was considered to be an *"Atonement,"* which would *"restore* [the violators] to the *Public's Favour* and *Confidence."* Selflessness became the most reliable indication of virtue, and the various programs to reduce importations and to increase manufactures provided a specific vehicle for such self-denial. After decades of ambivalence and uneasiness about the moral implications of the prosperity that their work produced, the colonists had an unfamiliar sense of righteousness about the conduct of their livelihoods. "An Action performed from no View of Advantage, but of that Advantage which [one's] Country might reap from it, cannot possibly involve [one] in Guilt."[22]

After the organization of the nonimportation programs, the colonists moved from one extreme to the other in their moral self-assessment. From being victims of luxury, idleness, and vice, they changed into the foremost defenders of virtue, taking up the torch of republican virtue which had been struck from the hands of the Corsicans. "The Eyes of All *Europe,*— nay of the whole World are fixed upon us. Heaven itself cannot be disinterested in the Event of the present Contest." Like Pym and Hampden, the Americans "stood forth in defense of their invaluable rights," and so the colonists seemed "truly to be the legitimate descendants of these glorious ancestors." Because they exposed their fortunes and lives "for the salvation of their country," the "patriotic Non-Importers" were compared favorably with "the heroes and demy gods of antiquity" and the barons of Runnymede. Perhaps the strongest mark of the colonists' self-congratulation was their readiness to compare the resistance involved in the nonim-

[21]Amos Adams, *A Concise, Historical View of the Perils, Hardships, Difficulties, and Discouragements Which Have Attended the Planting and Progressive Improvements of New England . . .* (Boston, 1769), p. 65; "Monitor II," Rind's *Virginia Gazette,* 3 March 1768.

[22]Salter, *A Sermon,* p. 12; *To the Tradesmen, Farmers, and Other Inhabitants of the City and County of Philadelphia . . . September 24, 1770* (Philadelphia, 1770); *Maryland Gazette,* 18 May 1769; *South Carolina Gazette and Country Journal,* 5 June 1770; "Coriolanus," *New York Mercury,* 27 August 1770.

portation movement with the virtuous self-denial of their ancestors. The preacher of the artillery sermon of 1770 spoke of "the plainness and simplicity of our ancestors with respect to their manner of living," and he pointed out that, even if a simpler life were not a political necessity, "the banishment of this vice [luxury] from among us, would be attended with great advantages to us as citizens." One writer managed to find both ancestral and republican similarities for the colonists' virtue. "The *Americans*, whose forefathers left their native land to avoid oppression, and, with much labour, cultivated a wilderness, and in it established *English* Liberty in its native purity, will not tamely submit to be slaves—No—Thousands would, with the celebrated *Brutus*, rather die free, than live a life of slavery."[23]

In order to enforce the restoration of American virtue, the organization of the nonimportation movement relied on visible and ritualized community participation. The basic action needed for the implementation of the movement was the signing of an agreement by a community's inhabitants which committed them to the boycotting of various imported articles. The agreements usually contained an explicit moral obligation to foster industry and frugality and to discourage luxury. They were often discussed as means for the transcendence of ordinary social distinctions in the community in order to give corporate interests primary importance. People could contrast their cooperation with the actions of the violators of the resolutions, who were "Parties audaciously *counteracting* the *united Sentiments* of the *whole Body* of the People." Care was taken to show that the merchants were cooperating in the public interest. Alexander McDougall, a leader of the Sons of Liberty in New York, wrote from jail that the merchants of the town had "chearfully sacrificed their private Interest to the public Good." The subscribers to the nonimportation agreement in New York claimed that they sought "to meet, and associate with People of all reputable Ranks, Conditions, and Denominations" in order to defend their rights.[24] In Boston a meeting called to discuss the enforcement of the agreement was thought to be the largest public gathering ever held there.

Because it depended on community participation and justified itself by invoking the public interest, the nonimportation movement gave people a strong sense of group awareness and public legitimacy. People who abided by the agreements applied the extralegal punishments of boycott and ostracism to persons guilty of violations against the agreed terms of

[23]*To the Inhabitants . . . of Philadelphia . . . July 14, 1770* (Philadelphia, 1770); *Pennsylvania Chronicle*, 4 June 1770, 12 September 1768, and 23 November 1767; *Proposals for Erecting and Encouraging a New Manufactory* (New York, 1770); Samuel Stillman, *A Sermon Preached to the Ancient and Honourable Artillery Company . . .* (Boston, 1770), pp. 25–26; "Filius Americani," *Pennsylvania Gazette*, 1 February 1770; "Cincinnatus," *Boston Gazette*, 11 July 1768.

[24]*South Carolina Gazette and Country Journal*, 5 June 1770; Alexander McDougall, "To the Freeholders . . . ," *New York Gazette*, 12 February 1770; *New York, February 27th, 1770: Forasmuch as It Is Manifest . . .* (New York, 1770).

nonimportation. Virtuous men were obligated to inform others of their vice. "If there should be found among us *any*, who shall *break through* these Resolutions, while your Danger is so threatening; it becomes *every honest Man*, to *knock* at your Breast, and warn you, like the Light on the Edystone, of the Rocks on which you are likely to split." The "public" was no longer simply the inhabitants at large, but rather "every person who values Liberty." By publicizing the names of violators of the agreements and by demanding confessions of them, the patriots were able to acquire a flattering conception of their own virtue; the stronger the denunciations of the violators and the more contrite the confession, the greater the self-esteem and group identity of the person who conformed to the agreement. A shopkeeper in New York who refused to abide by the agreement was labeled "an Enemy to his Country, a Pest to Society, and a vile Disturber of the Peace, Police, and good Order of this City." Alexander Robertson, who was accused of smuggling proscribed goods into New York, was denounced in terms which almost denied him recognition as a member of society. "It is not to be doubted, but that all Ranks and Degrees amongst us both of Men and Women, will unite in all legal Means to shew their just Abhorrence and Detestation of such scandalous Practices, that they will avoid any Connections and all Intercourse with him, treat him on all Occasions with the Contempt he deserves, regard him in the odious Light of an Enemy to his Country." Robertson apologized for his misdeed and promised that he would never again "attempt an Act contrary to the true Interest and Resolutions of a People zealous in the Cause of *Virtue* and *Liberty*."[25]

The virtuous alternative to the violator of the agreements was found in dozens of newspaper accounts about such patriots as college graduates who appeared at commencement dressed in American homespun, or about virtuous young ladies who assembled before dawn to make "exactly 92 skeins of choice linnen yarn." (An element in the colonists magico-political numerology, 92 signified the number of representatives in the Massachusetts Assembly who refused to obey the directive of Lord Hillsborough, secretary of state for American affairs, that they rescind their Circular Letter.) The ritualized performance of these activities encouraged people to interpret them as signs of a rising virtue in America. Women played a key role in these expressions of industry and frugality because they were thought to have a determining influence on the fashions and therefore the luxury in American society. Women's supposed irrationality inclined them to admire "shadowy Ornaments" rather than those "Qualifications

[25]"Libertus et Natale Solum," *South Carolina Gazette*, 14 September 1769; *To the Free-holders, Merchants, and Tradesmen and Farmers of the City and County of Philad. . . .* (Philadelphia, 1770); *New York, July 20th, 1769: Advertisement of Greater Importance to the Public . . .* (New York, 1769); *Advertisement of Great Importance to the Public . . .* (New York, 1769); Alexander Robertson, *New York, June 23, 1769: To the Publick . . .* (New York, 1769).

which are substantial and really useful." If American women were to become simpler in their dress and entertainment, they would aid public virtue both by their frugality and by their example. "It will place them in the most conspicuous point of view; will make them shine with a superiour and more durable lustre, and will yield a higher and more genuine pleasure than the short liv'd pageantry of extravagance, and idle show."[26]

Many discussions of the nonimportation movement urged more fundamental reforms than the simple reduction of consumption, which relied on the motto Save Your Money, and You Save Your Country. It was argued that the preservation of virtue and the stage of social and political development at which the colonies had arrived demanded a basic reorganization of the provincial economies so that they could be self-sufficient. These arguments resembled earlier "provincial mercantilism," but, instead of emphasizing the need for a better balance of payments for the colonies, they sought to protect themselves from corruption by means of a simpler way of life. A letter which appeared in the *New York Gazette* (one supposedly written by a Virginian), said that the change from an economy based on staple exports to a balanced economy might result in a reduced income, but that it would "render us happy, and be a sure means of preserving our Liberty, which to us is of much higher Value than Riches." The author thanked the "British Ministry as the best Friends to the Colonies," because their tyranny "has opened our Eyes; we now see that we can live within our selves; that our present Wants may be supplied, by importing only a few Articles from Great Britain; and that in a very short Time, we can live without them."[27]

Some writers, notably John Dickinson, argued that it was impossible for "a country of planters, farmers, and fishermen" to become manufacturers. Most of the advocates of domestic manufactures would not have disagreed with Dickinson's point that America could not become a significant exporter of manufactured goods. What they encouraged was a system of manufactures that was sufficient to free the Americans from their dependence on the importation of necessities. The emphasis of the domestic manufactures movement was on the production of cheap cloth. An advocate of woolen manufactures assured his readers "that some little alteration in our system of agriculture, and a few years application to the most essential manufactures, would supply us with all the necessaries of life." Some writers worked out this notion of self-sufficiency in terms that recognized the need and advantages of an extensive internal market. America's advantage lay with "a trade like that of China founded on the internal interchange of the manufactures of its various provinces, lying as

[26]"Philander," *New York Gazette*, 10 April 1769; *Newport Mercury*, 14 and 28 December 1767; "Phileleuteros," *New York Journal*, 31 December 1767; *The Female Patriot, No. 1: Addressed to the Tea-drinking Ladies of New York* . . . (New York, 1770).

[27]*Pennsylvania Gazette*, 31 December 1767; *New York Gazette*, 16 July 1770.

those of America do under various climes." It was not to the advantage of America, so this argument ran, to engage so extensively as previously in external commerce if by its subordination in a colonial situation "the profits of our labour are to derive to others." By reorganizing their economic life around self-sufficiency and simplicity, the Americans had an opportunity to remove themselves from the usual cycle by which societies began to decline after they had attained greatness and prosperity; this lesson was available to anyone who took "a transient view of the many revolutions and vicissitudes that have happened in the world, how the seat of liberty, religion, power and empire has circulated from place to place; and at the same time considers the luxury and venality of the *European* governments, the ambition and foolish spirit of the great, the poverty and discontent of the commonality."

Such appeals for self-sufficiency were usually couched in terms of the sublime natural promise of America. The colonies were "the American Canaan," where men could "eat Bread without Scarceness, and . . . lack nothing"; the inhabitants of such a land were "ashamed to be dependent on other Countries for Manufactures." Because God had made nothing in vain and had endowed men with liberty, which was "the virtuous Enjoyment and free Possession of Property honestly gained," he had "undoubtedly furnished all Nations with the Means of defending their natural Rights," which in the case of the Americans meant that he had provided them with the means of self-sufficiency.[28] Much of the appeal of this projected national self-sufficiency, however, depended on its tacit promise of straitened prosperity, for the identification of a protean economic life with independence would again focus attention on the destructive potential of the self in economic life.

The colonists hoped that the nonimportation movement would eliminate some of the moral problems that they associated with their work. By disciplining themselves, they sought to raise their self-esteem and to establish a secure basis of social legitimacy. The commercial life of America would remain under the influence of mercantilist thought in its estimation of the society's economic health. But the prosperity of a self-sufficient America would be moderate and therefore less corrupting. In such a setting men's work would lack the selfishness that had so long characterized it. The genuine pleasures to be had from participation in such measures of political resistance as the nonimportation movement derived from the sense of community solidarity which they provided as an alternative to the usual preoccupation with individual interests.

[28]Dickinson, *Letters*, p. 11; *New York Mercury*, 27 April 1767; *Pennsylvania Gazette*, 4 August and 29 December 1768; *New York Gazette*, 25 December 1769; "Anglus Americanus," *Pennsylvania Chronicle*, 27 March 1769; "A Son of Liberty," *Providence Gazette*, 19 March 1768; "American Whig #5," *Boston Gazette*, 6 June 1768; *Maryland Gazette*, 20 April 1769.

The Triumph of Selfishness

On 20 April 1770 Parliament repealed all of the Townsend Duties except that on tea. This action had an immediate weakening effect on the nonimportation movement and eventually led to its abandonment. The near-unanimity of the colonies' opposition to the Duties broke down as men weighed the economic advantages of renewed trade against the political need for continued resistance to parliamentary taxation. (This disjunction of political and broadly conceived cultural reform was part of a process of conceptual compartmentalization of life into economic, social, and political spheres, a process which Gordon S. Wood has linked with the search in the 1770s and 1780s for a new and explicit constitutionalism.)

Opponents of the continuation of the nonimportation movement argued that the political purpose of securing parliamentary respect for colonial liberties could be served better by the refusal to import duties goods than by ineffective boycotts of all English goods. Advocates of a "prudent" course of action toward England accepted the colonies' economic dependence as inevitable. "An Agreement not to import Articles, which were free from Duty, and which, it was notorious, the Colonies could not long do without, was as imprudent and absurd, as for a Man to make a Vow not to eat or drink, until he had accomplished a certain Thing, which he was very uncertain of effecting Time enough to prevent starving." Though they agreed with the political goals involved, people who wanted to end the nonimportation movement appeared to have little commitment to the moral and economic reform which was an integral part of the movement. The chief spokesmen for this view were merchants who felt that other people's sense of virtuous patriotism had come at their expense. They were willing to abide by a boycott of tea because it was still duties, and they chided people who questioned the merchants' virtue while the critics themselves continued to import wine and foreign sugar despite the duties on them. The advocates for an end to the nonimportation resolutions cast themselves in the role of sensible and responsible men of affairs, "eminent for their caution, prudence and good sense," in contrast to "those warm spirits who have been for some time past inflaming the city into an ill-timed rash resolution." Merchants who had been attacked as "infamous, base, treacherous, faithless, sordid, or infamously inclined Persons" by the local committee of merchants reminded the public that colonial prosperity depended on them. Merchants whose business was hurt by the nonimportation movement claimed that people "who are most violent for the Continuance of the Non-importation Scheme . . . happen in general to be Men little or not at all interested in the Trade, and who are carrying on other Branches of Commerce."[29]

[29]"Philo-Veritas," *Pennsylvania Gazette*, 2 August and 19 July 1770; *New York Mercury*, 27 August 1770; *To the Public . . . July 25, 1768: Pacificus* (Philadelphia, 1768); *Maryland Gazette*, 2 August 1770.

Supporters of nonimportation were accused of being "violent Pretend-ers to Patriotism" who combined their hypocrisy with a tyrannical irra-tionality. Their false patriotism resembled that of Cromwell, Ireton, the thirty tyrants of Athens, and "the decemviri of Rome." William Henry Drayton of South Carolina, later a patriot but at this time probably the most outspoken critic of the illiberal righteousness of the members of the nonimportation movement, attacked them as "false prophets." " 'Tis not because a man is always bellowing, Liberty! Liberty! that he is to be ex-alted into the rank of patriot! The liberty of acting contrary to public pro-fessions, is what our modern patriots aim at."[30]

Because of these attacks on the expression of patriotism, the unanimity which had been an essential goal of the nonimportation movement became an impossibility. Further difficulties with cooperation arose as people in various cities became suspicious that the inhabitants of other cities would import goods in violation of the resolutions and sell them while the demand was artificially high. John Mein, a pro-administration printer in Boston, had seen from the start that such fears could wreck the movement, and he had published the records of importations into Boston in a way which seemed to show that the merchants there were not abiding by the agree-ments. By 1770 suspicions were acute because each commercial com-munity feared that another one would break the agreement and secure a jump on the market. The accusations of one city against another filled the newspapers during the summer of 1770, and they showed that where com-merce was concerned it was unwise to depend on people's public virtue and self-denial to discipline their actions for very long. The merchants' com-mittee of Albany gave reasons that were typical of those elsewhere for eliminating their nonimportation resolutions. "The Agreement operated no longer to any other Purpose, than tying the Hands of *Honest* Men, to let *Rogues, Smugglers*, and *Men of no Characters*, plunder their Country."[31] All men presumably had a right to plunder the country.

Not everyone wanted to end the nonimportation movement. The wave of denunciations which followed each supposed defection showed that for many people the moral importance of the movement remained after the brunt of the duties had been removed. But the commercial imperatives were such that a few determined opponents of the movement had it in their power to divide and wreck the program. When the colonists tried to ac-count for the failure of their efforts at reform, it was clear to them that the prevailing selfishness was the cause. "As Unanimity strengthens, so Divi-sions, and intestine Broils, will certainly weaken any Community where

---

[30]"Talionis," *Pennsylvania Chronicle*, 6 August 1770; *South Carolina Gazette*, 28 Decem-ber 1769, 13 July 1769 ("The Merchants of Charleston") and 12 October 1769 ("Freeman")

[31]*New York Mercury*, 20 August and 3 September 1770; "J.P., a Farmer," *New York Gazette*, 30 July 1770; *Maryland Gazette*, 2 August 1770; "Philadelphus," *Pennsylvania Chronicle*, 8 October 1770; *An Address to the Merchants, Freeholders, and All Other the Inhabitants* . . . (Philadelphia, 1768).

they happen, and give the common Enemy an Advantage. If so, how melancholy is it to behold (at a Time when Unanimity is most necessary) among the Inhabitants of the City of New-York, such Heats, Animosities, scurrilous Scriblings, and hard Reflections, as tend to irritate and disturb each other; when you ought to be unitedly joined to oppose your Enemies."

The charge of selfishness was laid especially against the upper class. People who sold their liberties "for a Mess of Potage" were described as a wealthy minority of "a few high-flying scoundrels" or "Men who have soar'd so high as to attract the Admiration and Esteem of all the virtuous part of Mankind." This populist note figured in the attacks on Drayton, who was asked by the mechanics on the nonimportation committee "whether he really can claim any merit from his possessing an estate not obtained, or obtainable, by his own industry." The criticism directed against such people was that "the Few ought to give Way to the Many." After the repeal of the Townsend Duties, selfishness took the form of greed and envy in a commercial situation. "There is a most pernicious and destructive opinion too prevalent amongst mankind, and our fellow citizens have imbibed a large share of it, which is this, that they are not to sit still, as they call it, and see others making their thousands, &c. though they are doing of it in a way which is utterly subversive of all the blessings of society—not considering that the very same method of reasoning might be made use of, to justify a man's going on the highway."[32]

This type of selfishness was thought to be most characteristic of merchants. As early as 1768 someone, possibly John Dickinson, had warned that Townsend had shaped his revenue plan in a way—unlike the case of the Stamp Act, which "hurt all parts of the populace and so all opposed it"— that set the patriotism of merchants against their own private interests. Not all merchants were distrusted, but any merchant who claimed that the needs of his business required him to violate the nonimportation resolutions was liable to be grouped with the "commercial vultures," "these commercial Hectors" who followed self-interest in defiance of the "universal concern" for virtue and liberty. The conduct of business took on connotations of contemptible and antisocial behavior. Advocates of the policy of easing the limitations on trade were accused of having "*sordid* dispositions," which prevented them from transcending "the *narrow* bounds of *self*" and instead compelled them "to *triumph* in their dexterity to gain a few *farthings*." Shopkeepers especially could not be relied on for reasonable behavior; they were "Creatures of muslin intellects whose brains are addled by being violently mixed and always turned round within the narrow circle of a store." "The Landholders, Artificers, and independent Free-

---

[32]"A True Friend of Liberty and Unanimity," *New York Mercury*, 2 and 16 July 1770; "Mechanicks of the Committee," *South Carolina Gazette*, 5 October 1769; "The New York Inspector," *Pennsylvania Chronicle*, 20 August 1770.

men," in contrast to the merchants, came to be looked on as the "proper source" of patriotism.[33]

The judgment of the patriots was that the deviant merchants should adhere to the traditional standard of public virtue, that the interests of individuals ought to be sacrificed for those of the whole society. People who ignored this principle were obviously indifferent to the needs of the public welfare and sought instead "to render the united Interest of the whole Community subservient to the *partial Purposes* of Commerce."[34] The expression of such attitudes destroyed people's confidence that they were working together for the public good. At first they attacked greedy merchants as scapegoats for their loss of an opportunity for reform, but eventually the failing was seen to be deeper and more widespread, a perpetuation of long-established vices.[35]

An allegory entitled "Ship News Extraordinary" recounted the failure of the nonimportation movement in terms of a merchant voyage and showed how selfishness replaced virtue among the colonists and led to America's ruin. The ship *America* was bound for the "Cape of Good Hope" with a cargo on which the owners had risked their entire estates, and every man on board had taken as large a venture as he could afford because the voyage would make his fortune. Soon after the ship sailed some sailors noticed that they had left clothing and tobacco ashore and insisted that the ship return to port so that they could collect them. They refused to change their demands even when told that the cargo would be ruined if they returned. The rest of the crew argued with them that everyone's interests were involved.

Surely they would sooner relinquish their imprudent Design of returning, than the certain Advantages that encouraged them to persevere in their Course; that every One on board was much in the same Situation with them, it being remarkable, that in the Hurry of leaving Port, when the *Wind and Tide served*, every man of them had left *some of his Effects behind*; they were entreated, therefore, in the most tender Manner, to have some Pity for their *Fellow Sailors*, . . . for the Owners, in whose Employ they had been brought up, and had always sailed, and who had always treated them as their Children; and for themselves, who were so much interested in prosecuting the Voyage.

Despite these pleas, the wayward sailors refused to work on the ship until it had put about. The short-handed vessel was obliged to return to port,

[33]David L. Jacobson, "The Puzzle of Pacificus," *Pennsylvania History*, 31 (1964): 406–18; *To the Free and Patriotic Inhabitants of the City of Philad. . . .* (Philadelphia, 1770); *New York Gazette*, 5 June 1770; "A Freeborn American," *Pennsylvania Gazette*, 12 May 1768 and 24 May and 11 October 1770.

[34]"Citizen," *Pennsylvania Gazette*, 11 October and 25 January 1770; "A Son of Liberty," *New York Gazette*, 21 May 1770.

[35]Alan Heimert, *Religion and the American Mind from the Great Awakening to the Revolution* (Cambridge, Mass., 1966), chap. 9; Gordon S. Wood, *The Creation of the American Republic, 1776–1787* (Chapel Hill, 1969), pp. 65–69, 106–8, 418–19.

where a British man-of-war broke loose from her moorings, ran down the *America*, and sank her. Only the mutinous sailors survived, and they were jailed for damaging the king's ship. With nothing to call their own, the owners of the *America* "lost their Spirits, finding now, that the strictest Industry they could use in procuring Intelligence, the greatest Wisdom they could exert in executing them, could not save them from Ruin, while they cherished, within their Bosoms, as it were, those who counteracted and betrayed every Effort of their Diligence, Understanding and Virtue."[36]

Readers of this allegory would have recognized that each individual concealed such treason within his breast. The allegory demonstrated the characteristic confusion of the Revolution, that of hopes for material welfare with those for virtue; as it turned out, feelings about property were both the occasion for action and the cause of its failure. The allegory also revealed the difficulty of working virtuously in a commercial society. When it was cooperative, work redeemed a society in crisis, but when it was selfish the energies released by work were not only asocial but destructive of society.

In its reform efforts the nonimportation movement relied on abnegation and thereby demonstrated the difficulty of treating work in the context of virtue. The situation itself—one of political resistance and later of wartime patriotism—was suited to conceptions of social harmony, and virtue and community participation could be imputed to the existing structure and conduct of work on the basis of the public interest embodied in the political situation. But in the aftermath of the Revolution, when the dangers posed by men's normal acquisitiveness and selfishness were no longer overshadowed by those of external events, the matter of the tension between personal and public definitions of prosperity came to the fore again.

[36]*New York Gazette*, 29 January 1770. The allegory was also printed in *Pennsylvania Gazette*, 25 January 1770.

EPILOGUE

REPUBLICANS ARE ECONOMIC MEN

I N THE COURSE OF THE AMERICAN REVOLUTION, partly as a consequence of disillusionment, but more important as a result of the new political and commercial necessities born of independence, economic valuations of work gained a prominence they had previously lacked in public discourse. For example, in the spring of 1784, while the problem of the disposition of the western lands and hence decisions about the course of economic development in the new nation were before the Continental Congress, Thomas Jefferson and George Washington corresponded about the desirability of a canal which would connect the Potomac River with the Ohio. Both viewed the canal as worthwhile, even though it would foster commercial life. Jefferson declined to speculate "whether commerce contributed to the Happiness of mankind." "All the world is becoming commercial," he wrote, and it was impossible for the United States to keep itself apart from such a trend. "Our citizens have had too full a taste of the comforts furnished by the arts and manufactures to be debarred the use of them." American political necessities required the country to "endeavor to share as large a portion as we can of this modern source of wealth and power." Washington agreed that it was idle to speculate about the dangers of a commercial society when America already was one. "From Trade our Citizens *will not* be restrained, and therefore it behoves us to place it in the most convenient channels, under proper regulations, freed, *as much as possible*, from those vices which luxury, the consequence of wealth and power, naturally introduce."[1] Experience with the nonimportation movement and wartime profiteering had shown that local attempts at virtuous self-denial were unlikely to be successful, and, even if they were enforced, competition with other political entities required resources which only commerce could provide. The demands of the political situation, combined with the frailties of Americans themselves, required that commerce be embraced, not simplified and restrained.

This realistic and, in the context of previous aspirations for reform, pessimistic appraisal of American social development had been voiced before the Revolution, when accommodation of the Continental Association to the needs of war was under debate. In 1774, when the Continental Congress had drawn up the Association, there had been little disagreement over its necessity, and attention had focused on the way in which its economic effects on Britain would influence Parliament's policy toward the colonies. A year later, however, when the nonexportation provisions of the Association came into effect and after Parliament had passed a general restraining act on all colonial trade except that of four provinces (New York, Delaware, North Carolina, and Georgia), argument arose over whether or not such limitations on access to financial resources were appropriate when war supplies were needed. Nonexportation went into effect on schedule, but the debate revealed that expectations of social and economic reform had diminished and that the issue had become what Gordon S. Wood has termed "the debate over the virtue of the people." Some members of the Continental Congress, most often those of New York, played down the necessity of virtue and contended that the best way to acquire needed supplies was to mobilize the desire for gain. Arguing against them were several representatives of the plantation colonies who saw the Association as an opportunity for domestic reform, especially in the encouragement of domestic manufactures. But the prevailing opinion fell between these extremes and held that, while Americans had virtue enough to submit to short-term economic limitations for patriotic purposes, they could not be expected to alter their way of life in any fundamental way except politically. This cautious confidence in American virtue, combined with an expedient interest in intercolonial unity, determined the decision not to allow exportation, for it would have provided some colonies with unfair economic advantages and thereby would have fostered jealousy in the others.[2]

Experience with the previous nonimportation movement had lessened hopes for moral and social reform; simultaneously, however, repressive

[1]Thomas Jefferson to George Washington, 15 March 1784. and Washington to Jefferson, 29 March 1784, *The Papers of Thomas Jefferson*, ed. Julian Boyd, 18 vols. to date (Princeton, 1953–), 7: 26, 51; George Washington to Benjamin Harrison, 10 October 1784, *The Writings of George Washington*, ed. John C. Fitzpatrick, 39 vols. (Washington, D.C., 1931–1944), 27: 474. These items are cited in Joseph Dorfman, *The Economic Mind in American Civilization, 1606–1865*, 5 vols. (New York, 1946), 1: 247–51.

[2]John Adams, *Diary and Autobiography of John Adams*, ed. L. H. Butterfield, 4 vols. (Cambridge, Mass., 1961), 2: 137–40, 191, 193, 210–14; John Adams to James Warren, 19

British measures after the Boston Tea Party, especially the closing of the port there, had led Americans to associate their commercial prosperity with the success of their political resistance and thus to cast American economic life in a more favorable light. Restraints on trade became a symptom of British corruption, while American hopes for freedom focused on revival of a vigorous commercial life. In effect, Parliament, by using commercial restrictions to impose its rule in the colonies, conferred a patriotic legitimacy on the prevailing patterns of work in the American economy. Thus the donations received by the Boston town meeting to relieve those in economic difficulty as a result of the Boston Port Bill were used to employ the colonists "in their several occupations." Allegiance to ancestral virtue required that America be prosperous. "Of what value are our lands and estates to us, if such an odious government should be established among us? Can we look with pleasure on the inheritance left us by our ancestors, or on the fields cultivated by *our* industry? When we reflect that all our labours have made them only a more inviting prey to our enemies, will not the vine-yard of Naboth be ever in *our* minds?" The qualms about the structure and conduct of American commerce which had been evident during the late 1760s were lessened, and the self-imposed restrictions of the Continental Association became less an exercise in criticism of American social development than an affirmation of virtuous independence from Britain.[3]

Throughout the late colonial period many Americans had tended to identify the public interest, at least partially and often equivocally, with commercial prosperity. As in the case of provincial mercantilism, this view could be combined with the traditional social values of industry and frugality to confer legitimacy on actions. Owing to the preoccupation with strategic and political concerns during the Revolution, however, the attention paid to the social aspects of work diminished. The problems of commerce were seen as more strictly economic ones, in which matters of morality and

---

and 20 October 1775, *Warren-Adams Letters*, ed. Worthington Chauncey Ford, 2 vols. (Boston, 1917), 1: 146, 156; cf. Carter Braxton, *An Address to the Convention of the Colony of Virginia* (Philadelphia, 1776). These items are discussed in Gordon S. Wood, *The Creation of the American Republic, 1776-1787* (Chapel Hill, 1969), pp. 93-97. See also Arthur M. Schlesinger, *The Colonial Merchants and the American Revolution, 1763-1776*, Atheneum ed. (New York, 1968), pp. 569-76; Bernard Mason, "Robert R. Livingston and the Non-Importation Policy: Notes for a Speech in the Continental Congress, 1775," *New York Historical Society Quarterly*, 44 (1960): 296-307.

[3][Robert Carter Nicholas], *Considerations on the Present State of Virginia Examined* (Williamsburg, 1774), p. 31; John Trumbell, *An Elegy on the Times* (New Haven, 1775), pp. 5, 8, 13; *A Letter from Tom Bowline . . . Dec. 20, 1773* (New York, 1773); Boston Town Meeting, *The Committee . . . Oct. 25, 1774* (Boston, 1774); Boston Committee of Correspondence, *Gentlemen: The Evils Which We Have Long Foreseen . . . June 8, 1774* (Boston, 1774); Massachusetts Provincial Congress, *In the Provincial Congress, Cambridge, December 10, 1774: To the Freeholders* (Boston, 1774); Charles Chauncey, *Christian Love, as Exemplified by the First Christian Church in Their Having All Things in Common . . .* (Boston, 1773), p. 13; William Gordon, "A Discourse Preached December 15th, 1774, Being the Day Recommended by the Provincial Congress," in *The Pulpit of the American Revolution*, ed. John Wingate Thornton (Boston, 1860), pp. 210-13.

individual social legitimation became less important. American behavior in the wartime economy was especially disillusioning because selfishness in economic life seemed ineradicable, yet commerce was essential for the success of the Revolution. All types of economic activity seemed to provide opportunities for injustice. "Does it not seem [a minister asked his congregation in 1777] as the whole country was contaminated with a spirit of selfishness? . . . And yet, how ready is every one to excuse himself from blame, and cast the fault upon others—When perhaps, the greater part, if not all who are any ways concerned in trade, whether in Town or Country, are either in a greater or less degree promoters of this internal oppression." Complaints about the wartime economy dealt with the disruption of accustomed economic arrangements, especially the severe rise in prices and costs; laborers could charge high wages, farmers could withhold goods from market, and merchants could demand high prices for goods. Measures for the regulation of prices and wages were initially popular because they promised to control these abuses, but, when they proved ineffective and even added to the duress, they became the source of additional bitterness. Benjamin Rush's comments to the Continental Congress in 1777 revealed the growing sense that the problem was an economic one, not a matter of deficiencies in virtue. "It is a common thing to cry aloud of the rapacity and extortion in every branch of business etc. among every class of men. This had led some people to decry the *public Virtue* of this country. True Sir there is not so much of it as we could wish, but there is much more than is sometimes allowed on this floor. We estimate our Virtue by a false barometer when we measure it by the price of goods. The extortion we complain of arises only from the excessive quantity of our money." By the end of the Revolution it was apparent that market uncertainty in wartime and inflation caused by public spending had necessitated many of these actions, but this recognition also reduced the relevance of considerations about the social nature of work.[4]

The fiscal, monetary, and commercial situation of the United States after the War for Independence accentuated this need to apply economic

---

[4]Jonathan French, *A Practical Discourse against Extortion* . . . (Boston, 1777), pp. 19-20. Rush's remarks are cited in Richard B. Morris, "Labor and Mercantilism in the Revolutionary Era," *The Era of the American Revolution*, ed. Richard B. Morris (New York, 1939), pp. 99-100. See also William Gordon, "The Separation of the Jewish Tribes after the Death of Soloman, Accounted for, and Applied to the Present . . ." [1777]; George Duffield, "A Sermon Preached in the Third Presbyterian Church in the City of Philadelphia" [1783]; and Nathaniel Whitaker, "An Antidote against Toryism, or the Curse of Meroz" [1777], in *The Patriot Preachers of the American Revolution*, ed. Frank Moore (New York, 1862), pp. 182-83, 366-67, and 210-11.

On economic developments during the Revolution, see Morris, "Labor and Mercantilism"; Oscar Handlin and Mary Flug Handlin, *Commonwealth: A Study of the Role of Government in the American Economy: Massachusetts, 1774-1861*, rev. ed. (Cambridge, Mass., 1969), chap. 1; idem, "Revolutionary Economic Policy in Massachusetts," *William and Mary Quarterly*, 3rd ser., 4 (1947): 3-26; and Bernard Mason, "Entrepreneurial Activity in New York during the American Revolution," *Business History Review*, 40 (1966): 190-212.

analysis. The implications of this development for traditional valuations of work and for the conceptions about the relationship between self and society which they revealed were markedly evident in the dispute which took place in Pennsylvania in 1785 and 1786 over the rechartering of the Bank of North America, one of the most important discussions of the economic life of the new nation before that concerning the Constitution.[5] The Bank functioned chiefly as a source of commercial credit, and it had run afoul of the Pennsylvania legislature when it thwarted the creation of a second bank and refused to fund a large issue of public bills of credit. The Bank, its opponents asserted, "facilitates both public and private ruin." It encouraged that perversion of the purposes of commerce which prevailed when importation was a more profitable activity than exportation of "produce and manufactures." In particular, the Bank was blamed for the depression that had developed as a result of a credit shortage which accompanied the large increase of importations after the war. Opponents of the Bank refused to place all the blame for this situation on the imprudence of the inhabitants and insisted that the Bank had contributed to the problems by withholding funds from circulation.[6]

Yet the Bank's opponents only occasionally espoused a social valuation of work. Their arguments showed them to be committed to life in a market society, and the framework within which they evaluated their interests and judged the economic inadequacies of the Bank was a mercantilist one. "To cultivate these now jarring interests ["of the farmer, the mechanic, and the merchant"], and render them mutual, we must first propagate or import a greater number of people, that we may have labor of all sorts cheaper; we must encourage our own produce and manufactures; we must try to curb our luxury—to mortify our madness for trade and foreign wares. Our present manner of trading, if persisted in, must prevent us from ever being in any reputable degree, an independent or a commercial nation." The antagonists of the Bank saw it as a restraint on commercial development and recommended instead the creation of a public loan office. They did not hesitate to assert the need for commerce in America, both for reasons of political survival and for reasons of social development. "A civilized nation, without commerce," they argued, "is a solecism in politics." They used the social nature of man as an argument for the development of commerce, whereas previously it had been used to demonstrate the need to place social concerns before economic ones. The public interest was conceived chiefly in economic terms, and the most pressing need appeared to be the availability of credit for the farmer so that he could "improve or

[5]The significance of this debate for an understanding of postrevolutionary views on individual interests and the public good is shown in Constance E. Snyder, "Monopoly, Anarchy, or Compromise: The Bank of North America and the Common Good" (Seminar paper, The Johns Hopkins University, May 1968).

[6]Mathew Carey, ed., *Debates and Proceedings of the General Assembly of Pennsylvania, on the Memorials Praying a Repeal or Suspension of the Law Annulling the Charter of the Bank* (Philadelphia, 1786), pp. 67–68.

cultivate his estate." The drawback of the Bank was that it did not spread the benefits of credit wide enough. "Money of this kind [from a state loan office] operates as a *stimulus* to the borrower, to procure funds for repayment, whereby a spirit of industry is Excited. Add to this that a circulating medium is established, adequate to the necessities of the whole community; our exports increased; domestic trade enlivened; population promoted; and a revenue furnished to the state." This benign view of commerce, uncommon in America until after the Revolution, was combined with lessened expectations of public virtue, and the public good was seen as the sum of individual, chiefly economic, interests. "A few individuals in a nation may be actuated by such exalted sentiments of public virtue, as to sacrifice their own interests to the general welfare; but these instances must be rare; and professional men of every description are necessarily, as such, obliged to pursue their immediate advantage."[7] The situation which would make these personal interests least damaging to others was one of economic expansion. It was assumed that in a young nation with unlimited material resources the centrifugal expression of selfishness was less damaging socially than the centripetal. To think in such terms was to assume society to be a boundless entity in which economic activity shaped life—in the colonial period the domestic economy had been difficult to conceptualize because of an embracive notion of society; after the Revolution the matter was reversed.

Though Americans expressed greater equanimity toward commerce after the Revolution, fears about its most obvious result, namely personal wealth, remained. Its opponents charged that it was in the nature of the Bank to be dangerous because it had "no principle but that of avarice, which dries and shrivels up all the manly—all the generous feelings of the human soul. . . . The human soul is affected by wealth, in almost all its faculties. It is affected by its present interest, by its expectations, and by its fears." In the dispute over the Bank these concerns about the social and personal effects of wealth focused on the danger which concentrations of wealth posed for republican government, but they also indicated doubts about self-control in conditions of abundance, as in the case of the inability of the inhabitants to resist the luxurious imports which credit from the Bank made available. William Findley, the most voluble antagonist of the Bank, demonstrated this ambivalence toward wealth at several points in the debates in the Pennsylvania legislature. He warned against the political power which the Bank could exercise; "enormous wealth, possessed by individuals, has always had its influence and danger in free states." To guard against this danger he recommended that the state do what it could to enable everyone to become wealthy. "Wealth in many hands operates as many checks: for in numberless instances, one wealthy man has a control

[7]*Ibid.*, p. 127; [William Barton], *The True Interest of the United States, and Particularly of Pennsylvania* . . . (Philadelphia, 1786), pp. 1-2, 19, 27; *Remarks on a Pamphlet Entitled "Considerations on the Bank of North America"* (Philadelphia, 1785), p. 15.

over another. Every man in the disposal of his own wealth, will act upon his own principles. His virtue, his honour, his sympathy, and generosity, will influence his disposals and designs; and he is in a state of personal responsibility." Such an economic structure might well guard against the political dangers of wealth, but would it avoid the more personal consequences of its motive principle, "which dries and shrivels up all the manly—all the generous feelings of the human soul"? At one point in the debates Findley responded to the charge that his opposition to the Bank was motivated by a love of wealth. "I love and pursue it—not as an end, but as a means of enjoying happiness and independence."[8] Rather than assert his self-interest as a sufficient justification for his actions, Findley chose to identify them with the liberty of himself and others. Political considerations applied to a public interest which was still separable from that of individuals, while economic interests now corresponded to an interpretation of the public good as being composed of personal desires.

The defenders of the Bank shared with their antagonists many of these views about the benign nature of commerce and wealth, but they were more explicit in voicing them and less ambiguous about their implications. In marking the change from colonial social values, the most striking feature of their arguments was their forthright assertion that selfishness was not socially dangerous. The Bank's advocates no longer accepted the notion that gains in domestic commerce could come only at the expense of others. Thus they were not disturbed by the charge that officers of the Bank could use the money of others for their own advantage. "We must acknowledge, that this evil will in some degree prevail; for we know that nothing on earth is perfect. But must we forego a great advantage to all, because a greater advantage will result to a few?" The supporters of the Bank sought to defend their motives, not by arguing for their virtue, but by asserting that their motives were the same as those of others and no different from what could be expected in economic life. "Commerce is excited, directed, and carried on by interest. But do not mistake this, it is not carried on by general universal interest, nor even by well informed national interest, but by immediate, apparent, and sensible personal interest." In their explanations of the value of the Bank, they associated the public good with the "general prosperity," the "security of property," and the "toleration of every man to pursue his own benefit in his own way"; the only restriction on self-interest was that it be compatible with the public good, which was implicitly the interests of other individuals and not an entity which subsumed them.[9]

The corollary of this benign view of the social effects of selfishness was that economic valuations of action were sufficient ones in discussions of

[8]Carey, *Debates*, pp. 66, 125, 128.

[9]*Ibid.*, p. 26; *An Address to the Assembly of Pennsylvania on the Abolition of the Bank of North America* (Philadelphia, 1785), p. 24; John Witherspoon, *Essay on Money as a Medium of Commerce* (Philadelphia, 1786), p. 56.

work and its consequences. Economic rationality and opportunities for its exercise were now presented as the best means to avoid those wrongs to self and society which had formerly been identified with commercial life itself. A prosperous trade tempted people into irrational extremes of consumption and debt, but these individual follies entailed their own punishment and therefore did not require restrictions for the "sober and discreet." Similarly, such restraints on the market as regrating and engrossing were treated as functions of credit availability and profit expectations and therefore were considered inappropriate for social valuations. On the contrary, it was implicit in the arguments of the defenders of the Bank that the economic nature of commerce should determine its practice, and they referred to the distress caused by wartime efforts to enforce social valuations of work in commercial life as a demonstration of their point. Economic rationality and economic justice were becoming barely distinguishable. From this perspective the most important relationships among men were economic. Credit replaced virtue as the principle of public action.

Credit, in a commercial sense, is the confidence which people place in a man's integrity and punctuality, in fulfilling his contracts, and performing his engagements. . . . From this view of the matter, it appears that credit is a most valuable thing in society, it gives hearts ease, it gives wealth, 'tis a purse of every social virtue, it makes a soil suitable for the growth of public spirit and every public virtue.[10]

Such a shift in emphasis from social to economic valuations of work marked a change in views of the relationship between the self and society. The traditional fear of selfishness appears to have been moderated by a confidence in the durability of accustomed social and economic practices and institutions. The price of this confidence was a diminution in moral considerations that were publicly applicable to work.

The rhetoric of American self-evaluation throughout the eighteenth century wove together complaints about declension and expectations of reform. This tension corresponded to a persistent inability on the part of Americans to establish a relationship between the self and society which was both descriptively accurate for their work and psychologically satisfying for their self-respect. The most troubling experiences arose from membership and participation in a commercial society. Most of the changes that accompanied the expansion of market activities resulted in a marked betterment of people's lives. Commerce provided access to a wide range of technological resources and material comforts. Increased wealth gave men greater opportunities for the sheer pleasures of consumption and

---

[10]Carey, *Debates*, pp. 89–90, 105; Peletiah Webster, *A Seventh Essay on Free Trade and Finance* (Philadelphia, 1785), p. 3; *idem, An Essay on Credit in Which the Doctrine of Banks Is Considered . . .* (Philadelphia, 1786), pp. 3, 5; *Address to the Assembly of Pennsylvania*, p. 6; Witherspoon, *Essay on Money*, pp. 29–34.

ownership. The economic orientation of much of the population could change from subsistence to gain. But this gain could take place only in a peculiar context, a market society in which goods, labor, and land were for sale as commodities, and hence a society in which the members' most important relationships seemed to be economic ones. In a market society some individuals could gain while others did not; personal gain often came at the expense of others. The dark side of prosperity reflected men's antagonism.

Commerce could lead men to wrong themselves as well as others. The colonists subscribed to the idea, basic to European thought, that there was a tension in human nature between man's reason and his passions. Though they considered the faculty of reason to be a characteristic which distinguished man from other earthly creatures, they believed that his passions usually controlled his behavior. This conception of human nature bore directly on the relationship between the self and society. The public interest consisted of the harmonious organization of the interests of autonomous, rational individuals. This harmony constituted the colonists' sense of community, and its vagueness made them all the more concerned about its preservation. The public interest could not be simply the sum of individual interests, because it would then have an irrational basis. It was assumed that each society had a proper order, but in fact people knew only about the sources of that order—virtue and reason—and were confused about the nature of the order itself. Thus the public good was often negatively defined as the absence of selfishness. It was impossible to give legitimacy to gain which came at the expense of others, because by definition such action violated the harmony of interests of the members of society. Self-respect required conviction of the existence of harmony between private pursuits and public interests.

In opposition to the rationality of communal interests stood the particularity of individual interests, and commerce unleashed men's selfish passions. The greater the opportunities for action were, the wider the scope for irrationality was. Recommendations of industry testified to the conviction that fulfillment of the self required the exercise of reason for the control of the world and juxtaposed this ideal against the destructive potential of individual action. Yet the economic order thus created threatened to submerge the self in its demands for action in an overelaborate structure and the excess of gratifications which it provided.[11]

Thus the way in which Americans thought about work revealed their values concerning the general issue of the relationship between the self and society. The most obvious feature of their ideas about work was their persistent moralizing about it. They thought of society as a moral realm in which men's actions were accountable for their justice. Selfishness could

[11]For an analysis of these themes in responses to nature and civilization, see Leo Marx, *The Machine in the Garden: Technology and the Pastoral Ideal in America* (New York, 1964), chap. 2.

not be excused as the unavoidable response to social and economic imperatives; such moral neutrality would have destroyed their sense of community
and undercut their self-esteem.

In apparent contradiction to their preoccupation with the social consequences of work, the colonists assumed that society was composed of
economically autonomous individuals. This autonomy consisted of a willingness to assume the responsibility of self-preservation and to accept the
consequences of one's economic activity. Liberty depended on the individual's control over the fruits of his industry; slavery was a condition in
which men lacked this control over property, with the result that slaves
were idle, self-indulgent, and dependent on others for their survival. Given
this association of autonomy and rationality, certain aspects of economic
thought, especially the monetary measurement of the utility of work and
the tendency to provide a strictly economic account of men's motivations
in work, had the potential to provide an alternative basis for the legitimization of work. Economic utility was a measure of the rationality of men's
work, yet it ignored the traditional ethical issue of the relationship between
the self and society. For reasons discussed above, however, this alternative
basis was not implemented. In the course of the eighteenth century the
focus of concern in discussions of work tended to shift from individual imperatives for work to the institutional context in which it took place. Thus
both anticommercial feelings and acceptance of a market economy became
more explicit. Moral questions about work remained significant, but considerations about the economy were increasingly separable from those
about society, though the disjunction between economy and society,
was less complete than that between society and politics.[12] Developments in
British (especially Scottish) social philosophy reinforced this change with
the theory that the unhindered expression of individual interests was
naturally harmonious, and thus the irrationality of motivation became
dissociated from the distrust of self.[13]

American public expression, especially during the Revolution, indicated
that, despite the increased prominence of economic valuations of work,
the colonists were still anxious about the individual and social consequences of work. It is a puzzle for the modern reader of these materials
that more affirmative values, ones which actually legitimized the prevailing
behavior, were so seldom expressed. Intellectual elements were available
for a less normative and more empirical understanding of work. It was
hypothetically possible to substitute an economic analysis of men's work
for an ethical one, an account which would have accepted the fact that

[12]On the separation of ideas about society and politics in the early republic, see Wood,
Creation of the American Republic, p. 608.

[13]Elie Halévy, *The Growth of Philosophic Radicalism*, trans. Mary Morris (London, 1952),
chap. 1; Duncan Forbes, " 'Scientific' Whiggism: Adam Smith and John Millar," *Cambridge
Journal*, 7 (1954): 643–70; Daniel J. Boorstin, *The Lost World of Thomas Jefferson*, Beacon
ed. (Boston, 1964), pp. 140–51.

men's acquisitive appetites determine economic life and that society is therefore the open-ended result of their satisfaction. It is indicative of American views on society and human nature that, after the Revolution, when such ideas became more widely expressed, they were the result of pessimism about the possibility of a moral relationship between the self and society. This pessimism was balanced, however, by an optimism about the ability of society, when regulated by wise men, to weather the activities of selfish men.[14]

[14]Yet the traditional concern about the corrosive effect of economic activity on individual morality and social order continued to be voiced in the early national period. See Fred Somkin, *Unquiet Eagle: Memory and Desire in the Idea of American Freedom, 1815–1860* (Ithaca, 1967), chap. 1; Charles L. Sanford, "The Intellectual Origins and New-Worldliness of American Industry," *Journal of Economic History*, 18 (1958): 1–16; cf. Samuel Wales, *The Dangers of Our National Prosperity* . . . (Hartford, 1785). For an indication of the continuation into the industrial era of aversion for the values of economic life, though with important modifications in its implications for self-respect, see Michael Zuckerman, "The Nursery Tales of Horatio Alger," *American Quarterly*, 24 (1972): 191–209.

INDEX

159

Library of Congress Cataloging in Publication Data

Crowley, J   E   1943–
    This Sheba, Self: the conceptualization of economic
life in eighteenth-century America.

    (The Johns Hopkins University studies in historical
and political science, 92d ser., 2)
        Includes bibliographical references.
        1. Christianity and economics.   2. Work.
3. Labor and laboring classes—United States—History.
I. Title.   II. Series: Johns Hopkins University.
Studies in historical and political science, 92d ser., 2.
BR115.E3C76   301.5'5   73-19334
ISBN 0-8018-1579-7